Inequity in the Global Village

# Inequity in the Global Village

## Recycled Rhetoric and Disposable People

Jan Knippers Black

Kumarian Press

*Inequity in the Global Village: Recycled Rhetoric and Disposable People*

Published 1999 in the United States of America by Kumarian Press, Inc.,
14 Oakwood Avenue, West Hartford, Connecticut 06119-2127 USA.



*Production and design by The Sarov Press, Stratford, Connecticut.*
*Index by Barbara J. DeGennaro.*
*The text of this book is set in Adobe Sabon.*

Printed in Canada on acid-free paper by
Transcontinental Printing and Graphics, Inc.
Text printed with vegetable oil-based ink.

∞ The paper used in this publication meets the minimum requirements of the American National Standard for Information Sciences—Permanence of Paper for Printed Library Materials, ANSI Z39.48–1984.

---

**Library of Congress Cataloging-in-Publication Data**

Black, Jan Knippers, 1940–.
Inequity in the global village : recycled rhetoric and disposable people / Jan Knippers Black.
p. cm.
Includes bibliographical references and index.
ISBN 1–56549–100–9 (cloth : alk. paper). — ISBN 1–56549–099–1 (pbk. : alk. paper)
1. Income distribution. 2. Social justice. 3. Capitalism. 4. Competition, International. 5. Economic history—1990– I. Title.
HC79.I5B598 1999
339.2—dc21 99–29730

---

04 03 02 01 00 99 6 5 4 3 2 1 First Printing 1999

# Dedication

*TO THE MOSTLY* unsung heroes and heroines around the world who, often at great personal risk and sacrifice, have undertaken to make their communities and their countries more hospitable to the humblest and most selfless of their neighbors — among the hundreds I have known and admired:

- Maria Arancibia de Rosas, former president of the Federation of Mothers' Centers of Población "La Victoria" of Santiago, Chile
- Amílcar Méndez, founder of SERJ, promoting human rights for indigenous communities, Santa Cruz del Quiché, Guatemala; elected a member of congress in 1995
- Creuza Maciel, formerly of the human rights organization Servicio Paz y Justicia of Argentina and Brazil, who works with abandoned and delinquent children in Rio de Janeiro
- Jaya Arunachalam of Madras, founder of India's Working Women's Forum
- Veena Nayyar, president of the Women's Political Watch in New Delhi
- Diana Chuli, writer and founder of the Women's Forum of Albania
- Elizabeth Sequeiros, founder of an organization promoting literacy and basic education in Mozambique
- Zeke Mphalele, South African novelist and civil rights advocate
- Hsiu-lien (Annette) Lu, founder of human rights, feminist, and democracy movements in Taiwan, and most recently Senator and Magistrate
- Lydia Villarroel, founder, and Sabino López, community organizer, of Center for Community Advocacy, assisting farm workers in the Salinas valley of California
- Nancy Pettis, founder and president of VOICE International (Voluntary Organizations Initiatives in Central and Eastern Europe and Eurasia), Washington, D.C.

# Contents

# Preface

*THIS BOOK HAS* been inspired in large part by an extraordinary incongruence between what I have seen and experienced around the world in the past few years and what has been reported by the mainstream media, and to a large extent by academia as well, about this new post-Cold War order. As in the aftermath of hotter wars, we have seen a great deal of posturing and preening, of the claiming of credit and bounty as well as the higher moral and theoretical ground. It could hardly be surprising that a multifaceted imbalance would be one of the outcomes of a long war.

Of course there is much to celebrate in the ending of the Cold War for peoples on both sides of what was strangely and arbitrarily labeled a great East-West divide. To the new freedoms enjoyed in the "East," there is a certain resonance in the West, as well. Those who fail to appreciate this book may fruitfully call me foolish, but they would get little mileage now out of trying to label me subversive. The days of schoolchildren ducking under their desks in mock nuclear attack drills and civil defense specialists plotting the instant evacuation of major cities seem now to belong to a distant and mysterious — almost comical — past. Few people of any country with normal hormones and no vested interest in weapons systems could fail to appreciate the ending of the Cold War, but we dare not be blinded by such appreciation to the dangers of the course on which we have embarked.

Since orthodox economics — formerly the dismal science — has joined political science and most of the other standard social science disciplines in the cheerleading squad, it remains for someone (I'm not alone, but not exactly caught up in a stampede either) to point out that there are losers in this new game, a great many of them. And for ever greater numbers, the path we are on leads off a bluff.

It would be difficult to sum up in a few words what this book is about—I have been calling this my "book about everything"; but it seems worthwhile to issue some disclaimers as to what it is not. It is not a current events book — a snapshot of the world at a particular point in time. Nor does it aim to be a comprehensive collection of data or history of a period. It employs theory and aggregate data but does not rely on them; rather it is richly textured with human drama. It is a very personal book. I want to pass on to you, my readers, what I have seen and heard and experienced of this all-encompassing decade of transition, of kaleidoscopic change for good and for ill, leaving no part of the world, no species and no culture, untouched.

In this endeavor, I will draw upon the analyses of various scholars and schools of thought no longer playing in prime time as well as the more recently circulating ideas and concerns of environmentalists, feminists, and community builders. But more immediately I will draw upon observations and insights of people around the world of various classes, sectors, professions, and relationships with fate, those who reap the consequences of shifts in power, paradigm, and policy.

This book seeks to highlight linkages among trends that are seemingly divergent — even contradictory — and that are generally treated in isolation: democratization and the dissolution of states; healthy economies and unhealthy peoples; arms control treaties at the summit but free-fire zones on city streets; a global village but one that is gated and guarded "for members only."

I will attempt to show that what lies at the base of these tightly linked trends and problems is not cultural difference or any lack of generosity on the part of Mother Nature, but rather a yawning gap in wealth and thus power both among and within states, the product of a capitalist system run amuck, one that has escaped popular control and has come to dominate the public arena, a system of speed-of-sound mobility of money and immobilized political leadership. The gap will most likely continue to grow exponentially until it is confronted by a globally coordinated policy U-turn or a global financial system meltdown.

The international development thrust that followed upon the close of World War II leaned heavily on technology and money to solve global problems; but neither is in itself a solution. Together they constitute a large part of the problem. Whatever else is required, it is clear that the solution to widespread poverty and growing gaps lies in some combination of insight and empathy, political will and social responsibility.

This is an irreverent book. There is surely something here to offend almost any reader. But I dare hope that the insights offered, gleaned from thoughtful people of many nationalities and cultures, will help us to understand where we are and where we are headed so that we might more readily plot a course toward where we want to be.

# Acknowledgments

*FIRST, I WOULD* like to acknowledge the hospitality and intellectual stimulation of St. Antony's College, Oxford University, where my work on this book was completed. I am grateful to Herminio Martins and Michael Aris of St. Antony's and to Barry Gills of the University of Newcastle-upon-Tyne for reading and commenting on portions of the manuscript. I also appreciate the encouragement and ideas of my colleagues and students at the Monterey Institute of International Studies, particularly my graduate assistants Kirea Drayton, Kiara Tsoukkou, Miguel Castrense, Marian Hart, and Peter Zutz.

I appreciate as well the journals, magazines, and newspapers that have carried my work in recent years. Some vignettes or passages in this book draw from or build upon articles previously published in *The Review of Social Economy* (Chap. 22), *NACLA Report on the Americas* (Chap. 16), *The Manchester Guardian Overseas Weekly* (Chap. 11), *Latin American Perspectives* (Chap. 15), *Contemporary Review* (Chap. 21), *In These Times* (Chaps. 1, 4, 7, 18), *Z Magazine* (Chaps. 8, 10, 19, 20), and *USA Today Magazine* (Chaps 12, 13, 14). Parts of the introduction to Part V appear in my chapter in Brad Roth and Gregory Fox, eds., *Democratic Governance and International Law,* Cambridge University Press, 1999.

Finally, I must thank my husband, Martin C. Needler, who constantly nurtures and refines my ideas and serves better than any computer as my punctuation-and-spell-check.

Fez, Morocco

Chapter 1

# Introduction: No Place to Call Home

*THE GREAT AMERICAN* poet Carl Sandburg once said that his least favorite word in the English language was "exclusive." Sandburg would have been most uncomfortable at this turn of the century, because exclusivity is among the hallmarks of the new global village. For ever growing numbers, citizenship has become a privilege rather than a right, and even those who are fortunate enough to claim citizenship somewhere can claim no right to make a living. The Third World nationalism of the sixties, invoked to build nations from the fragments of antagonistic tribes and language and religious groups, has given way in the 1990s to the state-wrecking nativism of the imploding Second World. Moreover, economic shocks and increasing income gaps — downsizing and outsourcing and burden-shifting — are deepening chasms among ethnic groups in nations old and new, of First World and Third, and in many countries tensions are further aggravated by the accelerating influx of immigrants and refugees.

Much of what constitutes the post-Cold War order — from revived tribalism and religious fundamentalism to spreading poverty and pestilence and the casual juxtaposition of beggars and kings — is as new as the nineteenth century. But some features of this new order, especially those associated with global togetherness, are truly new. I will seek in this book to highlight those features, to show how they relate to each other and to explore the obstacles and options they pose to those who would make the world a more hospitable place for people and other living things.

## Second-Coming Capitalism

The reigning and virtually unchallenged economic paradigm most commonly known as neoliberalism is indeed "neo" enough to have Adam Smith, the socially progressive father of nineteenth-century liberalism, fuming and sputtering in his grave. In its most extreme form, it relies on twenty-first-century technology and bureaucracy to re-impose nineteenth-century social relations.

I call this system Second-Coming Capitalism in that it represents the return of an older, Spencerian kind of capitalism that had been superseded, especially after World War II, by a socially more responsible, government-regulated, mixed economy with all-inclusive service and social welfare provisions. Moreover, fortified by technological breakthroughs, global reach, and concentration of economic power, it has returned in a more virulent form, like a bacterium that has developed resistance to antibiotics.

With Second-Coming Capitalism, I allude also to a comment attributed to President Reagan's first Secretary of the Interior, James Watt. Urged to preserve America's forests for the benefit of future generations, he allegedly said something like, "What's the point? The Second Coming of Christ might be any day." Translated into economic policy and corporate behavior, this means at the very least borrowing from future generations — allowing for a feeding frenzy with respect to production and consumption and depletion of scarce resources. It means, in other words, "There may be no tomorrow; get yours now!"

## The Unemployed State

Second-Coming Capitalism has a lot to say about what the state must not do — plan, regulate, tax, coddle — but says little about what ordinary voters and taxpayers may have hired the state to do. Thus, in much of the world, the state itself, whether built on conquest, on colonial legacy, or on some concept of ethnic apartheid, has lost its job. Whatever the inclinations of its leaders, the state is no longer able to carry out what was seen a few decades ago as its primary function — that of serving as the focus of popular sovereignty. That is, the state cannot protect its citizens from the vagaries of a global marketplace or give them a voice in the externally rendered decisions that seal their fate. Nor can it preserve for their use the essential life-sustaining resources of the national territory. Like the colonialists of centuries past, today's second-coming capitalists deplete, despoil, and depart. The only reliable guardians of any ecosystem are those who do not have the option of leaving.

The fragmentation that threatens the state from within is a response in part to the threat to the state from without — that of the denationalization, or out-sourcing, of economic decision making. Global concentration of economic power seems now to have the gravitational force of a black hole. Moreover, both the new nationalism and the new internationalism are exclusive. New states are being carved out as if by a cookie cutter. Ethnic minorities that don't fit are discarded like so much excess dough.

## A Cookie-Cutter World

One might have thought that the inspiration for a new world order at the turn of the twenty-first century would be the progressively integrating European Community. Instead the model appears to be that of Highland Papua New Guinea, where every valley has its own semi-autonomous *wontok* (one talk, or language group).

The most popular souvenir of the former Soviet Union, the matryoshka, the hollow wooden doll that has ever-smaller dolls within, now seems prophetic. The stripping away of the republics that constituted the Soviet Union may have been only the first step in the dissolution of the Russian Empire. In the Russian Republic itself, the costly and perhaps unfinished battle over Chechnya is only the most direct and most violent of many secessionist movements. Other non-Russian minorities, like the Tartars, have demanded states of their own. Meanwhile, irredentism persists in distinct regions of Georgia and Moldova, and in Latvia and Estonia, ethnic Russians and Poles alike face loss of citizenship.

We cannot be sure we have seen the end of the violent breakup of Yugoslavia, as each republic has minority settlements within it. Having freed themselves at such great cost of Serbian dominance, Croatians must now deal with the secessionist elements of their own Serbian minority. The people of Bosnia-Hercegovina have already paid a terrible price for their claim to statehood. We can hope that the worst of the "ethnic cleansing" among Serb, Croat, and Bosnian communities is now past, but short-sightedly self-serving policies on the part of local and distant political leaders are simply shifting the conflict farther South.

By peaceful means, Czechs and Slovaks have gone their separate ways. Monarchs-in-waiting, in casinos and spas along the Riviera, learn the languages of their ancestors and pray for a draft. In Europe, at least, the pace of national disintegration appeared to have slowed by the mid-1990s, but it may be too soon to send the map-makers home. Meanwhile capitalists returned from exile to homelands they scarcely knew to exchange hard currency for political office.

Back in the West, the secessionist movement in Northern California had been taken less seriously than it was meant, but America is by no means immune from the malaise of the nation-state system. The most serious secessionist movement in the United States is that of the rich. And the withdrawal of resources has left impoverished ethnic minorities to fight among themselves for the scraps.

The United States is in no immediate danger of fragmenting into regions or states. We are all carpetbaggers now. At the time of the last great depression, there was a sort of diaspora — out of the collapsing centers of industry and commerce and back to the homesteads of Tennessee or Texas or Iowa. That will not happen next time around; there are precious few homesteads to run to. But the society is fragmenting nonetheless, between heavily armed ghettoes and fortified suburbs, between those inside double-bolted doors and those left out on the street.

In the Third World, the failure of the nation-state is all too apparent: insurgency in the Andes, racial and communal strife in North Africa and South Asia, urban anarchy in the most rapidly modernizing countries, rural destitution in the most backward, and in some places — Somalia, Rwanda, and Albania, for example — all of the above. That is not to say that the contemporary nation-state system doesn't work — all systems work for somebody — but it certainly fails to protect the interests of ordinary people. Nevertheless, atomization into mini-states, even if it could take place without violence, would promise little relief. As everybody with a family tree to swing from faces off against everybody else, one is tempted to look beyond the disintegrating imperial states and the proliferating mini-states to something on the order of world federalism.

A couple of decades ago, I asked a distinguished professor of mine if a single world government might not be better than the anarchy of the nation-state system. "Perhaps," he said, "but where would the refugees go?"[1] That question becomes ever more urgent as people everywhere become more closely integrated into, and dependent upon, a global economic system over which they have no control — a system that uproots people and then discards them, and leaves ever more people competing for ever fewer jobs.

## A World of Refugees

I had occasion in the early 1990s to visit one of the camps in Hong Kong that warehoused Vietnamese boat-people. The Whitehead camp was no charitable operation; it was a high security detention center, run by the colony's corrections department, surrounded by barbed wire and spikes. The inmates, of both sexes and all ages, were guilty only of seeking refugee status — a status that most had already been denied. And this, mind you, was in British-ruled Hong Kong, *before* the much feared Chinese takeover. If a people are to be judged by the way they treat the most helpless among them, the plight of the Vietnamese boat-people and of other refugees does not speak well for civilization on the eve of the twenty-first century. For a number of reasons — famine, war, tyranny, economic disintegration — the ranks of refugees around the world are swelling rather than shrinking; and governments are becoming ever more hard-nosed about it. No part of the world is raising a torch and issuing an invitation, as the United States and other Western Hemisphere states once did to the "huddled masses" of Europe.

Europe itself now rejects at least 80 percent of its asylum applicants. After a half century of taunting the Soviet Union and its allies to "let their people go," West Europe now shrinks in horror as the floodgates open. Italy, a major exporter of people at the turn of the last century, found itself in the 1990s doing battle against thousands of Albanians fleeing their homeland. Borders were closing all over Europe in the early 1990s as hundreds of thousands of Bosnians sought refuge; and while East German thugs terrorized the refugees and foreign workers in their midst, West Germans, feeling overtaxed, seemed to be trying to figure out who to give East Germany back to.

The United States occasionally mustered outrage at the treatment of refugees elsewhere, but throughout the 1980s the US government detained Salvadorans, Guatemalans, and Haitians and shipped them back to their oppressors. More than twelve thousand Haitians were forcibly repatriated in the early 1990s on the claim that they were economic rather than political refugees, even though more than two thousand civilians had been killed by the military regime that toppled elected president Jean-Bertrand Aristide in 1991.

Perhaps the greatest show of cynicism on the part of the United States with respect to refugees has been the use of refugee camps and so-called humanitarian aid on the borders of Honduras and Nicaragua, Thailand and Cambodia, and Pakistan and Afghanistan to sustain guerrilla wars. Likewise, whether the United States wins or loses in its foreign crusades, it always seems surprised to find that the ethnic minorities it has co-opted and used as proxies (Meo tribesmen, for example, or more recently, Kurds) are among the losers — the homeless, stateless debris of war.

The Palestinian plight is only the most enduring example of mistreatment of the stateless and misappropriation of the refugee issue in the Middle East. Nor is the Asian record impressive. Japan still denies citizenship to native-born persons of Korean descent; and the Koreans have yet to reunite families divided at the 38th Parallel several wars ago. Apart from countries generating refugees and apart from refugees who can be used to strategic advantage, would-be receiving countries do not receive. Thailand for a time made a practice of dragging leaky boats bearing Vietnamese refugees back out to sea; and along with the other ASEAN states, it has turned a cold shoulder to the Burmese of the repressed democracy movement. Australia is in the process of establishing a new detention center for Vietnamese in the harsh desert outback.

Perhaps it should not be surprising that it has been the world's poorest countries, mostly African ones, that over the last decade have absorbed the greatest number of refugees. The richest countries seem inclined to stay that way by taking foreign money and resources in and keeping the people out. Even as the numbers of refugees grow — some sixteen million in the late 1990s, more than forty million counting the internally displaced and dispossessed — the funds available from public and private sources for relief and resettlement are dropping off sharply; and national policies with respect to immigration or even temporary residence are becoming ever more restrictive.

## Comparative Disadvantage

Those fortunate enough, however, to be citizens of temporarily rich countries should not be lulled into a sense of security. What First World peoples increasingly have in common with those of the Third World is vulnerability. Most people in most countries, of First World or Third, are entirely dependent for their livelihoods on decisions made in faraway places in accordance with the needs of capital, not of labor. And that capital is eminently mobile, while labor is not. Jobs may vanish, as men and women are replaced by machines, or they may move halfway around the world in search of lower wages or taxes, leaving entire communities devastated. The same forces that for the money-movers dictate comparative advantage leave the rest of us with comparative disadvantage — the inability to produce what we would consume or to consume what we produce.

Governments, even popular ones — no, particularly popular ones — seem as helpless as their constituents to interfere with the mechanisms and maneuvers of the free-wheeling global money market. In late 1998, stunned by the ongoing reverberations of the year-old Asian crisis, world leaders finally took note of the destabilization wrought by unregulated hot money — portfolio investment, currency speculation, hedge funds — upon financial markets. But such leaders have yet to take note of the destabilization so wrought downmarket, upon families and communities.

As capital whips around the world at the speed of sound, job-seekers have no choice but to try to follow. To the extent that workers are able to chase after capital, however, they do so bereft of the rights of participation associated with citizenship. As "guest-workers" or worse yet—"illegal aliens," or political or economic refugees — they are not likely to be able to vote, or to organize politically or bargain collectively, and all too often they are exploited and abused.

Even where capital carves out a temporary home in the Third Word, it is likely now to be in an export-processing zone where capital enjoys a sort of extra-territoriality — beyond the reach ordinarily of union organizers and tax collectors, and unavailable for forward or backward linkages to stimulate other sectors of the local economy. In these zones of *maquiladora* industries, workers may become "guest-workers" in their own countries.

## New Venues for the Homelands Policy

After more than a decade of deterioration almost everywhere in the terms of exchange for labor, it is as if the homelands policies finally being abandoned in South Africa were coming to characterize the global system. Afrikaner leaders had maintained that they were not denying civil rights and political participation to Black citizens, because those Blacks who worked in South Africa's cities and mines and lived in outlying townships and work camps were actually citizens of some distant and resource-free homeland.

Like selective citizenship, residential segregation in First World as well as Third has become so pronounced that whole towns become "servant quarters," in effect, for more affluent neighboring ones. And based on income rather than racial or ethnic exclusivity, such segregation encounters little opposition. Visiting one of the havens in Connecticut for money collected in New York and earned in Bangkok or Bangladesh, I was told that the major local issue was whether or not to subsidize housing for teachers, as they could not afford to live within a reasonable commute of the schools.

Gated and guarded communities become ever more common in the US, as elsewhere. On South Carolina's Hilton Head Island, only the highway is public. Those who work in the island's resort and retirement villages are bussed through the guarded gates in the morning and out in the evening.

One of the very positive developments of the last several years has been the spread of democracy — or at least of the institutions and rituals that have come to be associated with it; but this is happening in part because economic interests are less threatened now than they were two or three decades ago by the formal processes of democracy. That is, global concentration of economic power is such that elected leaders have very little latitude in economic policy-making anyway; and elite interests are well served by allowing elected governments to absorb the blame for policies punishing to the poor.

## The Globalization of the Cargo Cult

Though the ruling elite of the world system have assumed no formal structure and adopted no single site, it appears that we are very close now to having a single world government, at least for the essential roles of economic policy-making. If rule-making processes are as yet indiscernible, the administrative ones have clearly been delegated to the international financial institutions, with the International Monetary Fund (IMF) assuming the most visible role. Whatever its creed or constituency, no indebted government — and most are now deeply indebted — dares to defy the IMF, because a state can be stripped of capital as if by thieves in the night.

The same kinds of leverage are increasingly applied to governments beneath the nation-state level, as is abundantly clear now in the United States. While the bankruptcy of the US federal government may be obscured indefinitely by military and corrections-system Keynesianism and by a range of taxing and borrowing options, the vulnerability — even desperation — of US state and local governments is ever more apparent. Along with national and local governments in Africa, Asia, and Latin America, state and local governments in the United States have fallen back on a modernized version of the "cargo cult."

In the manner of South Pacific islanders exposed suddenly to modern air transport and conspicuous consumption, they build landing strips in hopes that riches of exotic origin will come to rest on their turf. And along with ever more elaborate landing strips, enticements include golf courses, industrial parks, tax holidays, and suppressed wages. Some local governments have even become desperate enough to compete for disposal sites for people and things – i.e., prisons and toxic waste dumps. Despite rhetorical and ritual nods to self-help, such a "race to the bottom" development strategy promotes and rewards the skills of hustlers and punishes precisely those who would empower local communities to set their own goals and use their own ingenuity to build from the bottom up.

## Austerity: The Solution or the Problem?

In public affairs, it seems that the easiest way to solve a problem is to redefine it. When the international financial institutions were created at the close of World War II, austerity, or doing without, was seen as the problem to be overcome; now it is being touted as the solution.

The IMF and the creditors it represents have insisted that a government, to pass their test of creditworthiness, must be "structurally adjusted" to run like a business; that has meant underpaying workers and overcharging consumers and taxpayers in order to generate maximum profits and privileges for a few. And while government is run like a business, business is run like a war — e.g. "we had to destroy this village in order to save it." The larger banks and corporations feed insatiable appetites by consuming the smaller ones — stripping assets and downsizing employees in order to channel even more capital in the short term into dividends and CEO bonuses and perks.

Austerity, as a debt service strategy, has usually meant lower wages and longer working hours, higher prices and interest rates, fewer subsidies and services, less protection of domestic enterprises and less regulation of foreign ones, greater emphasis on export promotion, currency devaluation, and a fire sale of public assets. It stands to reason that the working or would-be working classes who saw no benefits from the foreign loans are the ones who are obliged, through their sacrifices, to service the debt. If the state-holding classes who borrowed and spent the money actually had to pay it back with interest themselves, the game would surely grind to a halt.

One "business-like" measure that has been promoted universally has been privatization. At the same time that prospective tax revenues are lifted off by speed-of-sound capital flight, governments are stripped of the services that potentially pay for themselves and left with empty coffers and unmeetable needs. But privatization of gains is only half of an equation — a hybrid of Eastern and Western economic models — the other half of which is socialization of losses. "Risk" capital, invested first in political campaigns, runs no risk thereafter, as bad private investments become public debt.

Privatization extends to politics as well. Parties and popular movements with platforms and programs, or at least public policy goals, are being replaced by pollsters and image-makers and media czars, and the value of elections appears to be inversely related to their costs. The privatization of politics serves to reinforce the unemployment of the state. In the immediate post-World War II period, when scholars were laying out rationales for the public underwriting of private overseas investment, it was argued that democracy would mitigate the extremes of free-market distribution; now it is argued, or at least implied, that the requirements of the free market must temper the extremes of democracy.

## Buddy, Can You Paradigm?[2]

The First World rationales of the mid-century postwar period were soon overtaken and discredited by events. Far from mitigating an increasingly transnational brand of capitalism, democracy in much of the Third World was obliterated by it. In the shadow of crushing counterrevolution, scholars from some of the best Latin American universities elaborated a development paradigm of their own, featuring economic nationalism, that came to be widely adopted throughout the Third World.

Much has changed in the decades since. Third World leaders had been gaining voice for a time in the 1960s and 1970s, and Third World movements were gaining momentum; but in the 1980s First World interests, those with the most to gain or the most to lose materially in Third World operations, rebounded with great force. Where the disadvantaged had mobilized in pursuit of structural change, the advantaged struck back with structural adjustment. Development perceived as maximizing production has taken an awful toll on the environment. Abrupt shifts of national boundaries, trade patterns, and investment capital have left millions on the move or at the mercy of foreigners, creating new categories of the deprived and displaced. The economic shocks that devastated Africa and the Western Hemisphere in the 1980s, Eastern and Central Europe and Eurasia in the early 1990s, and East and Southeast Asia in the late 1990s, with reverberations in "emerging markets" on every continent, threaten to reverse recent democratic gains and continually to deepen class and ethnic antagonisms around the world.

The Cold War rationale for the containment of social action has been swept away, but so has the only development model that promised social equity. What was once a dialogue between North and South has become a monologue in which the nature of participation is determined less by region than by function in a global economic system, but one in which most people, whether from North or South, have no audible voice. The evangelists of globalization gained market monopoly with the doctrine of market infallibility and with the conviction that full global integration of markets was not only universally beneficial but also inevitable and inescapable. There was no alternative, no opting out.

Whatever else might be required to transform this brave new world order, it is clear that one requirement will be a revolutionary new paradigm in the social sciences. Such a paradigm must shun the East European-style "workers' state," which pits the same people as workers against themselves as consumers. But it also must shun the US model of each against all, of the individual against society. It cannot rely on economic nationalism in a world so interdependent and one in which nationalism too easily dissolves into ethnic slaughter, but neither can it be internationalist in the traditional sense, in which people expect national governments to represent their interests.

Above all, the new paradigm will have to devise a means whereby popular organizations can spread across borders, bypassing the "receivership"[3] apparatus of the state to confront global economic power with global people power. Meanwhile, people who have lost all else may come to find strength and security in their commitment to each other. To the extent that national governments turn their backs on their own people, local governments and communities have no choice but to take up the slack. And as material resources shrink, communities can and must begin to turn obstacles into assets. While the global village can afford to waste and discard people, the local village cannot. Those who have been marginalized — prevented from fulfilling their full potential — because they were too young or too old, or of the wrong gender or color or religion or nationality, must be liberated from alienation or dependence and empowered to contribute to community well-being. At any rate, if exclusivity has become the watchword of national and international power systems, then it is from the grassroots that the ideal of inclusiveness must spring again.

## Notes

1. Professor Ted Couloumbis, then of the School of International Service, American University, Washington, D.C., more recently of the University of Athens.
2. This expression is borrowed from Professor Emeritus I. L. Claude of the University of Virginia.
3. The term is borrowed from Professor Jorge Nef of the University of Guelph, Ontario, Canada.

# Chapter 2

# Marketing Snake Oil and Theory

*The size of the market for snake oil depends on the size of the snake peddling it.**

*Among the things that "have-nots" have not is a public forum.*

*ARCHEOLOGISTS DISCOVERED* long ago that the most promising place to dig for the major temple of a particular era was directly beneath the major temple of the subsequent era. Consecutive waves of conquerors have chosen to construct the sacred places of their new civilization directly over the ruins of the old. Is it any wonder, then, that in the heart of so many of the sacred sites and best-preserved historic districts around the world, one finds the golden arches of McDonald's hamburgers. McDonald's now has establishments in more than one hundred countries, an empire that would have been the envy of Genghis Khan.

For those who would understand and/or promote international development, the end of the twentieth century must be seen as both the best of times and the worst of times. The United Nations Development Programme (UNDP) reported in 1997 that poverty has fallen more in the past fifty years than it had in the previous five hundred. Life expectancy and infant mortality rates have improved markedly over the past quarter century, largely as a consequence of the spread of modern medical and sanitation practices. Child death rates in developing countries have been cut in half since 1960 and malnutri-

* The epigrams opening chapters and parts are by the author, drawn from "Black's Laws of Public Affairs and Paradoxes of Development," an ever-growing list begun in 1982. A list of 243 laws and paradoxes appears in J. Black, *Development in Theory and Practice: Paradigms and Paradoxes* (Boulder: Westview Press, 1999).

tion rates have declined by almost one-third. It is estimated that oral dehydration therapy alone saves more than a million children annually and perhaps a few million more have been protected by inoculation from a variety of diseases.

The International Food Policy Research Institute reported that food production increased on average 2.6 percent each year between 1961 and 1985 while annual world population growth dropped from a high of about 2 percent in the early 1960s to 1.6 percent in the mid-1980s. UNDP figures show an increase in per capita food production in developing countries of 22 percent between 1980 and 1997, despite a 3 percent decline in Sub-Saharan Africa. Meanwhile, human fertility rates had fallen over the last quarter of the twentieth century by 40 percent. The proportion of children in the developing countries who were underweight declined from 41 percent in 1975 to 22 percent in 1996. UNICEF (United Nation's Children's Fund) has seen increases in school enrollment — from less than 40 percent of school age children in the 1950s to some 70 percent in the mid-1980s — as one of the greatest achievements in the developing world. Literacy rates reportedly continued their climb as well. Between 1970 and 1995 the worldwide adult illiteracy rate was nearly cut in half, from 57 percent to 30 percent.

## Development's Mixed Message

Juxtaposed with such indicators of progress are equally well-established indicators of retrogression. Some of these indicators represent the negative effects of indisputably worthwhile endeavors. Overpopulation, for example, owes much to the spreading benefits of modern medicine. Others, like rural landlessness and urban unemployment, are attributable to long-term trends, like the spread of export-oriented agribusiness and capital-intensive technology, that have been beneficial to some and damaging to a great many others. And finally, there are shorter term trends, like international capital flows, that turned extremely disadvantageous for Third World countries in general and the Third World poor in particular in the 1980s.

Much of the bad news at the beginning of the 1990s had to do with economic growth trends that, having been positive for most of the previous twenty to thirty years, turned sharply negative in the 1980s. World GDP growth rates dropped in the late 1980s, from 4.3 percent in 1988 to 3.0 percent in 1989 to 1.0 percent in 1990.[1] During the last half of the 1980s in Latin America and the Caribbean, Africa, and much of Asia, foreign aid and new loans and investments did not begin to compensate for the amounts flowing, as debt service payments, from those areas into the coffers of First World banks. The terms of trade for traditional Third World products also declined sharply. Commodity prices worldwide plummeted in the 1980s and GDP dropped by 8 percent during the decade in Latin America and by 20 percent in Africa.[2]

The US Agency for International Development (USAID) reported that 70 percent of the world's ninety-five least developed countries suffered overall economic decline in the 1980s. Faltering growth rates meant falling wages and rising unemployment. In times of economic decline, the affluent are far better able to defend their share of income and assets, so the belts that are tightened will be those already around the narrowest waists. Such belt-tightening normally takes the forms not only of wage freezes, layoffs, and foreclosures, but also of cutbacks in subsidies and services and protections for workers and consumers. UNICEF reported that the world's thirty-six poorest countries slashed budgets for education and health by 25 percent and 50 percent, respectively, during the last half of the 1980s. Food production also fell in most of those countries. Infant mortality worsened in two-thirds of them. Overall life expectancy declined in a few, and diseases thought to have been eradicated, like smallpox and polio, reappeared.[3] Changes consistent throughout most of the world in budget priorities and other areas of economic policy left no doubt that the debts incurred in the 1970s, in many cases by military dictatorships, were being serviced in the 1980s by the classes and sectors that benefited least from the loans.

What is one to conclude from such seeming discrepancies with respect to progress and retrogression, apart from the fact that one can "prove" anything one wishes with statistics? How should we explain aggregate data showing long-term gains but short-term losses, increasing production but also increasing hunger, increasing educational levels for increasingly unemployed work forces? It may be that standards of living are improving for the majority of the world's population over the long term, although that remains subject to dispute on various grounds, subject most decidedly to some means of coming to terms with the contradiction between ecological limitations and the production and consumption requisites of an economic growth model, and subject finally to policy decisions yet to be made. At any rate, the short term is the term we live in, and, in the short term, living standards are definitely intolerable for a growing absolute number in the Third World, and since the 1980s, in the First World as well.

Economic recovery between 1987 and 1993 was such as to register, in accordance with World Bank criteria, a decline from 34 percent to 32 percent in the proportion of the people in developing countries living in income poverty. However, it is estimated that the actual number of income-poor people increased by almost 100 million during that period from 1.2 billion to 1.3 billion, and the number appeared to be growing in every region except Southeast Asia and the Pacific. According to the human development index drawn up by the UNDP, living standards declined more in thirty countries in 1996–97 than in any other year since the UNDP's *Human Development Report* was first issued in 1990. The average incidence of income poverty for Eastern Europe and the offspring states of the Soviet Union increased sevenfold between 1988 and 1994, from 4.7 percent to 32 percent. The number of people in the region who had become impoverished increased from 14 million to more than 119 million. Oxfam, one of the major international relief and development agencies, maintains that in cereal grains alone, the world food supply offers 2,200 calories per person per day; yet more than 840 million people are chronically hungry.

## Progress on a Zig-Zag Course

Advances in living standards since the dawn of the industrial revolution have not followed a steady course, nor have they been uniform across geographic and cultural regions. Advances in some areas have come at the expense of decline in others — in colonial or neocolonial centers, for example, at the expense of colonized or client states. And periods of progress have been interspersed with periods of retrogression, consequent not only to the creation of wealth through technologically more efficient exploitation of material and human resources but also to development of social and political mechanisms for equitable allocation of responsibility and benefit. The distribution of progress and retreat in poverty reduction across time and region during the second half of the twentieth century is represented in Figure 2.1 at right.

Following on the widespread, and in some regions very deep, recession of the 1980s, the 1990s have appeared to most analysts (and more important, to creditors and investors) to be a decade of recovery. In fact, growth in some regions and countries had been dramatic enough to inspire talk of economic miracles and to cause creditors and others in a position to set conditions and exercise leverage over state policy to insist on a uniform set of policy changes generally known as economic restructuring or structural adjustment. The miracles were gushers of foreign currency coming in as bankrupt governments staged going-out-of-business sales. It might have been guessed that if the prescriptions were the same (i.e., bleeding) for countries whose ills were as diverse as those of Haiti, Mexico, Russia, and South Korea, the needs being met were not those of the patients but rather of the doctors.

Such restructuring is designed to attract capital as credit or investment. As countries, all undergoing the same process, compete for capital, obligations and offerings to creditors take precedence over obligations to domestic constituencies. These policy changes, which have had the effect of shifting costs downward on the social pyramid and benefits upward and outward, to foreign stakeholders, have sharply increased the already growing wealth and income gaps between regions and countries and within them.

In 1994, the ratio of the income of the wealthiest 20 percent of the world population to that of the poorest 20 percent was 78 to 1, up from 30 to 1 in 1960. Globally, the number of billionaires increased between 1989 and 1996 from 157 to 447. The net worth of the world's ten wealthiest individuals amounts to more than 1.5 times the total national income of all of the least

FIGURE 2.1: Progress and Setbacks in Income Poverty Reduction Since 1950

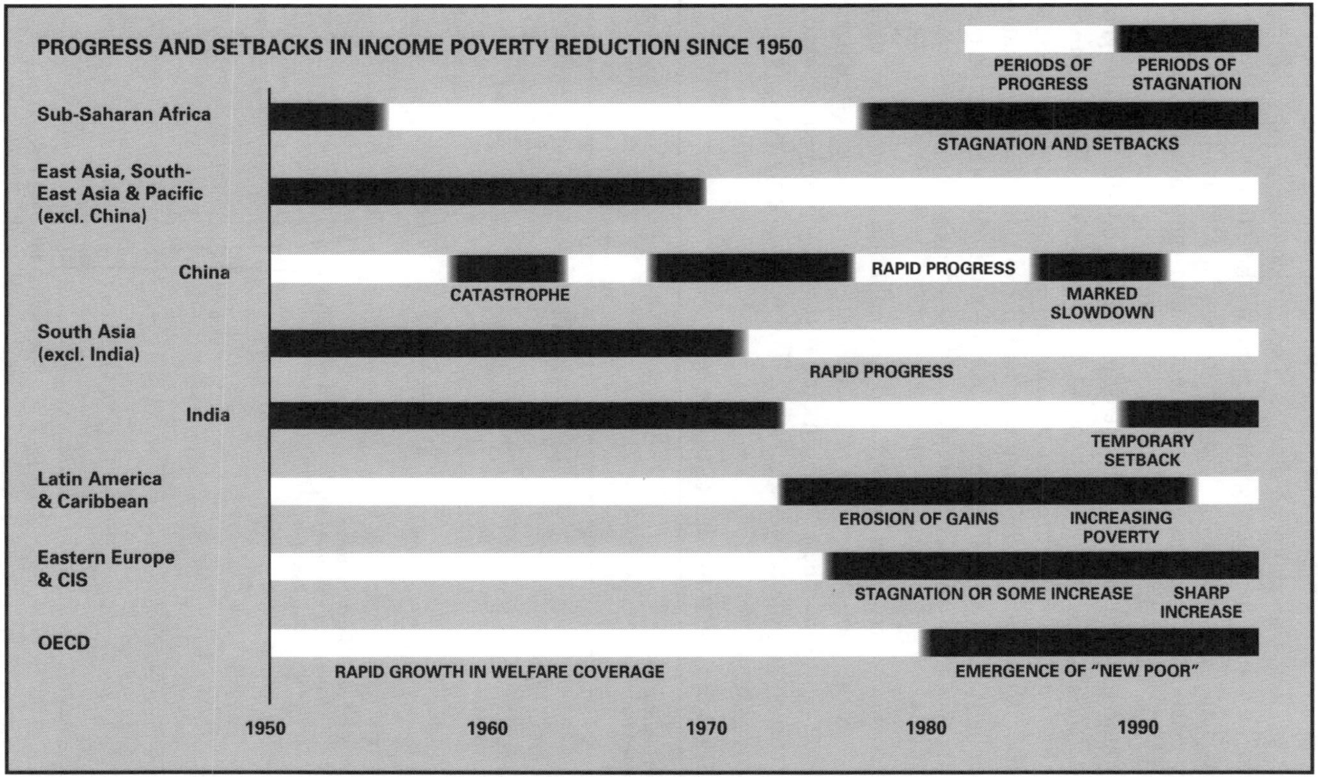


*Source: Human Development Report 1997*. Copyright © 1997 by the United Nations Development Programme. Used by permission of Oxford University Press, Inc.

developed countries, as designated by the UNDP. In Mexico, where in the late 1980s and early 1990s economic miracles alternated with economic meltdowns, the holdings of the richest individual among many new billionaires is equal to the combined income of seventeen million poor Mexicans.[4]

Nor was such income disparity limited to the Third World. Pockets of poverty had been growing in the developed world as well since the early 1980s, particularly in the United Kingdom and the United States. By the early 1990s more than 100 million people in the industrialized countries were found to be income poor. In the United States, one-fifth of the aged and one-fourth of the children live beneath the poverty line. The boom of the 1990s had come largely at the expense of workers, most of whom were earning less in real wages in 1997 than they had in 1989. In fact, wages had been essentially flat in the US since the 1970s. The minimum wage bought less in 1998 that in 1968 and fewer employees had adequate health insurance or pensions [5]

Income poverty is generally found in combination with other deprivations, since the poor are less able to defend their rights to services, to personal security, even to the "best things in life" that we used to believe were free, like relatively unpolluted air and water. The water supply per capita in de-

FIGURE 2.2: Global Income Distribution

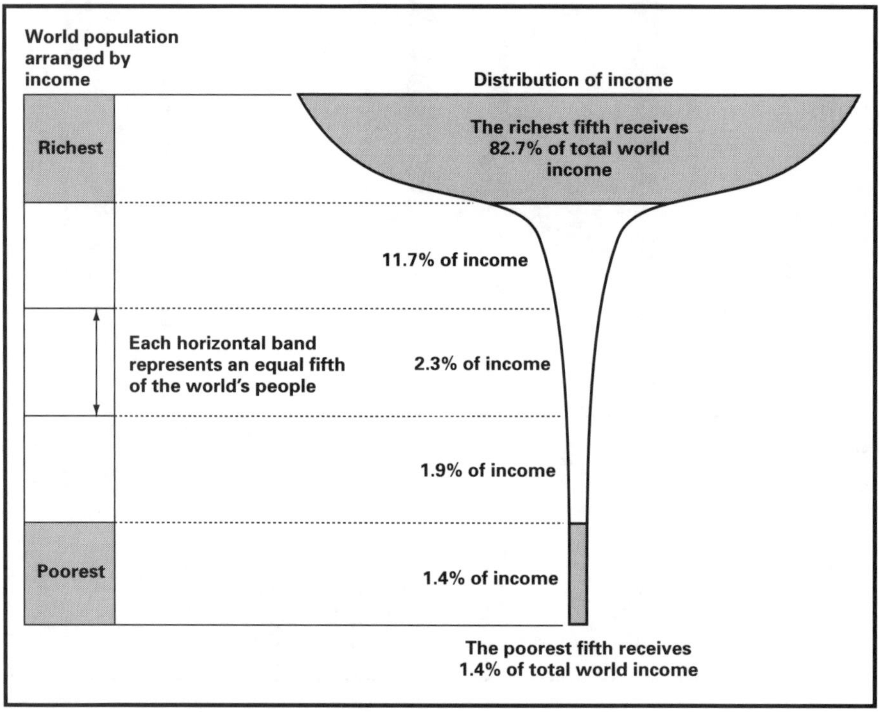


*Source: Human Development Report 1992.* Copyright © 1993 by the United Nations Development Programme. Used by permission of Oxford University Press, Inc.

veloping countries is only a third in the late 1990s of what it was in 1970, and 40 percent in those countries lack proper sanitation.

More than a billion people in the Third World lack adequate shelter, and worldwide it is estimated that 100 million are homeless. In New York City alone, 250,000 people have sought public shelter at some time in the past five years.[6] Education and health care are among the services that have suffered from recent changes in the dominant economic model. Between 1990 and 1993, Zambia spent thirty-five times as much on debt payment as it did on education.[7] In developing countries, seventeen million people die each year from curable infections and parasite diseases. HIV/AIDS afflicts another twenty-three million, fourteen million of them in Sub-Saharan Africa, where half the population lacks access to medical services. In the United States, where more money is spent on health care than in any other country, more than forty-seven million people are effectively denied care as they lack health insurance.

Worldwide, some 800 million people lack access to health care. Many, especially in Eastern Europe and the offspring states of the Soviet Union, are newly deprived. Malnutrition and premature deaths of both children and adults are on the rise. In the Ukraine average daily caloric intake dropped precipitously from about 3,500 in 1989 to 2,800 in 1994. By 1996, the new Moscow stock market was up 150 percent, making it one of the world's most attractive emerging markets.[8] (That was before it crashed in 1998). But new cases of diphtheria among Russian children had increased twenty-nine-fold, from five hundred in 1989 to fifteen thousand in 1993. Cases of orphaned or abandoned children were also rising steeply. Children were entering the orphanages at the rate of 30,000 a year, amounting to 160,000 institutionalized by 1998.

School enrollment rates have dropped in that region and violent crime, on the rise almost everywhere in the past two decades, has increased even faster there. Crime rates have tripled, for example, since 1989 in Hungary and the Czech Republic.[9] Rising crime in turn means rising demand for police and prisons, which are even more costly than teachers and schools with which they compete for funds from shrinking public budgets. Since 1994, the United States has had more than a million people in its prisons, the highest per capita rate of any industrialized country. The American Association of State Colleges and Universities reports a five hundred-dollar-per-student decline between 1980 and 1995 in state appropriations for public universities and colleges, largely a result of increased state costs for prisons and health care.

## The Bursting Bubble Boomerang

From the mid-1980s to the mid-1990s, the model held up to the rest of the world by public and private international financial institutions and other economic pacesetters was that of the East Asian tigers and their Southeast Asian cubs. The model was that of export-led growth, said to owe its success in large measure to liberalization and deregulation. In fact, the tigers had based their export industries on domestic markets that were well-grounded and protected by extensive government regulation.

It was not until the economic meltdown of 1997 was well underway and many governments had been reduced to desperation that foreign creditors, foreign investors, and the IMF were able to get the degree of openness — that is, the freedom from oversight and regulation — that they sought. But major measures of liberalization in the mid 1990s brought an influx of foreign capital, including fickle portfolio investment. Crisis, it turns out, is not a product of too little foreign investment, but of too much. When it became clear that some of these economies were overheated, that credit was overextended, with foreign debt outstripping service capacity, fickle foreign money took flight, leaving local currencies exposed to speculative pressure.

The meltdown that was soon to pull under a whole region of export-oriented and thus highly interdependent economies began with the devaluation of the Thai baht in mid-1997. The contagion of capital flight, currency devaluation, and crashing markets spread quickly to South Korea, Indonesia, Malaysia, and Hong Kong, and all too soon to less exposed but still vulnerable Japan.

In the months following the Thai devaluation, some $110 billion, by World Bank estimates, drained out of the four countries most severely damaged by the crisis. Over a two-year period leading to the fall of 1998, the South Korean economy had shrunk by 45 percent, that of Thailand by 50 percent, and that of Indonesia by almost 80 percent.

Asian trade amounts to about one-third of global trade. It would be naïve to imagine that an Asian crisis could somehow be geographically contained. In fact, hot money jitters ricocheted to other emerging markets in fall 1998, draining banks and stock markets in Russia, Turkey, Brazil and South Africa. The crisis even caused gyrations and tense moments on Wall Street. In the aftermath, both London's *Financial Times* and the *Neue Zürcher Zeitung,* voice of the Swiss banking system, called for controls on the movement of capital.

The Chinese had been saved from the worst fallout of the crisis by a healthy disregard for Western financial advice, but there was fear in the West that the competitive devaluations in their neighborhood might tempt the Chinese to devalue as well. It had begun to dawn on Western makers and enforcers of financial policy that now that they were invested everywhere, the continual deflation of non-Western currencies and economies might not always serve their interests, particularly when, as in the case of China, it was not clear where the bottom might be.

Jeffrey Sachs, the intellectual father of shock therapy, had already disavowed some aspects of it and, along with Milton Friedman, joined the chorus calling for reform of the IMF. As Japan's recession deepened, previously unyielding enforcers of monetarism were urging Japanese leaders to adopt Keynesian strategies for reflating the economy. In fact, leaders everywhere had come to see that the current system is dangerously volatile.

There was optimism in some quarters that resurgent regionalism might begin to crosscut rather than to reinforce global instability in trade and finance. Some European leaders were beginning to resist the pressures of the money movers; and the awarding of the Nobel Prize in economics in 1998 to Amartya Sen, whose work has highlighted maldistribution and unfairness, argued well for a major paradigm shift. But it is not clear that those seeking to protect their own investments will come to understand that a stable system calls for confident consumers and, by extension, regularly paid employees. Income insecurity and inequality are not moral issues only; they are major sources of economic disequilibrium.

The UN-affiliated International Labor Organization reported in 1998 that a record one billion people, one-third of the global workforce, were unemployed or underemployed. This was in large measure a consequence of the Asian meltdown and its spreading reverberations; but it also reflected a sharp deterioration in the 1990s in employment levels and wages throughout the former Soviet sphere (excepting Hungary and the Czech Republic) and increased levels of unemployment even in Europe. More generally, it reflects a short-term profit-centered interpretation of productivity and efficiency that dictates continual downsizing to the point of dumbsizing — in which there are too few employees to get the job done.

## A Failure of System or of Theory?

What, then, has gone wrong, and what is to be done? It might be argued that attention to the problem has been insufficient, but the body of literature on Third World development has been growing exponentially for several decades. It has been argued, on the one hand, that the Third World suffers from too little modernization and, on the other, that it suffers from too much modernization. Certainly some of the ideas, institutions, and technologies diffused from the centers of industrialization to less developed states and areas have been beneficial, appropriate, and sustainable while others have not.

It has been argued that deteriorating terms of trade for primary products was the major problem, but an increasing infusion of manufactured products into the export mix of a number of Third World countries has not necessarily enhanced their bargaining positions or their trade and payments balances. It has been argued that the main problem was a simple lack of capital, but a surfeit of capital flowing from North to South in the 1970s and early 1980s became the prelude for a voluminous current in the other direction. The poorest nations continue to pay more to the multilateral financial institutions — not to mention to private creditors — than they are receiving in aid, and their interest payments alone exceed expenditure on health and education.

US development assistance has been shrinking fairly steadily since mid-century, both in absolute terms and as a percentage of GNP. Nevertheless, overall disbursements of official development assistance (mainly from Japan, Canada, and Western Europe) increased steadily until the 1990s. Assistance from the twenty-one richest nations amounted to more than $55 billion in 1996, though in 1997 that figure dropped to $47 billion, or 0.25 percent of combined GDP, proportionally an all-time low. Aid from multilateral and nongovernmental sources has grown steadily, adding perhaps another $40 billion annually to the total. And both official and nongovernmental agencies as well as community-level popular organizations in recipient or client states have proliferated. Why, then, do the prospects for Third World development, for the shrinkage of poverty and of income gaps, look so dismal at the close of the twentieth century?

Even the World Bank, after almost two decades of using credit to leverage policy changes disadvantageous to the poor and crippling of essential government services, has begun to sound repentant. At its annual conference in June 1997 in Montevideo, bank Vice President Shahid Burki called for reducing the gap between rich and poor, combating unemployment, and increasing public investment in health and education. World Bank President James Wolfensohn, opening the annual joint meeting of the World Bank and the International Monetary Fund in October 1997, called for giving top priority to reducing global inequity, both within and between countries. "The challenge of inclusion," he said, "is the key development challenge of our time."[10] Likewise, the Inter-American Development Bank (IDB) in its annual report for 1996 noted that the benefits of globalization have been unevenly distributed. See Figure 2.3 at right.

How are we to explain such a disappointing outcome at this juncture of an enormous international development effort? Should we attribute it to 1) failures? 2) lies? 3) discontinuity between motives and outcomes? 4) factors external to the development effort? The answer, of course, as will be explored in the ensuing chapters, is all of the above and more. But it should be borne in mind that there is no such thing as a system that doesn't work. All systems work for somebody. (Otherwise they would cease to be.) Perhaps what is not working here is theory.

## The Emergence of a Development Dialogue

The process of development — by any definition — might be judged timeless, but the "business" of development, as we know it in the late twentieth century, is in large part an outgrowth of the exaggerated skewing of world resources in the aftermath of World War II. The fact that, as George Kennan, intellectual father of US "containment policy," noted, the United States had about 50 percent of the world's resources and only 3.6 percent of the world's population made "security" (maintaining the disparity) the overriding concern. Moreover, the devastation of Europe had left the United States without trading partners. Such concerns dictated not only the nature and objectives of development assistance, but even the operative definition of development itself. Where big bureaucracies and major investments were to be involved, development would be seen almost exclusively in terms of the use of resources, including people, in the pursuit of material production and economic growth rather than, for example, the regeneration of resources and the cultivation of local self-sufficiency for peoples previously rendered dependent.

The earliest and most massive disbursement of US aid, then, was for the

**FIGURE 2.3: Uneven Effects of Globalization**

UNEVEN EFFECTS OF GLOBALIZATION
*Policymakers face challenge of ensuring equity*

| WINNERS | LOSERS |
|---|---|
| East, S.E. Asia | Africa, Latin America |
| Productive output | Employment |
| People with assets | People with no assets |
| Profits | Wages |
| Skilled workers | Unskilled workers |
| Adaptive firms, workers | Rigid firms, workers |
| Techno-specialists | Primary producers |
| Creditors | Debtors |
| Those not dependent on public services | Those dependent on public services |
| Large companies | Small companies |
| Men | Women |
| International markets | Local communities |
| Global culture | Local culture |

*Source: Inter-American Development Bank Annual Report 1996* (Washington, D.C.: Inter-American Development Bank, 1996).

reconstruction of Europe. Subsequently, the US expanded its horizons, offering to Latin America and to African and Asian states then emerging from colonialism less in the way of resources but a great deal more in the way of advice. Development aid for the Third World came wrapped in the assumption that underdevelopment would be erased if the poor and tradition-bound were to embrace Western technology and entrepreneurialism.

In time, the European and other industrialized countries joined and surpassed the United States as donors of aid. They have generally shown less concern over security issues, but equal concern for promoting trade and investment opportunities for their own nationals. In the meantime, however, a community of development scholars and practitioners had come into being, many of whom had worked at the grassroots level and had their own notions of what development is, or should be, about. There was also a mushrooming throughout the world of locally based popular organizations, pursuing their own interests.

To many of these non-governmental organizations (NGOs), development came to mean empowerment — the generation of skills, of individual and collective self-confidence, and of effective, locally based, problem-solving techniques. They found that development, to be meaningful to the disadvantaged majority, must encompass equity as well as accumulation, choices and opportunity as well as occupation and sustenance, a sense of self-worth and dignity as well as national pride, and some degree of control over personal, community, and national destinies.

For a time, particularly in the 1960s and 1970s, the needs of the disadvantaged in the Third World appeared to coincide with those of would-be nation-builders and of national capitalists who sought protection from transnational competitors. That coincidence of interests constructed a forum for those in academia as well as in government and non-governmental development agencies who took exception to the prevailing paradigm.

Dependency theory, springing from the most developed of the Latin American states but spreading to other Third World regions, particularly where industrialization was making headway, was based on assumptions directly challenging to those of First World architects and purveyors of development policy. Among them: Causes of underdevelopment are not found in national systems alone, but rather in economic relationships between dominant and dependent states. Both within and among states an unregulated market tends to exacerbate existing inequalities.

World systems theory, like dependency and its European-based forefather, Marxism, rejected the idea that what is good for the goose is necessarily good for the gander. It focused, however, on transnational private sector strategies and economic centers rather than on government policy and political metropoles. Long before post-Cold War globalization made it so readily apparent, world systems theory pioneer Immanuel Wallerstein argued that the essential struggle was not between rich and poor states but rather between rich and poor classes in a global society.[11]

Such contrarian theories (theories countering those of the most powerful states and economic interests) began to lose their Third World patrons with the military counterrevolutions of the sixties and seventies and were further disabled by the depression of the 1980s, but the collapse of socialist regimes that signaled the end of the Cold War was their coup de grâce. Right too late or too soon, the prophets who warned of resource and policy denationalization and of the globalization of systematized inequality were left without defensible turf from which to take a stand.

## Unconditional Surrender and Paradigmatic Monopoly

With the collapse of the Soviet Union and of what passed for socialism elsewhere, US Cold Warriors were quick to claim victory. The winner in this case, however, was not a country or set of countries, but an economic system complete with its ruling elite, its legitimating myths, and its high priesthood.[12] That system was not just capitalism, but what I have designated second-coming capitalism — a socially pre-modern version bulwarked by postmodern technology.

Second-Coming Capitalism, emerging triumphant, has demanded unconditional surrender, not just of socialism in its extreme forms but also of most traces of popular participation in economic decision making — of the many variations of state planning and regulation, state-run enterprise and protected domestic industry and of social services and benefits and other elements of the welfare state — products of more than a half century of political development engineered by national governments. And surrender has generally been forthcoming. It seems that no array of weapons has been quite as threatening to governments as the trillion dollars sloshing around, changing hands every day in global currency markets, beyond the control of any government. Every currency is thus left vulnerable to speculative manipulation. Capital operates in a sellers' market, with fixed conditions as to its availability, and governments are forced to compete for its favors.

Such globalization of economic power and planning has meant also a level of hegemony in the realm of ideas unprecedented perhaps since the era of scholasticism. It is not in spite of the importance of a general development paradigm or of the serious implications of the growing gap, but rather because of them that most literature on the subject remains so arid, so nearly devoid of debate. That is not to say that there is no dissidence or heresy. So long as there have been spokesmen of the "haves" proclaiming that trends and policies in their interests were in the interest also of "have-nots," there have been defenders of the "have-nots" having the nerve to say "not so." But one of the things the "have-nots" have not in times like these is a forum.

It has commonly been argued that wealth and income gaps are not problems in themselves so long as the losses of the poor are in relative terms only, not in absolute ones. But at least since Aristotle, political scientists have been pointing out that political power and the distribution of wealth are interdependent. As power is relational, a relative loss of income means an absolute loss of power, and an ever more uphill struggle for the deprived and oppressed, of First World and Third, in the pursuit of effective participation and social justice.

The ever-increasing concentration of economic power includes, as Noam Chomsky and Edward Herman have documented so well,[13] the power to limit the parameters of public debate. The role of legitimization of power systems once played almost exclusively by religion is now shared by academia and the media; and the holders of the largest stakes cannot afford to be indifferent as to how the role is played.

The kind of economic devastation that followed the final cataclysms of the Cold War in the region of its epicenter got a long head start in Latin America. The debt crisis of the early 1980s left Latin American leaders at the mercy of creditors and currency speculators. The state itself, as a representative of a sovereign people, was so weakened that any line of policy, or even rhetoric, that smacked of economic nationalism threatened to set off a stampede of fleeing capital.

The surrender of economic policy-making seemed not to be a matter of choice, but it nonetheless demanded explanation and justification, which was scripted in neoliberal terms. Dependency theorists might claim that this turn of events had validated their analysis of the problem; but in a globalized economy — that is, without economically defensible borders and without an alternative market or credit source — they were left without politically feasible solutions.

## From Liberalism to Neoliberalism

As elaborated in 1776 by Adam Smith, liberalism was a progressive proposition, designed to redistribute wealth and opportunity from opulent courts and colonizers monopolizing trade under a system known as mercantilism to a new class of merchants and entrepreneurs operating their own businesses; their interests and powers would be limited by competition and public regulation. Championed by an expansive Great Britain in the nineteenth century and the United States in the twentieth century, liberalism's qualifiers faded, leaving emphasis on the free flow of goods, services and capital across national borders. Smith's laissez-faire principle was reinforced by David Ricardo's theory of comparative advantage. That theory posited that states should trade the goods they could produce most efficiently for goods in which other states had the advantage. In colonial and neocolonial systems, the advantage accrued, of course, to mother countries, not colonies.

Development and modernization theory, prominent in the post-World War II United States, was a legitimate offspring of liberalism, and like its sire it served to explain and legitimate the seemingly limitless opportunities and responsibilities of an imperial power at its peak. Though its power center does not reside in a state, neoliberalism shares those circumstances and attributes of its forebears; but whereas development theory sought to strengthen state institutions, neoliberalism as expressed in policy tends to eviscerate them. Privatization of government enterprises or services that might bring in a profit has commonly been a condition for the extension of credit. These and other measures that have come to be known collectively as "structural adjustment" are in the context of neoliberalism both policy prescriptions and factors in explanation and prediction of economic growth and stability or its absence. It is also assumed that an economy restructured along the lines prescribed is a prerequisite for a smoothly functioning electoral democracy. It has been conveniently forgotten that in general the "opening" of Latin American economies coincided with the demise of democratic systems rather than with their return.

## Variations on a Theme: Cultural Causation and Clashing Civilizations

Apart from the "End of History" cheerleaders,[14] there are those who applaud the general manifestations of neoliberal globalization but seek to explain growing income gaps and the still abundant conflict and disorder. Finding ideology to have been defeated or superseded[15], they have been left to explain conflict, inequality, and socioeconomic change or the lack of it in cultural terms. Culture as explanation for differential reward and punishment in multicultural societies — local, national, or global — predates and underpins development and modernization theory. Having assumed that some cultures are more conducive than others to democracy and prosperity, researchers find the evidence of have and have-not cultural groupings to be compelling. In other words, the blame for poverty and powerlessness falls squarely on the poor and powerless.

Samuel Huntington, who had earlier professed that Third World modernization was both desirable and inevitable, in the 1980s suggested that non-Nordic cultures may prefer austerity, hierarchy, and authoritarianism to wealth, equity, and democracy. In the 1990s, Huntington addressed the enemy crisis and warmed the hearts of pessimists by arguing, in *The Clash of Civilizations,* that the most important distinctions among peoples are cultural, that the newly emerging axis in world politics is between the West and the rest. The civilizations he sees as most likely to pose future threats to the West are the Islamic and the Chinese.[16]

Renewed or intensified attention to cultural difference, often in the guise of immigration policy issues, is to be expected in the post-Cold War globalized market system as a means of diverting attention from issues of class difference — that is, difference in income and opportunity — and increasing inequity. At the peak of the Cold War, those who challenged economic orthodoxy risked being labeled traitors, and attention to economic issues was diverted through racism, sexism, and a moving target of enemy states. Even so, most states had some latitude for economic decision making, so debate on allocation of burden and benefit was difficult to suppress.

In the new order, debate on economic issues has been muffled not because it appears treasonous, but because it appears futile. Resource allocation is perceived to have been snatched away by the inexorable forces of the marketplace. But that does not mean that government will wither away or that those who compete for the benefits of stateholding will run out of anything to talk about. Even as actual cultural difference shrinks, awareness of it will be heightened by pervasive communications and population shifts, and it will become an increasingly useful topic for political theater — useful particularly as a means of keeping the resentment of the disadvantaged targeted on the desperate rather than on the privileged.

## The Left: Alive and Well and Living in the Center

With the end of the Cold War, the Right had lost its cover story, but the Left had lost something harder to come by; it had lost its dream. In the absence of clear options, political strategies and policy alternatives from the Left in the 1990s have been measured and modest.

The *dependentista* school has gone under deep cover. Fernando Henrique Cardoso, one of its founders, was elected president of Brazil as a born-again neoliberal. Osvaldo Sunkel, another founder, argues diffidently in *Development from Within* [17] for priority attention to the development of the domestic market. Andre Gunder Frank, noted earlier as a *dependentista*, has joined world systems scholars in the study of long cycles of history. He and others pursuing that line of investigation would agree with Huntington as to the importance of the resurgence of the Orient and of China in particular but would seek explanation in economic and political rather than cultural phenomena. Numerous political commentators, including Mexican Jorge Castañeda, have observed that the entire political spectrum of Latin America has shifted sharply to the Right in the 1990s, the outcome of learning through painful experience to see politics as the art of the possible.[18]

### International Political Economy and Globalization

In the 1990s, theorists of international politics and development increasingly came to focus on some aspect of economic globalization — its nature, causes, and consequences, its beneficiaries and its victims, and in particular the ways in which it has changed the relationship between public and private sectors. Most of those drawn initially to the study of globalization had been identified with dependency or world system models or with the broader field of international political economy and were concerned primarily with growing income gaps and other effects of the process they saw as detrimental to society generally. But the new focus has more recently drawn economists and others whose interests and concerns lie elsewhere and who take a more benign view of globalization and its consequences.

International political economy (IPE), coming into its own in the 1970s and 1980s, sought to recapture the scope of nineteenth-century concerns for the purpose of addressing late twentieth-century policy issues. IEP was not so much a new field as the re-establishment of continuity with an older one, born of concerns about industrialization not only of the Third World but also of the First.

The IEP agenda also included the analytical reconnection of economic and political factors. Like most weddings and mergers, however, the remarriage of political science and economics turned out to be an unequal one, one that is drawn toward safety in the seemingly technocratic economic side of the equation, tending to the political only in its willingness to ask embarrassing questions. Barry Gills and his contributors to a special issue of *New Political Economy* on "Globalization and the Politics of Resistance" are anxious to see that that hegemonic relationship does not develop again. Gills says, "We seek to reclaim the terrain of the political, sometimes lost in the first phase of the globalization debate, and indeed to make concrete strategies and concepts of 'resistance' central to our analysis of 'globalization.'"[19]

## A Strange Bedfellow

Those who would impose political restraints on the globally free-wheeling money-movers have found a powerful ally in a strange place. Through the shrewd practice of currency speculation, George Soros has become wealthy enough to field a stateless army of young idealists to confront governments of North, South, East, and West in the pursuit of his vision of a global public interest. In newly democratizing and non-democratizing (e.g., Burma) states, through his Open Society Institute, he has fought tyranny and corruption and championed transparent politics and free expression; and in the West he has challenged the "War on Drugs" and the war on immigrants. Now Soros, whose Quantum Fund has the best performance record of any investment fund over the past quarter-century, is calling for constraints on actors like himself. He sees the international regulation of markets — international economic co-operation to match the globalization of markets, including harmonization of policies on taxation — as the only means of correcting inequities and preventing a breakdown in the system.[20]

## Beating Economists into Plowshares: Views from the Field

The 1990s have seen the amassing of a great body of scholarly and normative literature inspired by needs and interests that run counter to those advanced by neoliberalism. This output, however, particularly of environmentalists, feminists, and advocates of grassroots community development has yet to generate a great debate, mainly because economists, who now enjoy unchallenged disciplinary primacy in the business of theoretical legitimization, have generally ignored it.

Between these concerns and neoliberalism as now advanced there is little common ground. From the perspective of environmentalism, the global village is being stripped of resources by deregulation, the new openness of markets, and hard currency debt service requirements. Globe-hopping investors take what they can of depletable resources then move on, leaving communities and ecosystems devastated.

### Environmentalism

The environmentalist perspective might in fact pose the greatest challenge to neoliberalism since its thesis of absolute limits is directly contradictory to that of an absolutely unlimited requirement of growth. It also has the advantage of freshness, of respectability (it remains more acceptable socially to hug trees than to hug poor people), and of a large and highly committed constituency, cross-cutting classes and generations. But the two approaches are not articulated. For the most part they are played out in different arenas, coming together only in "greenwash" — corporate public relations gimmicks to demonstrate concern for the environment. In other words, it is not through straightforward debate, but only through greenwash that the money movers and their apologists acknowledge the existence of an environmental challenge to their position.

### Feminism

Likewise scholars engaging in gender analysis, and advocates of the international women's movement, have noted that the front-line victims of the economic restructuring now sweeping the global village are women. Shrinkage of the public sector has cost women their best professional jobs at the same time that loss of family services, pensions, and benefits has expanded their responsibilities. While women are being squeezed out of the better-paying formal economy, they are being drawn in ever-greater numbers into exploitative informal sector work. Moreover, it is not only women's interests that have suffered in this new order but also women's values, particularly the value placed on collective responsibility as opposed to individualized self-indulgence. Major public and private institutions have made a point in recent years of making room for women, but not of reversing the policies so damaging to them.

### Community Empowerment

As governments, bound first to distant creditors, default on their debts to their own citizens, the newly displaced and deprived are discovering what the long-suffering have always known — that the last bastion of security is the community, a community organized and aware of the need for general commitment and mutual support. Theorists of grassroots development note that such awareness and commitment runs counter to the dog-eat-dog or all-eat-dog options suggested by neoliberal individualism. Moreover, globalization — the alienation, or distancing of decision making about priorities and livelihoods — presents a dire threat to the ideal of individual and collective self-sufficiency or "empowerment" that is the philosophical foundation of community development.

## The Human Rights Perspective: A Wide-Angle Lens

To the countercurrent approaches to explanation, prediction, and prescription, one might add the ontological screening of those whose focus of concern is human rights. Though human rights consciousness has not woven about itself, or become embedded in, a theoretical model, it has become a point from which to affix to the mind's eye a wide-angle lens.

The reign of terror to which the human rights mobilization of the late 1970s responded, a reign unleashed particularly by military regimes in Latin America, had come about as political democracy threatened to lead toward economic democracy. As economic policy appeared to be set primarily at the level of the nation-state, it was assumed that an equitable or at least tolerable standard of living could be expected as a byproduct of democracy. The objective, then, of the human rights movement was to stop the torture, execution, and other physical and psychological means of repression that stood in the way of redemocratization. A government of the people should then be able to assure the protection of other basic rights.

The 1948 Universal Declaration of Human Rights, however, had sought to establish a far more encompassing view of the rights deserving of universal protection. And Third World countries having had far less reason than the most highly developed of the Latin American states to invest hope in so-called democratic governments early on urged human rights organizations to adopt a broader view of their mission. That argument carried greater weight as local chapters of human rights organizations proliferated in the Third World.

With the recent spread of democratization or redemocratization, the broader mission previously assigned to democracy has reverted to the defenders of human rights. That is, as decision making has been removed from the province of state government and democracy has come to be defined in narrow terms of electoral process, basic economic and ecological rights (to food and shelter, potable water, and breathable air) increasingly come to be seen as human rights issues. It follows, then, that deprivation of such rights cannot be legitimated by governments no matter the rationale and no matter how such governments may have been conceived; and that protection of such rights cannot be entrusted to individual governments but must be the concern of the international community.

Mary Robinson, UN High Commissioner for Human Rights, concedes that the results of a half-century pursuit of human rights protection under the aegis of the United Nations has been underwhelming. She sees the gap between civil/political and socioeconomic interpretations as a major obstacle to effectiveness and she has committed her office to the promotion of a broad interpretation, embracing economic, social, cultural, and gender rights along with the civil and political rights more traditionally acknowledged in the West.[21]

If action is what is needed — and it clearly is — why all the fuss about a paradigm? Because action without understanding is at best futile, at worst dangerous to those it is meant to help. And understanding must start with an act of will, with withdrawing from the powerful the right to plausible deniability but also with denying it to ourselves. In fact the kind of wide-angle lens suggested now by a human rights perspective would seem to be required both for understanding the trends that constitute the new post-Cold War order and for ameliorating or reversing their most damaging consequences.

# Notes

1. United Nations, Department of International Economic and Social Affairs, *World Economic Survey 1991* (New York: United Nations, 1991), p. 10.
2. Inter-American Development Bank, *The IDB,* Vol. 16, Nos. 9–10 and 11, 1989; and Jeff Drumtra and Thomas George, "The 1980s: A Lost Decade," *Worldview,* Vol. 2:3, Fall 1989, pp. 8, 11–12.
3. Drumtra and George, *loc. cit.*
4. UNDP, 1997, *loc. cit.*
5. Op. cit. Julianne Malveaux, "Trying to Put the Dream Back in View," *San Francisco Examiner,* Aug. 31, 1997, p. D-2; "When Gephardt Speaks," (editorial) *The Nation,* Dec. 29, 1997, p. 3.
6. UNDP, 1997, *loc. cit.*
7. Larry Elliot, "Caught on the Horns of a Global Dilemma," *The Manchester Guardian Weekly,* July 7, 1996, p. 13. Former President Kenneth Kaunda told this author, in conversation at the Oxford Union, Oxford University, Nov. 10, 1997, that his government, in order to stop such a capital drain, had severed relations in 1986 with the IMF and cut debt payments service to 10

percent of foreign exchange earnings. Economic growth shot up to 8 percent the following years, but by 1989 the country was suffering from a liquidity crisis and was forced to submit once again to the IMF regimen.

8. Thomas L. Friedman, "Russians: Clear Destination, Unclear Map, Arrival Probable," *International Herald Tribune,* July 8, 1996, p. 8.
9. UNDP, 1997, *loc. cit.*
10. "Recomienda el BM, Reducir la Brecha entre Ricos y Pobres en América Latina," *Excelsior,* 1 de julio, 1997, p. 2-F; and Larry Elliott, "World Bank Warning of Poverty Time Bomb," *The Manchester Guardian Weekly,* Oct. 5, 1997, p. 19.
11. Wallerstein, *The Modern World-System: Capitalist Agriculture and the Origins of the European World-Economy in the Sixteenth Century (*New York and London: Academic Press, 1974).
12. Economics, now a religion, has heretics but no controversy.
13. Herman and Chomsky, *Manufacturing Consent: The Political Economy of the Mass Media* (New York: Pantheon Books, 1988).
14. Enthusiasts of the perspective assumed by Francis Fukuyama in "The End of History?" *National Interest,* Summer 1989.
15. To the evangelists of neoliberalism, ideology was a mental disorder found only on the Left.
16. Samuel Huntington and Myron Weiner, eds. *Understanding Political Development* (Boston: Little, Brown and Company, 1987), pp. 21–28; and Huntington, *The Clash of Civilizations and the Remaking of World Order* (New York: Simon and Schuster, 1996).
17. Osvaldo Sunkel, *Development from Within: Toward a Neostructuralist Approach for Latin America* (Boulder, CO: Lynne Rienner, 1993).
18. Jorge B. Castañeda, *Utopia Unarmed: The Latin American Left After the Cold War* (New York: Knopf, 1993).
19. Barry Gills, "Editorial: Globalization and the Politics of Resistance," in Gills, ed., *New Political Economy,* Special Issue, Vol. 2, No. 1, Mar. 1997, pp. 11–15.
20. "Beyond Chaos and Dogma," a dialogue between George Soros and Anthony Giddens, *The New Statesman,* Oct. 31, 1997.
21. Mary Robinson, "Realizing Human Rights," The Romanes Lecture, 1997, Sheldonian Theater, University of Oxford, Nov. 11, 1997.

# Chapter 2
# Suggested Readings

Bello, Walden, with Shea Cummingham and Bill Rau. *Dark Victory: The United States, Structural Adjustment, and Global Poverty.* Oakland, CA: Institute for Food and Development Policy, 1994.

Boulding, Kenneth. "The Economics of the Coming Spaceship Earth," originally published in Henry Jarrett, ed. *Environmental Quality in a Growing Economy.* Baltimore: Johns Hopkins University Press, 1968, pp. 3–14.

Cardoso, Fernando Henrique, and Enzo Faletto. *Dependency and Development in Latin America.* Berkeley: University of California Press, 1979.

Chomsky, Noam. *World Orders Old and New.* New York: Colombia University Press, 1994.

———. *Year 501: The Conquest Continues.* Boston: South End Press, 1993.

Daly, Herman, and John Cobb. *Toward the Common Good: Redirecting the Economy Toward Community, the Environment, and a Sustainable Future.* 2nd ed. Boston: Beacon Press, 1994.

Durning, Alan. *How Much is Enough? The Consumer Society and the Future of the Earth.* New York: W.W. Norton, 1992.

Frank, Andre Gunder, and Barry K. Gills, eds. *The World System: Five Hundred Years or Five Thousand?* New York: Routledge, 1996.

Greider, William. *One World, Ready or Not: The Manic Logic of Global Capitalism.* New York: Simon and Schuster, 1997.

Heilbroner, Robert. *The Worldly Philosophers,* 6th ed. New York: Simon and Schuster, 1992.

Henderson, Hazel. *Paradigms in Progress: Life Beyond Economics.* Indianapolis: Knowledge Systems, Inc., 1991.

Korten, David. *Getting to the Twenty-First Century: Voluntary Action and the Global Agenda.* West Hartford, CT: Kumarian Press, 1992.

Norberg-Hodge, Helena. *Ancient Futures.* San Francisco: Sierra Club Books, 1992.

Nussbaum, Martha C. "Nation, Function, and Capability: Aristotle on Political Distribution," *Oxford Studies in Ancient Philosophy.* (Supplementary issue), 1988.

Rist, Gilbert. The History of Development: From Western Origins to Global Faith (translated by Patrick Camiller). London: Zed Books, 1995.

Seligson, Mitchell A. and John T. Passi-Smith. *Development and Underdevelopment: The Political Economy of Inequality.* Boulder, CO: Lynne Rienner Press, 1993.

Smith, Adam. *An Inquiry into the Nature and Causes of the Wealth of Nations.* New York: Modern Library, 1937.

Tinker, Irene. *Persistent Inequalities: Women and World Development.* New York: Oxford Univeristy Press, 1990.

Wallerstein, Immanuel. *The Politics of the World-Economy: The States, the Movements, and the Civilizations.* Cambridge: Cambridge University Press, 1984.

Wilson, Richard A. *Human Rights, Culture and Context: Anthropological Perspectives.* London: Pluto Press, 1996.

Krujë, Albania

# Part I

# A Cookie-Cutter World: The New Nationalism

*There is no such thing as a system that doesn't work.*
*Every system works for somebody.*

*All weapons eventually fall into the wrong hands.*

*IN THE EARLY* 1990s, as old empires collapsed and new nations formed at a dizzying pace, Peruvian scholar Max Hernández likened the social ferment to a violent tornado that drives people to the "basement of their souls," there to cling to such pillars as religious or ethnic roots.

One of the most dramatic aspects of the transition to a new order has been the implosion of the Soviet Union and its sphere of influence. The new nationalism that was both cause and effect of that phenomenon is in many ways the inverse of the nationalism of the post-war de-colonization period, that is, of a state-wrecking rather than nation-building variety. Several minority nations within Russia are in open rebellion, and of the thirty-nine territorial entities that make up the new state one–third are seeking some kind of autonomy.[1] No matter how the new boundaries are drawn, there are other ethnic minorities within suffering discrimination and seeking a niche of their own. And the centrifugal forces that brought about the implosion of the Soviet Union have been operating in other regions as well.

The generalized scarcity, the substitution of symbolic sovereignty for real decision-making authority, the inability of government at any level to follow through on popular mandates, and the diversion of potentially constructive energies to a focus on ethnicity and ethnic apartheid that plagued the areas freed of Soviet hegemony have since spilled over to many other parts of the world; and the loosening of the superpower gridlock brought previously dormant ethnic conflict into relief.

## The Illusion of Sovereignty

As walls between twentieth-century empires came tumbling down, new walls between and within states and cities were going up, and separatism had become epidemic. Even older multiethnic states (e.g., Spain, Great Britain) not being downsized by disintegration were subject to devolution of powers or at least of responsibilities.

Intertribal warfare, endemic to some of the least modernized regions, like Papua New Guinea and Afghanistan, has been intensified by the encroachment of narco-trafficking and the easy availability of automatic weapons. UNESCO calculated in 1997 that there had been ninety armed conflicts around the world over the previous ten years.

Even as "independence" is stripped of meaning in the interdependent, or centrally planned, global village, it becomes ever more sought after. The geoeconomic forces that have trampled national boundaries — thus exposing the weakness of the guardians of those boundaries — have in turn unleashed new geopolitical forces, defined more often by ethnic myopia than by programmatic vision, to bombard and atomize states into particles ever smaller and more dependent on external resources. Unable to protect its citizens and their resources from the vagaries of a global marketplace or to maintain a monopoly on the use of force, states large and small find themselves competing with regional and ethnic separatists as well as with trans-national corporations and crime syndicates, and they begin to dissolve. Such centrifugal forces have been felt even among Caribbean mini-states, where Tobago is seeking to secede from its union with Trinidad, and Aruba, annoyed by the hegemony of Curaçao in the Netherlands Antilles, claimed independence in 1996.

Even in the Western Hemisphere's tiniest country, St. Kitts and Nevis, with forty-six thousand people living on two islands separated by two miles of water, the smaller partner, Nevis, filed for divorce in 1996. The real issue for St. Kitts and Nevis, as for many island mini-states, was offshore banking (whereby the bulk of the world's liquid assets hide from tax collectors).[2] But the fact that a handful of people on a large rock could pretend to national sovereignty demonstrates the devaluation of the concept of sovereignty and the fact that the latitude of "sovereignty" is determined by the global-level centrally planned economy in accordance with the needs of its weightiest players.

## The Illusion of Victory

Though the Cold War ended with a whimper rather than a bang, the post-war period has had much in common with the aftermath of other wars. Abrupt shifts of national boundaries, trade patterns, and investments, for example, have left millions on the move or on the mercy of foreigners. Like other wars, too, it has left a messy and confusing balance sheet for sorting out winners and losers.

One might have thought during the US presidential campaign of 1992 that the Reagan and Bush Administrations had been single-mindedly committed to international tension reduction and peaceful co-existence. In fact, it was through no fault of his own that Bush found himself at the outset of his presidency presiding over the demise of the Cold War. The Cold War ended because Gorbachev, more keenly aware than American leaders of its costs, opted out.

Bush administration officials, having been downright peeved about Gorbachev's "peace offensives," nevertheless claimed full credit for the termination of the Cold War, and further, claimed that the US had won it. By 1992 there was no disputing that the Soviet Union had lost the war. The empire had imploded and most of its shards were swiftly slipping from the Second World into the Third. It did not follow however that the US had won. Its frenzy of military activity in the immediate post-war period served only to set in relief the fact that the US had squandered its real assets in the accumulation of military prowess — by then a devalued currency.

In terms of the only convertible currency of the 1990s — economic strength — the nations that might be said to have won the Cold War are the ones that did not fight it. Having lost World War II, Japan and Germany were unable to participate in the arms races and military engagements of the Cold War.

The real winner of the Cold War, however, was not a country or set of countries but an economic system. That system was not just capitalism, but a particular pre-modern brand of it — pre-modern in that it rejects the equilibrium both of the social welfare state that had evolved in Europe and of the modernized feudalism of Japan. Second-coming capitalism is a Spencerian approach to enterprise wherein the fittest — the money-movers, or creditor cartel — are seen as rightfully free of obligation to nations or to any other human collectivity whereas the unfit — those whose labor or skills are not needed by the money-movers — are simply discarded. They are not necessarily entitled to citizenship anywhere, to land or work or shelter, to education or health care, community or culture.

With the new order, the expansion of spatial horizons that might have enabled us to concern ourselves with a bountiful and livable environment for future generations has been offset instead by a severe shrinkage of time horizons. Advances in technology and increases in productivity that might have allowed a crowded planet to accommodate its growing numbers have led instead to a new kind of exclusivity. And the accumulation of capital by the creditor cartel had become ever more efficient since the otherwise beached ship of state had been subcontracted as a receivership; its primary function has become that of making the collections necessary to maintain debt service.

## The Illusion of Peace

Those who dared to hope that the crumbling of the Berlin Wall would mean a more general liberation of the human spirit from political, ethnic, and other barriers were soon to be disappointed. The removal of the Cold War overlay that for so long had defined friend and foe and set priorities in line with the interests of the superpowers unleashed other energies, both constructive and destructive, opening political space particularly for those who might profit from more traditional rivalries.

Even as the Berlin Wall was being sold off in chunks to tourists, walls elsewhere were being reinforced. New tensions were rising in Cyprus, as Greek and Turkish Cypriots faced off along the island's UN-demarcated Green Line, and the Koreas, divided so many wars ago, escalated rhetorical hostilities across the 38th parallel. Over the course of the 1990s, tensions continued to rise in perenially divided Jerusalem, as Jewish settlements went up on what had been Palestinian land and in Bosnia's Brcko, which had come to be known as the Berlin of the Balkans.

In some cases, nationalism, though suppressed for half a century, remained vibrant. In the cases of Poland and the Baltics, it provided the getaway vehicle for escape from the Soviet sphere. In other cases, like those of Belarus and the Central Asian Republics, independence came by default, a consequence of empire implosion, and nationalism had to be fabricated from older threads. In all cases, however, there is a residue of ethnic tension that mocks all efforts to reconstitute statehood. All remnants of the Soviet Union now have large and largely persecuted Russian minorities within them; and other minority ethnic groups — those whose names do not coincide with the name of the Republic — have become acutely aware of their minority status.

In all cases economic hardship was both cause and effect, at least in the short term, of the breakdown and reconstitution of systems of production, distribution, and trade. In some cases, like that of Poland, transition was underway well before the break-up of the Soviet Union in that economies were already suffering from the worst of both worlds — the rigidities and disincentive to quality and service of the Soviet system and the debts, dependencies, and insecurities attendant to the emerging Western model.

In other parts of the world, hostilities that had been contained to some degree by the Cold War overlay flared anew. The relative inattention of the great powers left hostilities to be fed, as in Cyprus, by the rivalries of regional hegemons or in the Horn of Africa, where war is surely least affordable, by individual, fratricidal rivalry.

The most devastating showdown of centrifugal forces has been in the former Yugoslavia. Harboring at least seven major ethnic groups in six separate republics, speaking four languages, practicing three religions, and using two alphabets, a scarcely idyllic but reasonably well-functioning Yugoslavia was the very model of a post-World War II multiethnic nation-state. In addition to the republics of Serbia, Croatia, Slovenia, Bosnia and Hercegovina, Macedonia, and Montenegro, there were two autonomous provinces, Vojvodina in the northern region of Serbia, having a large Magyar (Hungarian) minority, and ethnically Albanian Kosovo, on Serbia's southwestern border.

Under Marshal Tito's firm but in many ways enlightened rule, the country managed to irritate the Soviet Union by being stubbornly independent and the West by being stubbornly socialist. For a time the country displayed considerable social and economic creativity and enjoyed relative prosperity. But situated on the Adriatic it could not aspire to strategic unimportance. So, after Tito's death, when the ambitions of regional warlords, particularly the revival of Serbian chauvinism, began to tear the country apart, the major powers that might have helped to patch it back together instead reinforced the centrifugal tendencies. By the mid-1990s, Slovenia, Croatia, and Macedonia had become independent, and Bosnia and Hercegovina had become a ward of the Organization for Security and Cooperation in Europe (OSCE), while an uneasy truce settled over its disputed zones. The rump of Yugoslavia consisted then of Serbia and Montenegro; and the Albanians in the Serbian province of Kosovo, having lost political autonomy and been subjected to new forms of discrimination and repression, had become restive.

It is not clear that we have seen the last of national decomposition and "ethnic cleansing" in the Balkans. Cease-fires and even elections cannot represent the endgame. UN Secretary-General Kofi Annan has said, with respect to Bosnia, "Issues of justice and peace are indivisible. Without justice, the healing cannot begin."[3]

Albanians, emerging from a half-century of discipline and sacrifice, were just beginning to learn Western ways of self-indulgence when the only capitalist bubble most had known — a pervasive pyramid scheme — burst. The government of Sali Berisha, a born-again neo-liberal, already was in trouble, following an unconvincing election and a clampdown on political opposition. It is hardly surprising then that, blaming the government for their losses in the pyramid investment scam, angry citizens took to the streets in early 1997. Social convulsion spread throughout the country, claiming some two thousand lives and forcing a change of government.

Even before the emergence of that crisis, the optimism of Balkan peacemakers had been tempered by concern about spill-over of unrest to ethnic Albanians elsewhere in the region, particularly in Macedonia and Kosovo. Unfortunately, the foresight and resolve on the part of the great powers and international agencies that might have forestalled the early unraveling of Yugoslavia continued to be missing-in-action when the challenge arose once again in the Balkan's southern tier. In Kosovo, by the fall of 1997, Serbian suppression of ethnic Albanian assertiveness was transforming a political movement for the reinstatement of autonomy into a guerrilla campaign for independence.

In a few short months, ethnic Albanian insurgency and Serbian counterinsurgency had turned Kosovo into another war zone. Throughout the year that followed, the conflict spread and intensified. Several hundred Kosovo Albanians were killed and several hundred thousand displaced, spilling over the border into already anarchic northern Albania or fleeing into the harsh, unwelcoming mountains, while the United Nations passed resolutions and NATO proclaimed in ever stronger terms its "readiness" to employ force against Serbian military and paramilitary oppressors.

In fact, as before, the United Nations lacked the jurisdictional autonomy, the structure and the resources to take the actions — e.g., a massive show of force on the ground early on — that might have headed off disaster; and the major powers aligned in NATO, in the absence of clearly defined "strategic" interests, lacked the will. Those powers may come through once again to play a role in peacekeeping, after the unequal contest of force has played itself out, but they have been unwilling to take the political risks of involvement in peacemaking.[4]

## Notes

1. Dr. Andrei Grachev, former press secretary and foreign affairs adviser to Soviet leader Mikhail Gorbachev, "Russian Society: Which Way Out of Communism?," Lecture, St. Antony's College, Oxford, Oct. 20, 1997.
2. Caribbean mini-states are reportedly laundering hundreds of millions annually from narcotics alone. On "Hot Money," a PBS Frontline production, Nov. 1, 1994, it was reported that more than 60 percent of the world's liquid assets reside offshore, 50 percent of them in the Caribbean.
3. Newshour with Jim Lehrer, PBS, April 5, 1997.
4. The author's views on this matter have been reinforced by several conversations in 1997–98 with Sir Marrack Goulding, who served the United Nations from 1986 to 1996, as Undersecretary-General, first for Peacekeeping, then for Political Affairs.

# Chapter 3

# Tinderbox in the Balkans' Southern Tier

*Violence results from power inequities. The only real solution to the problem of violence is the empowerment of would-be victims.*

*The pen is mightier than the sword, but not in hand-to-hand combat.*

*MIROSLAV, A SERBIAN* artist living in Macedonia, maintains that his adoptive country is relatively stable, like a car that has been teetering for some while on the edge of a cliff and has not gone over yet. As an artist, Miroslav is keenly aware of Macedonia's economic slump. Artwork is a luxury commodity — not in great demand in a country in the fifth year of economic decline.[1] Even a national prize-winning artist, as he is, has a hard time making ends meet where GDP has shrunk by 50 percent and unemployment is variously estimated at 30 to 50 percent.

As a Serb, Miroslav is frequently reminded also of the inter-ethnic tension that keeps the new state teetering. Born Yugoslav, he is now a foreigner in what was so recently a part of his country. His wife, Slaviça, a Macedonian journalist, believes that he might have been hired as a fine arts professor at the university had he not been born Serbian. Their six-year-old son is already developing an identity crisis. With his mother's family in Macedonia, he is considered a Serb. With his father's family in Serbian territory, he is called Macedonian.

Along with Serbs, Macedonia's population of two million has sizable minorities of ethnic Turks and Romanies, or gypsies; but the minority group that is the source of greatest concern is the Albanians, estimated by the Macedonian government at 23 percent of the population and by Albanians at about 30 percent.

## Geopolitics and the "Ancient Hatreds" Sham

Macedonians commonly point out that they did not opt out of the socialist system, or for that matter out of Yugoslavia. Independence was thrust upon them. So they do not understand the fears and resentments of the now restive Albanian minority, of the Greeks, whose economic embargo was dropped only in the fall of 1995, or of the Serbs, who until March 1996 did not recognize Macedonian statehood. In a September 1991 referendum, Macedonians voted overwhelmingly in favor of an independent and sovereign state, but by that time they had little choice; Yugoslavia was dissolving around them.

Yugoslavia did not dissolve, as so many pundits would have us believe, because of ancient hatreds. There are no hatreds older than the heads that carry them. Alfred Stepan, Oxford's Gladstone Professor of Political Science, has noted that at the time of its dissolution Yugoslavia's ratio of interfaith marriages was among the world's highest. It dissolved because of competing political ambitions — because, in the absence of Marshal Tito's strong, integrative rule, the center could not hold.

With an economy suffering increasingly from debt and squeezed by creditors, Yugoslavia's collective central authorities ceased to be able to respond to regional or local needs or otherwise to reward loyalty to the federal system. Thus, political space was opened wide for those who would promote their own fortunes by regenerating fear and prejudice and fanning the consequent flames of separatism. Foreign powers that should have known better reverted initially to old alliances and old games of "let's you and him fight" (German recognition of Slovenian independence ensured further unraveling). The UN, finally given a mandate for peacekeeping but not for peacemaking, arrived too late with too little and found that there was no peace to keep. Multilateralism, given its first real test in a post-Cold War world, flunked it.

Likewise, the unease with which some ethnic Macedonians now view the minorities, and particularly the Albanians, in their midst is new and has little to do with ethnic rivalries. Rather, it is about geopolitics and the fear that the Balkan wars of the nineties have not run their course, that they might continue to spread southward.

Along with Macedonians, resident diplomats, international relief and development specialists, and US and UN peacekeeping troops live with a watchful eye on Kosovo. This enclave within the Serbian rump of Yugoslavia, about fifty-seven miles from Macedonia's capital, Skopje, and just twenty-one miles from the border with Yugoslavia, is home to some 1.8 million ethnic Albanians, almost two-thirds as many as reside in Albania proper and 90 percent of the population of Kosovo.

Meanwhile the new tensions that have been building between ethnic Albanians and Macedonians since Macedonian independence have become focused on a particular domestic issue: the demand for an Albanian-language university. The Macedonian government was reportedly afraid to give in for fear that the university issue was merely representative of a much broader set of issues and that its spokesman might become a central figure in a larger movement. Through its intransigence the government was making of its fears a self-fulfilling prophecy.

## Macedonia's Downsized Dreams

In the streets of Skopje in 1996, one saw only grim faces. To explain their situations, Macedonians made jokes about surviving with no visible means of support, but the tension and exhaustion, depression and bewilderment, were no joke. Since pay-offs of the new economic order were narrowly distributed, most Macedonians did not understand why they had to give up benefits they had enjoyed in the past and felt that they had earned. Having worked at reduced pay for considerable periods on the understanding that their government would in return provide for their retirement and for other requirements, they did not understand how an extraneous body like the International Monetary Fund could come in and clamp a lid on the government's budget for social programs. Much of what remained or had been regenerated in the way of public service, cultural continuity, or social safety net had been sustained by foreign donors or international non-governmental organizations, but such assistance was expected soon to dwindle.

While so many contended with unemployment, others were overemployed because that was required to make ends meet or to get the job done in understaffed institutions. Vladimir had two jobs. His full-time job was as professor and director of the theater arts program at the state university. His part-time job — about twelve hours a day, he said — was as director of the Soros Foundation program in Macedonia.

Vladimir represents the third generation of his family in the theater arts and he hopes his generation will not be the last. Theater has enjoyed a kind of popularity in Macedonia comparable to that of poetry in Russia. As late as 1996, there were about twenty full-time professional theater groups in the country and many more part-time and amateur ones. But the tradition is now threatened with extinction. The state funding it had enjoyed in the past was to be slashed, and in a depressed economy private patronage would not begin to take up the slack.

Vladimir directed Albanian theater as well as Macedonian — in the Albanian minority community in Macedonia and in Albania itself — and he had been struck by the changing fortunes of his two peoples. At the end of the 1970s, when Macedonia was prospering, he found Albania a very grim place. There were no smiles. Everybody looked sad and exhausted. There were no cars on the streets apart from the black Mercedes of the party bosses. Poverty was extreme. Even in the mid-1990s, Albania's standard of living was scarcely comparable to that of Macedonia. The country's best actor, according to Vladimir, might earn the equivalent of US$100 a month, while Macedonia's would earn five times that. But after the political anarchy and economic collapse of 1991–92, Albania's situation had been getting better, at least in the cities, until the crisis of 1997, while that of Macedonia was getting worse. Just before the crash, Tirana seemed to be booming.

In fact, Tirana's boom of 1996 and the bust of 1997, with its ongoing reverberations, serve to highlight the economic recklessness and social irresponsibility to which the new order lends itself.

## Albania's Boys' Town: No Adult Supervision

Like a bower bird with a mobile nest, a young man in a Mercedes sports car convertible drove up and double-parked on the already chaotic street. He leaned on his car as he chatted with passing friends. Perhaps our bower bird was well-connected, because he seemed oblivious to the omnipresent security forces and to the traffic jam his well-feathered nest was creating. But after a half-century of discipline and sacrifice, anarchy and self-indulgence had become the order of the day in swinging, downtown Tirana.

Along the broad avenue that connects the plaza and the university, where a few years earlier there had been a forested park, there was now a forest of bars and sidewalk cafes. It seemed that every flat surface had a table on it. The cafes were well patronized, even in the daytime, by middle-aged men, but by dusk they had been liberated and overrun by the rap and acid rock set. On a long summer night the avenue was like the midway at a county fair — packed with strollers of all ages on feet, skates, and bikes, eating ice cream cones and weaving in and out of the patternless traffic of hay wagons, milk carts, and Mercedes.

The imposing pyramid built to serve as a mausoleum for Enver Hoxha, Europe's most durable tyrant, is occupied now, unapologetically, by the US Embassy. More importantly, its slopes now serve as a mammoth slide for neighborhood children. At the Europa Park Hotel down the street, where diplomats and major donors stay, the entire restaurant and courtyard had been booked, at the cost of $60,000, for a wedding party of over two hundred persons from Kosovo.

In the spacious main plaza, under the somber equestrian figure of the national hero, Skanderbeg, and the mosaic of women warriors gracing the facade of the National Museum, were merry-go-rounds, Ferris wheels, and other amusement park paraphernalia. Across the plaza beside the old mosque, what was so recently the Palace of Culture had become the Poker Salon, filled with the latest in gambling machines. Five years after the collapse of the old regime, Tirana was a house abandoned by stern parents and left in the hands of teen-age boys.

There was no renovation. The old was simply crumbling. Factories, government buildings, hospitals, schools, and hotels leaned wearily on skewed foundations, breezes whistling through broken windows, rattling unhinged shutters. Trash piled up on the streets. But new life was sprouting everywhere, like blades of grass pushing through cracked sidewalks. Elevators, telephones, streetlights and plumbing were unreliable, but kiosks and cafes grew like mushrooms along sidewalks and in parks, and some kind of construction seemed to be underway on all sides. And then there was the population explosion of Mercedes, truly remarkable given that at the beginning of the 1990s there were only about four hundred cars in the whole country. A theory popular among Albania's neighbors is that for every happy new Albanian driver, there is a very unhappy German pedestrian.

Landmarks of the new auto age were already appearing around the fringes of the cities in the form of Parsee-type car cemeteries. Here car corpses are stripped bare by flightless vultures who make good use of all parts. Most donkey carts now have cushy car seats for the driver, and horsepower has taken on new meaning as there are many versions of the horse-drawn car.

## Amid Scarcity, an Abundance of Bunkers

Against the beehive intensity of the city, the countryside, where 60 percent of the Albanian population lives, seemed frozen in time. Electricity and running water were in short supply. Some of the old mosques, abandoned a half century ago, were coming back into use, and new ones were appearing; but the predominant feature of the countryside and the most visible reminder of a particularly macabre recent past was the bunker. In a fit of paranoia, during the tenure of his Chinese advisers, Hoxha ordered that tens of thousands of bunkers (looking rather like beehive ovens or concrete igloos and as indestructible as African termite mounds) be strategically placed along roads and beaches and around fields and factories, villages and towns.

In the bad old days there were regular drills in which children had to leave their classrooms and peasants their fields to sit with guns at the ready in the stifling, sweltering heat of those makeshift ovens. A movie was being made about "Colonel Bunker," the engineer who was ordered to pave the country with these concrete monsters. Apart from cinematographic or archeological interest, their only value seemed to be as reminders that things could be — and indeed had been — worse.

Albanian history has been just one damn thing after another. After holding their ground for a millennium or so, the Illyrians, to whom modern-day Albanians trace much of their language and culture, were overrun by the Romans in 167 BC (I now suspect that the descendants of the ancient Greeks and Romans are alive and well and living in Albania. A young woman I met there might well have been the model for most of the statuary of the classical period). The Roman Empire was in control for some five hundred years, but with its decline Slavic tribes gained ground and central authority gave way to feuding warlords.

Apart from Skanderbeg's last stand in the mountain top fortress of Druja, the territory was brought under Turkish Ottoman control by the early fifteenth century and remained so until 1912. (During that time, in the late seventeenth century, the mischief-making Turks moved a major chunk of the population north and east to what is now Kosovo.) Brief spurts of independence before and after World War I gave way to the colorful King Zog, to Italian annexation, Nazi occupation, and finally liberation in 1944 by Albanian partisans led by the Communist revolutionary Enver Hoxha.

Under the tutelage first of Yugoslavia's Tito, until 1948, of the Soviet Union until 1961, of China until 1976, and thereafter on its own — an extremely rare attempt at autarchy — the regime accomplished near miracles in education and public health and transformed a traditional peasant economy into a semi-modern, largely industrialized one. The cost, in disruption, hardship, and repression, was awful, as Hoxha's forty-year rule proved once again that power not only corrupts but maddens.

## The Breech Rebirth of a Nation

Most Albanians attributed their country's status in the mid-1990s as Europe's fastest growing economy (with a growth rate in 1994 of 8.1 percent), to the remittances of exiles drawn by all-too-remarkable investment returns, but the fact that acceleration was starting virtually from a dead stop was surely also a factor. Many found the extreme scarcity that followed the cut-off of Chinese subsidies tolerable, if only because it meant also the departure of the despised Chinese advisers. But the collapse of the regime that followed Hoxha's death in 1985 and the subsequent implosion of the USSR brought real terror.

Writer Diana Chuli, whose novel on the period of transition is now required reading in secondary schools, remembers going out at 2:00 AM to stand in line for milk at a shop that did not open until 6:00 AM — and then being afraid to go out at all because gunfire filled the night and nobody knew who was shooting from where at whom. When the smoke finally cleared, the scene it revealed was a still life. Nothing moved. Factories, schools, offices — everything was closed.

When in 1992 Diana saw a man pruning a tree, she began to cry with relief; it was the first time in a year and a half that she had seen anyone working. The collapse of the old regime meant the release of some twenty thousand political prisoners; but transition and The Reform scrapped not only most previous legislation but also most in responsible positions who, for good or ill, had been entrusted with carrying it out. A whole generation of trained professionals were suddenly jobless — diplomats, scientists, doctors, teachers, and others — seen as tainted by having served the government at a time when the public sector was, in fact, the only sector.

Diana, whose stock in trade is irony, missed the jokes, the literary subtlety, even the creative cooking (What else was there to do for amusement?) of the worst years. Among the less inspired, nostalgia for the *ancien regime* was harder to come by. But that is not to say that the public was celebrating the arrival of freewheeling democracy.

## Democracy Balkan-style?

Like a number of recent elections in ex-Communist states, the reelection staged by Albanian President Sali Berisha and his Democratic Party on May 26, 1996, received less than rave reviews. Opposition leaders charged, and international election monitors confirmed, that the election had been marred by all manner of irregularities, including police harassment and intimidation of voters at the polls. Even the US and European Union governments that warmly supported Berisha's market reforms were embarrassed by the immodesty of his margin of victory. The ruling party laid claim to 122 of the 140 seats in the legislature.

The main opposition party, the Socialists, withdrew before the polls closed and were threatening to boycott the ten seats allotted to them. Participants in a street demonstration after the election, including a prominent leader of the women's movement, were beaten, jailed, and, in some cases, tortured. Even members of the ruling party who suggested negotiation with the opposition were threatened with indictment on ludicrous criminal charges. George Soros, underwriter of the Soros Foundation, was sufficiently concerned about the fragility of press freedom to offer a $100,000 loan to the leading independent daily newspaper.

Western governments and creditors clearly favored a resolution upholding both the Berisha government and the appearance of legitimacy, but all trace of legitimacy for that government crashed in early 1997 along with the pyramid investment scam. It was unclear whether the open distribution of weapons from military stocks was taking place at the behest of the government itself or of one or another element of the opposition; but pockets of anarchy spread throughout the country, interspersed with pockets under the control of one or another armed faction, and everything other than arms came to be in dangerously short supply.

Conflict subsided only with the arrival of relief supplies from the European Community and a few thousand troops to distribute them. Under the watchful eye of the European Community a coalition government was established. New elections on June 29 turned government over to the opposition

Socialists and a measure of peace was restored, at least temporarily, in the central part of the country. But the resources essential to economic recovery and particularly to the rebuilding of social infrastructure were not forthcoming.

By fall of 1998, Albania had once again been plunged into chaos. The assassination of a leader in the opposition Democratic party, the party of former president Sali Berisha, prompted that party to promote a coup attempt. The attempt failed to unseat the Socialist-led coalition government, but Prime Minister Fatos Nano, finding himself unable to form a new cabinet, resigned a month later. Meanwhile Albania, heralded in the mid-1990s as Europe's fastest growing economy, had slipped back to its earlier distinction as Europe's most impoverished country.

## The Kosovo Challenge

A major concern to those on the Balkans watch had long been that an insecure leader or a reckless opposition faction in Albania might be tempted to play the Kosovo Card. If the Macedonian government should then choose to divert attention from a failing economy by scapegoating the Albanian minority and negotiations between the Serbian leadership of Yugoslavia and the Albanian leadership of Kosovo should break down, repercussions would surely be far-reaching. As it happened, even as order began to be restored to Albania itself in 1997, Kosovo was coming apart.

Among his early moves to consolidate power in a greater Serbia, Slobodan Milosevic suppressed the autonomy that Kosovo had enjoyed under Tito's Yugoslavia. According to diplomatic sources in Skopje, Milosevic had agreed informally, in the mid-1990s, to the restoration of Kosovo's autonomous status, but the offer became moot as hostilities deepened. By early 1998 Serbian military forces were indiscriminately shelling and burning Albanian villages, and Albanian advocates of autonomy had been overtaken and overwhelmed by militants seeking independence.

After months of staging exercises, roaring about readiness, and, finally, threatening air strikes, NATO, in the person of US Special Envoy Richard Holbrooke, reached agreement in principle with Milosevic in October 1998 to the effect that the Serbians would withdraw a major portion of their troops from Kosovo; allow refugees to return to their homes; admit a two-thousand-member mission from the Organization for Security and Cooperation in Europe (OSCE) to verify that those things were happening and that relief workers were able to work unmolested; permit overflights to verify the safety of the OSCE mission; and schedule negotiations on the status of Kosovo.

The ink was hardly dry on the initial agreement before observers were reporting that Milosevic was not in compliance, and NATO demonstrated the extent of its resolve by extending the deadline for compliance. The UN

Security Council, with Russian and Chinese abstentions, sanctioned the OSCE mission and the NATO surveillance overflights but withheld sanction of the use of force to punish noncompliance. The upshot may yet secure the honor of the US and NATO, but it is not likely to secure a long-term peace for Kosovo's Albanians and the Balkans southern tier.

Potential parallels to the unhappy and unresolved fate of Nagorno-Karabakh, the Armenian enclave in Azerbaijan, have not been missed; but the threat posed by conflict in Kosovo is even more open-ended, given the large Albanian minority in Macedonia scattered across the territory between Kosovo and Albania, and the small but well-connected Serbian minority in Kosovo. Moreover, the appetites of Serbian leadership are not necessarily sated; and there remains a possibility of spillover from unfinished business farther north, among Serbs, Croats, and Bosnians or of the spread of hostilities South and East into Greece and Bulgaria or even Turkey.

# Notes

1. Conversations with Miroslav and others cited in this chapter took place in 1996.

# Chapter 4

# The Spillover of Suppressed Nationalism: Poland and the Baltics

*Ethnic chauvinism is a distraction.*
*The leader who can claim a majority based on*
*policy consensus doesn't need it.*

*We are all either carpetbaggers or migratory laborers now.*
*Some can live anywhere they want to. Others just want*
*a place to live. But all of us have lost our moorings.*

*THE LOOSENING OF* central controls within the Soviet bloc and even within the Soviet Union itself initiated by Gorbachev gave encouragement to opposition forces in client states, like Poland's Solidarity trade union, and to displaced elites and silenced intellectuals in irredentist or nationalistic republics, especially the Baltic states. The long denied national self-determination that eased the chaos of transition for those who identified as Lithuanian, Latvian, and Estonian did not apply, however, to the large minorities of ethnic Russians in those states. They faced new forms of discrimination and at least partial loss of citizenship rights. In the Baltics, as elsewhere, it seems unlikely that any strategy for economic revitalization will hold promise in the absence of an acceptable formula for peaceful coexistence among disparate ethnic communities.

Poland joined NATO in March 1999; on March 31, 1998, the country began official negotiations for joining the European Union as well. That is not surprising, since political and economic transition have maintained a steady course if one overlooks the extraordinary influence of the Roman Catholic Church; and, after a severe dip in the early 1990s, the economy has rebounded with a force that is being called a miracle.[1]

Industrial production was up by 7 percent in 1995, making Poland the first Soviet-bloc country to return to the pre-reform production levels of 1989. Poland's place at the head of the pack seems appropriate in that it was the first of the communist states to be swept into the twister of transition.

## Poland at the Vortex: Just a Little Brawl Among Friends

One evening in the summer of 1987, patrons of a sidewalk cafe in Cracow's Renaissance-era market square were distracted by a brawl in their midst. In a most uneven match, a young lout apparently possessed of all his physical faculties was beating and kicking another youth who appeared drunk. My husband and I had witnessed similar fights on the two previous evenings in Warsaw, and on those occasions as well, onlookers, rather than breaking up the fight, simply joined in, aiming a kick or punch at the drunk. When we asked why no one came to the aid of the victim, our Polish companion responded that the fight was "just among friends."

Such brawling seemed particularly incongruous juxtaposed against a tradition of exquisite courtesy, which was still abundantly in evidence. But with a few days of exposure to an economic system so user-friendly that the simplest tasks of securing food and shelter seemed almost impossible, one could begin to understand why people might spend their spare time beating up their friends. Patience had been stretched to the limits, and frustration was manifest toward the Soviet Union and all testimony of its influence in Poland, as well as in seemingly uncritical reverence for all things Roman Catholic and Western. The very reasonable assumption that most of what they read in the government press was untrue was accompanied by the dangerous assumption that its opposite (e.g., that most Americans were thriving under Reaganomics) must be true.

What Poles understood very well, however, was their own political situation, rife with subtleties and paradoxes. The government of General Wojciech Jaruzelski had negligible popular support, but in practical terms that was not the issue. It was well understood that if Poland had the government its people truly wanted, the Soviets would send tanks. So the game was to expand social and economic freedoms without pushing the Russians too far. At least, that was the game as seen by most Poles and by the Solidarity trade union — which, in fact, was not only a trade union but a general representative of economic, social, and political interests of workers and the middle class alike.[2]

For the Jaruzelski government, the game was more complicated and more subtle. To some extent, the government was yielding to popular demands for greater freedoms and hinting that it would like to do more but could not without provoking Soviet counter- measures. To Moscow's hard-liners it argued that concessions were preferable to the economic, political and public relations costs of repression, and in fact were in keeping with the new Gorbachev approach. Moreover, the government hoped that a policy of selective concessions would split Solidarity by appealing to moderates in the movement.

Pawel Spiewak, an editor of the respected underground journal *Respublica*, which in September 1986 was given permission to publish openly, was well aware of the government's game. But he believed that the opposition stood to gain more than the government from any change that expanded the margins of free expression.

The Soviets were themselves somewhat unsure about whether concessions would weaken or strengthen opposition sentiment, and unclear about how far they could allow Poland to develop in its own direction before they lost control and had a military security problem on their Western border. Nevertheless, many staunch opponents of the Polish government admitted reluctantly that Mikhail Gorbachev was their best hope for further liberalization — even though they found it incongruous to view any Soviet leader as a source of anything other than oppression.

Another factor in this complex set of relationships was the United States. Poland was in such a weak position in international trade, and had become so indebted, that US economic credits played a vital role in the economy. Thus the Polish government had to take into account the views of Washington as well as — though not as much as — those of Moscow.

The final part of this equation was the Roman Catholic Church. Many commentators have pointed out the importance of Roman Catholicism to the national self-image of Poles, helping define the country's identity in relationship to Orthodox Russia and Protestant East Germany. And the enormous national pride in having a Polish pope intensified both that identity and its significance. The government had tried at one time or another to divide the church and weaken links with the pope as well as to discredit the Church as an institution and to intimidate its leaders, but all to no avail. Jaruzelski knew finally that he had to be attentive to the wishes of Rome as well as to those of Moscow and Washington.

## Between East and West

The dynamic of political confrontation as it evolved in Poland in the 1980s found more counterparts in the West than in the Soviet bloc, and both sides in this struggle looked to the West for inspiration and ideas. For example, the Polish military, in drawing up contingency plans in 1980 for the imposition of military law, reportedly sent envoys to Turkey to study the model employed by that country's armed forces. Solidarity, meanwhile, established links with repressed dissidents in a number of Western countries. A Solidarity group visiting the US arranged a meeting with South Africans struggling against apartheid, and in 1986 a delegation of Chileans organizing against President Augusto Pinochet paid a visit to Solidarity leaders in Poland. Economically, as well, Poland was in the late 1980s rather like a transitional zone between East and West, but Western influence and Western links did not constitute an unmixed blessing. It seemed, in fact, that Poland had acquired the worst of both worlds: Eastern inefficiency and Western debt.

On the whole, state enterprises were disasters in terms of efficiency and service to the public. Small private businesses, a concession achieved partly by Solidarity's efforts, helped to absorb the energies of the post-war population bulge and to mitigate economic rigidities and bottlenecks of the sort found elsewhere in Eastern Europe. But such essentials as housing and telephones were scarce, and salaries remained shockingly low in the face of a steady inflation. A university professor, for example, earned the equivalent of about $80 a month.

As early as the mid-1980s, some of Poland's economic woes were attributable to Western-style austerity measures imposed by creditors and their collection agency, the International Monetary Fund. Nevertheless, the waiting in line required for almost any transaction resulted not so much from shortage of goods or facilities as from shortage of incentive to serve. The feature of the working-class state most readily apparent to outsiders was that while employees saw little to gain in performing their job well, they also saw little to risk in performing it poorly. Thus the job itself became the worker's stock in trade. A waitress might eventually take your order or a hotel clerk may assign you to a room in return for humble entreaties rather than holding out for a bribe, but no service or transaction was simply routine.

The late years of the Jaruzelski government were not a time of great optimism for most Poles, as the struggle settled into a kind of waiting game. Even so, the Polish people have a well-earned reputation for quixotic efforts and almost fanatic nationalism. No one who had followed the accounts of Polish soldiers on horseback charging tanks, or who had seen the medieval center of Warsaw, reconstructed brick by brick after having been bombed to rubble, would have hastened to discount prospects for Solidarity.

## At the End of the Tunnel: Refracted Light

Solidarity was indeed to have its day, even to elect the world-renowned leader of its heroic struggle, Lech Walesa, to the presidency. But free of Russia and the Soviet Union did not mean free. Economic policy continued to be dictated from beyond the country's borders. Policy-making ceded to Western creditors and international financial institutions was carried out to the benefit of foreigners with little regard to the immediate needs of the Polish people. The early 1990s were years of desperation, in which what had been a highly industrialized economy came to a virtual standstill. Real GDP fell sharply in 1990 and 1991, while inflation levels exceeded four digits. In 1992, Poland became the first country in the region to resume economic growth. By 1994, the annual GDP growth rate had reached 5.5 percent — the highest in Europe except for Albania — and inflation had dropped back to double digits.

The rebound was made possible in large part by Western bank write-offs of half of Poland's $13 billion debt and by total investments between 1989 and 1996 of $6 billion, advantages that countries getting a later start on the restructuring track could not expect to receive. Even in Poland, the miracle did not appear from all perspectives to have been of heavenly origin. It left between two and a half and three million members of the labor force officially unemployed and another two to three million operating in the unorganized, unprotected informal sector. And inflation was rising at an annual rate of 22 percent.

Little wonder that by the time the decline had bottomed out and the economy had begun to grow again, Walesa and Solidarity had been popularly discredited and a reconstructed former Communist party had been elected to power. But even the Communists were unable to rebuild the essential elements of a public sector or to mend the gaping holes in the social safety net or otherwise to compensate the new underclass of losers in the reconstructed marketplace. As if to bracket the period of transition and to mock its original protagonists, the Gdansk shipyard, where the liberation struggle was launched, was shut down in March 1996, leaving 3,600 workers without jobs.

## The Baltics: Economic Deadlock and Resurgent Nationalism

Each of the Baltic capitals has in its heart an old city, dating to the Middle Ages. Old Vilnius exhibits, in particular, the golden age of the Polish-Lithuanian kingdom, while Riga and Tallinn retain their Hanseatic character. Each of these cities also manifests the architectural exuberance and quirkiness of the turn-of-the-twentieth-century Art Nouveau period.

On a sunny day, Riga can be particularly resplendent. Beyond the winding, cobbled streets of the old city, the newer city sports self-important boulevards and lush, manicured green parks, generously sprinkled with statuary. The unwary visitor, however, in the early 1990s, was likely to get lost; all street names honoring heroes of the socialist revolution had been changed, but the changes on city maps were not yet reflected in actual street signs.

Patriotism, or nationalism, in the Baltics is rooted in historic precedent, marked by ethnic difference, and reinforced by several years of sustained resistance. The Baltic states have historically looked West, across the sea, rather than East toward Asia, for trade and cultural relations. The languages of Latvia and Lithuania have no counterparts in Europe, East or West; they are traceable directly to proto-Indo-European. And Estonian, of the Finno-Ugrian family, finds close kinship only with Finnish and very distant kinship with Hungarian.

Above all, Baltic nationalism has been honed by resistance, and it is manifest in anger. Resentment, not simply of the former Soviet government, but of Russians generally, is remarkably widespread; it was reminiscent of the attitude toward Germans found in Europe in the 1950s.

## Lawlessness and Uncertain Legitimacy

The transition has brought pockets of lawlessness to virtually all of Eastern Europe's new states. A common feature seems to be the new, emboldened mafia. In each of the capitals my husband and I visited in 1992, we were told to avoid the largest and most modern hotels because those hotels had become the sites of mafia activity. We were told, for example, that two people had been shot to death the previous week in the restaurant of the luxurious, new Hotel Belarus in Minsk.

The more general and more remarkable problem, however, was not of international lawlessness, but of confusion about which rules and which authorities or institutions should enjoy legitimacy. The customs official who boarded our train at the Polish border demanded to know how much money we were carrying in what currencies, but when we asked why he needed to know, he looked perplexed, shrugged, and walked off in frustration. A Belarusan border guard demanded our visas with an officiousness suggestive of Stalin, but en route to Lithuania there was no check even for train tickets, much less for visas. Entering Latvia, a guard uninterested in visas or passports welcomed me with a souvenir bullet from his gun.

In Vilnius, the Prime Minister's foreign affairs adviser, a Lithuanian-American who had just completed a degree at the Monterey Institute of International Studies in California, confirmed that with a melange of old and new, sometimes contradictory, legislation in place and with officials and institutions representing both old and new regimes, it was very difficult, even for those in government, to sort out who and what were legitimate. And the uneven gains and losses of the transition contributed to instability. In fact, the nationalist neoliberal government this woman served had lost its majority the previous day to a communist-led coalition, a response, in part, to the hardships faced by peasants whose collective or cooperative farms were being dissolved so that land might be returned to the private owners from whom it was confiscated almost a half century ago.

Restitution of private lands that had been confiscated by the Soviet government from the small pre-war aristocracy did not sit well with the majority of Lithuanians, whose standard of living had plunged as a consequence of the hyperinflation and economic dislocation that accompanied restructuring. State farms were disbanded early on, and new political leaders sought to appease practicing farmers by allotting each farming family its own private plot. The number of private farmers jumped from seven thousand in 1991 to seventy-three thousand in 1993. But the new farms were for the most part too small and ill-equipped to be self-sustaining. Disruption in state agricultural production was one of the reasons for a decline of 50 percent in GDP between 1989 and 1992. (The economy did not begin to grow again until 1994, when it grew by 0.6 percent.)

Like several other Lithuanians with whom we spoke, the foreign affairs adviser registered her distrust of the intelligence and security agencies. Some reorganization had taken place, but the personnel was scarcely changed. Some five different agencies assumed responsibilities with respect to parliamentary and government offices. Elected leaders, she said, assumed that their phones were tapped.

## When Nothing Works

If the phone taps worked, they may have been just about the only thing about the telephone system that did. As elsewhere in the ex-Soviet sphere, pay phones used the kopec coin; but the kopec, made worthless by hyperinflation, was no longer in circulation. International calls were likely to take all day; they had to be routed through Moscow and booked up to five hours ahead; and there was always a queue.

For political and economic models as well as financial support, Lithuanian nationalists look to Scandinavia, and particularly to Norway. Even so, the loss of the Russian market — due primarily to Russia's economic crisis rather than to political factors — had been a terrible setback. Shops in Vilnius and Kaunas seemed well enough stocked, but among the new, privately owned ones there was little specialization and prices were arbitrary. (Soviet champagne, for example, might cost the equivalent of $2 or $20, depending on whether the price was cited in local or in hard currency.) Many of them seemed to be peddling whatever Uncle Rimas had in the attic.

For public institutions of higher education the squeeze of the transition was particularly tight. An academic administrator at the University of Kaunas told us that he would not be able to support a family on his salary (about $40 a month); after a day at the university he puts in several hours of work on the family farm, where he and his wife share a house with her parents, her brother and sister-in-law and their three children.

## Unwilling Service

Latvia's capital, Riga, had a look of prosperity to it, but when it came to service — or the lack of it — the old ways usually prevailed. As we had found elsewhere in the New East, dining out was a challenge. Local contacts assured us that the bouncers who guarded the doors of every restaurant merely wanted big tips; but the fervor with which they blocked entrances made it appear that they had already been tipped by the service staff inside to keep the pesky patrons out. Standards of service in Tallinn were not necessarily higher, but it was clear that once they bounce the bouncers, it would be ripe for a boom in tourism. At least within the maze that is the old city, Tallinn has the ambiance of a small town (a small town, that is, of the Middle Ages).

Businessmen who had established joint enterprises in architecture and construction in several of the former Soviet republics said they had located their headquarters in Estonia because, under Finnish "hegemony," Estonia had made greater progress than the others toward the realization of a free market. The fact that they had been offered the very comfortable premises of what was previously the headquarters of the communist party for their offices seemed to indicate on the part of Estonian authorities a remarkable openness to foreign investors — either that or an interest in tapping their telephones.

The businessmen maintained that the crunch would come for all of the Baltic states when they ran out of oil reserves, because they lacked the foreign exchange to buy more. Another problem for those new states was highlighted by a fresh-faced young German who confided that he was using the easy access between Finland and Estonia to bring precious metals out of Russia. The red tape was exhausting, he conceded, but the enormous profit margins made it worthwhile.

## The Unwelcome Russians

Given their almost unquestionable embrace of the global "free market," the new or newly sovereign states of Eastern Europe seem extraordinarily vulnerable to carpetbaggers. But the even greater threat to statehood is that embodied in the ruin that was relatively open and prosperous Yugoslavia. Like Yugoslavia, each of the new states has ethnic minorities within it.

For Estonia, as for Latvia, the most serious short-term problem is that of national identity and citizenship. The plight of the Russian soldiers still billeted in 1992 in the country — more as exiles rather than occupiers, soldiers deserted by their state — who had recently come under attack from Estonian civilians, was only the tip of an iceberg that threatened to sink the battered ship of state. In response to the concerns of ethnic Russians throughout the Baltics, Yeltsin had announced a decision to lengthen the timetable for withdrawal of Russian troops.

Approximately 30 percent of Estonia's inhabitants are ethnically Russian. Those who came as bureaucrats may well be able to defend their interests, but most came as factory workers; they constitute an underclass, held in contempt, and now lacking the protection of citizenship. A "grandfather clause" has been devised to exclude residents who arrived after 1939. More recent arrivals were required to pass a literacy test in Estonian to vote for delegates to the constitutional assembly.

Latvians likewise seemed determined to expel, or exclude from citizenship, or at least to limit political participation by the one-third of the population of Russian descent. Even in Riga, where Russian ethnics account for perhaps 80 percent, we saw anti-Russian demonstrations and placards telling Russians to "go home."

As in Estonia, citizenship has been denied to those who were not Latvian or descended from those who were Latvian before the Soviet invasion of 1940. And applicants for naturalization have been required to take an examination in Latvian history and language that they were not expected to pass.

In June 1998, under pressure from Russia and the European Union, Latvia passed new legislation that granted citizenship to children born in the country since independence in 1991. Adults, however, among the ethnic Russians, remain stateless, unable to vote or even to travel. Instead of a passport, they are entitled only to a document asserting that they are stateless.

## Social Order and Ethnic Exclusion

In the Baltic states, where the prevailing law and source of authority from one day to the next was often a mystery even to those most highly placed, order seemed to rise from the bottom up, from social inertia or family necessity or habits of meeting hardship with stoicism and civility. Such habits of social order at street level bode well for the process of transition. But in North Central Europe, as in most of the rest of the former Soviet sphere, transition has generated such economic dislocation and such a dramatic retreat from widely accepted standards of fairness as to bring the agents of restructuring into disrepute and to bring former Communists back into office by electoral means. If such leaders dare to adopt policies that deviate from contemporary Western economic orthodoxy, the process of transition may be threatened by Western intransigence. The process remains threatened, also, in the Baltics, by failure to establish workable mechanisms for peaceful coexistence among ethnically disparate communities, and particularly for accommodating participation by the now persecuted Russian minority.

## Notes

1. Economic miracles are about rising from the dead. The prior destruction of the economy is an essential element in generating a miracle.

2. When political freedoms have been suppressed, almost any institution or organization that dares to be critical can become the center of an opposition movement.

## Chapter 5

# Empire Implosion and Independence by Default: Central Asia and Belarus

*The more important the decision,*
*the fewer and less well informed will be*
*those involved in making it.*

*Dictatorship is a frame of mind —*
*the vindication of an attitude, not one-man*
*rule but a license that makes petty dictators*
*out of everyone who serves the system.*

*UNLIKE THE RESTIVE* Baltics, the Central Asian Republics did not secede from the union. The union seceded from them. Dissolution was decided by the leaders of Russia, Belarus, and the Ukraine on the basis of more narrowly drawn nationalism or political ambitions, and announced summarily to the stunned populations of other republics. That is not to suggest that there is now nostalgia for union; but the ethnic tensions simmering now are more generally a result, rather than the cause, of independence.

## Rediscovering Ethnicity in Central Asia

A problem shared by all of the new republics of this cultural area, stretching from the Himalayas north to Russia and from the Caspian Sea east to China, is the threatened unraveling of the social fabric. Ethnic blending has been underway on a grand scale at least since the Muslims swept through in the eighth century, but the cultural area as it has evolved over the past two centuries is as much an extension of Siberia as a vestige of the Silk Route.

More than 40 percent of the population of Kazakhstan is ethnically

Russian and another 10–20 percent is other than Kazakhi. The capital, Almaty, is 70 percent Russian. In other cities as well, Russian is the dominant language. Nevertheless, the momentum now runs toward the building of a Kazakhi, rather than a multicultural, new state, including the adoption of a national language that only about one-third of the young people speak.

On November 9, 1997, Kazakhstan officially moved its capital from Almaty to Akmola, a quiet town of 300,000 750 miles north of Almaty. Critics are referring to Akmola, where Siberian winds howl for ten months out of twelve and where one hundred residents had died in the previous year from the cold, as a Potemkin Village. The official rationale for moving the capital is that Akmola is more central, but analysts believe that the move was designed to dilute the strength of ethnic Russians who are a majority in the North and to discourage them from seeking support from Russia.[1]

It is hardly surprising that Russians, who profited for so long from forward discrimination, would be unenthusiastic about seeing the tables turned or that the long suppressed Kazakhs might see merit now in reverse discrimination. But even some opinion leaders of Kazakhi descent are troubled by the new discrimination against Russians in education and employment. The editor of the reputable journal *Science of Kazakhstan*, for example, lamented that the country was beginning to suffer from the "brain drain" of well-educated Russians.

Elsewhere across the Silk Route the ethnic mix is different, but variation and tensions are just as great. The Kyrgyz constitute scarcely half the population in the republic that bears their name. Stalin used Central Asia as a dumping ground for peoples he found troublesome in other areas, so along with the ethnic Russians and Uzbeks in Kyrgyzstan there are sizable communities of Ukrainians, Germans, and Crimean Tartars. A young teacher, ethnically Tartar, who worked with the US Peace Corps in the Kyrgyzi capital, Bishkek, told me that her ethnicity had never been a matter of much interest before, but that the recent increased attention to her distinctiveness was beginning to make her uncomfortable.

## Belarus: A Nation Stillborn?

The new order in Belarus came about neither through rebellion against Russian hegemony, as in Poland and the Baltics, nor through default as in the cases of Macedonia and the Central Asian republics. Rather, it came about through conspiracy with Russian leadership against Gorbachev and his vision of a new confederative, social democratic order for the Soviet Union as a whole. Thus, the new order in Belarus turned out to be remarkably like the old and to be strongly linked to the new disorder that was Russia.

## Time Travel

Illustrative of those links, both to the past and to Russia, is the Berlin to Moscow "express," a Russian train that my husband and I took overnight to Minsk in 1992. The express was not simply slow, it was a voyage backwards in time. But it made up in local color what it lacked in speed and comfort. The only refreshment to be had was Russian tea, prepared in a small ceramic pot and dispensed by the all-purpose attendant. The attendant *babushkas* appeared to be homesteading in their sleeping cars and to assume a proprietary attitude toward them, particularly the restrooms, which they generally kept locked.

Sleep would have been impossible, but at any rate a waste, given the entertainment that filled the wee hours. Shortly after the train crossed from Poland into Belarus, the cars had to be jacked up — one or two at a time — to be refitted with wheels that operated on the narrower Russian gauge. The jacks that lifted the cars some six feet off of the rails were hydraulic, but most of the subsequent adjustments, which took more than two hours, were make by male and female "grease-monkeys," who crawled into the pits under the rail cars with crowbars and screwdrivers and hammers from their lunchbox-size tool boxes.

## Assets and Liabilities

Minsk, in times past a mostly wooden city in the path of too many conquerors, reveals little of its history. With its broad avenues and leafy parks, it wears a placid face. At the farmers' co-op market, one could see tired shoppers waiting in long lines to buy eggs at subsidized prices, while a few free-marketers standing nearby offered the same eggs without the wait, but at prices few could afford. We were told that there was a seasonal shortage of sugar, but we saw no evidence of generalized shortage or panic buying or other manifestations of the trauma of transition so recently reported from Russia.

Among former Soviet Republics, Belarus had more than its share of productive agriculture and potentially profitable industry. Thus in 1992 it also had more than its share of visiting businessmen, hustlers, and would-be investors, Western and Eastern. Surprisingly few of them were American. (Most of the Americans we saw in Minsk were evangelicals who had packed the municipal stadium for a revival meeting.) The chairman of the political science department at the University of Minsk, who does risk analysis on the side, said that American businessmen come and find that the phones don't work and leave. Chinese businessmen, he said, come and find that the phones don't work and stay to design a new telephone system. The Chinese were, in fact, designing centralized switchboards for ministries, hotels, and other establishments.

Another thing Belarus has more than its share of is military divisions. The Soviet front-line forces previously deployed to Poland and East Germany pulled back to where the second line of defense had been established in Belarus — and there they remained. With some 250,000 military personnel, a ratio of one soldier for forty-three civilians, according to leaders of the Belarus Peace Committee, Belarus in 1992 had the largest military concentration of any republic in the new Confederation of Independent States (CIS). For better or worse — and civilian analysts and policymakers were ambivalent as to which was the case — this massive array of force remained without a mission. There were no "strategic objectives" either for Belarus alone or for the CIS, although CIS forces had intervened in Georgia, Moldova, and elsewhere. (In the case of Moldova, there seemed to be agreement at least on the importance of maintaining access to its cognac.)

What was unmistakably clear to civilian leaders was that maintenance of such a military establishment could be very expensive and that subjecting it to deep budget cuts could be dangerous. Russian leaders indicated recognition of the problem when they came through with a major grant to support the troops in Belarus.

## A Belated and Reactive Nationalism

Belarus gained its independence by executive fiat, without political struggle, and the Old Guard remains largely in control. With links to and, in some areas, dependence upon Russia still strong, patriotism in Belarus until recently lacked the fervor that was apparent in the Baltics. Even among scholars who hail from elsewhere, there are opportunities as well as challenges that come with independence. University professors, for example, while braced for a cutback in funding (the system was previously supported by the Soviet central government) find new fulfillment in being consulted regularly on proposed legislation, and some are tempted to become candidates for elective office. But the plan to make Belarusan (a Slavic language related to Russian) the official language is disconcerting to the approximately 80 percent of the population who have come of age speaking Russian and are not fluent in Belarusan. Nor did the issuance of a Belarusan currency inspire much enthusiasm. Most shunned it initially in favor of *real* money, by which they meant rubles.

Complacency about Belarusan national identity began to give way to consternation and finally to assertiveness after 1994, when Alexander Lukashenko was elected to the presidency. Former head of a collective farm, he proved to be unreconstructed in both political and economic dimensions.

Lukashenko rode to power on a wave of revulsion against corruption.[2] But it soon became clear that he had plans of his own for short-circuiting legal process. By dubious means, including an election boycotted by the better-educated and more Westernized urban voters, he ensured that the parliament would be dominated by a Communist-Agrarian Party alliance supportive of his policies.

Even before the elections of 1994, investments from the West had been mostly fluff — McDonald's, Phillip Morris, Coca Cola. But Lukashenko's open rejection of Western-inspired structural adjustment strategies led to a credit freeze and an economic meltdown. Scarcities appeared, most acutely of heating fuels during a cold winter, and prices rose five-fold between 1994 and 1996.

## A Crumbling Crutch

Such hardship might have been endured with little more than standard grumbling had not Lukashenko chosen also to engage in a direct affront to nationalist sentiment. He signed an agreement of confederation with Russia that was to mean Russian subsidization of energy costs in exchange for more or less open borders for trade. What else it might mean remained unclear (currencies and basic economic legislation were to remain distinct); but that very lack of clarity, along with the autocratic approach to the agreement, generated widespread protest, including a demonstration by some fifty thousand on the streets of Minsk in the spring of 1996. A crackdown on such protest came into effect in April and pressure continued to build. A carefully controlled referendum in November extended Lukashenko's presidential powers, and in 1997 he was using the expansion of NATO — to embrace neighboring Poland — as a rationale for further tightening of political controls.

Increased attachment to and dependence upon Russia made Belarus all the more vulnerable when Russia, in August 1998, after a growth spurt, expressed particularly in a booming stock market, took another plunge.Like most of the Central Asian Republics, Belarus has the material resources on which to build a national economy and is in the process of constructing a national consciousness; but again like the new states of Central Asia, it has made a mockery of democratization and appears far removed still from domestic tranquillity, not to mention civility and social harmony.

## Notes

1. "New Capital Gets a Chilly Reception in Kazakhstan," *The International Herald Tribune,* Nov. 10, 1997, p. 5.
2. Corruption has been a theme useful to second-round electoral candidates in most of the newly independent states, since the opportunities for private enrichment at public expense so abundant in economic restructuring have not gone wanting.

## Part I: A Cookie-Cutter World: The New Nationalism Suggested Readings

Bardhan, Pranab. "Method in Madness? A Political-Economy Analysis of Ethnic Conflict in Less Developed Countries." Economics Department Working Paper. University of California, Berkeley, 1996.

Bennis, Phyllis and Michael Moushabeck, eds. *Altered States: A Reader in the New World Order*. Brooklyn, NY: Olive Branch Press, Interlink, 1993.

Bideleux, Robert and Richard Taylor, eds. *European Integration and Disintegration: East and West*. London: Routledge, 1996.

Chomsky, Noam. *World Orders Old and New*. New York: Columbia University Press, 1994.

Dunn, Seamus, and T.G. Fraser, eds. *Europe and Ethnicity: World War I and Contemporary Ethnic Conflict*. London: Routledge, 1996.

Helleiner, G.K. "Conventional Foolishness and Overall Ignorance: Current Approaches to Global Transformations and Development." In C. Wilber and K. Jameson, eds. *The Political Economy of Development and Underdevelopment, 5th ed*. New York: McGraw-Hill, 1992.

Hitchens, Christopher. *Hostage to History: Cyprus from the Ottomans to Kissinger*. New York: Verso, 1997.

Hoyer, Hans. *Open Minds: Reflections on Human Development and South-North Issues*. Colombo, Sri Lanka: Plan International, 1996.

Kumar, Radha. *Divide and Fall? Bosnia and the Annals of Partition*. London: Verso, 1997.

Kulchik, Yury, Andrey Fadin, and Victor Sergeev. *Central Asia After the Empire*. London: Pluto Press, 1991.

Lake, David A. and Donald Rothchild, eds. *The International Spread of Ethnic Conflict: Fear, Diffusion, and Escalation*. Princeton: Princeton University Press, 1998.

Leffler, Melvyn. *A Preponderance of Power*. Palo Alto: Stanford University Press, 1992.

Nef, Jorge and H. Wiseman. "The Second World: A New Periphery?" *Worldscape* 4 (1), 1-4, 1990.

Ro'i, Yaacov. *Muslim Eurasia: Conflicting Legacies*. London: Frank Cass, 1995.

Rupesinghe, Kumar, with Sanam Naraghi Anderlini. *Civil Wars, Civil Peace: An Introduction to Conflict Resolution*. London: Pluto Press, 1998.

Udovichi, Jasminka, and James Ridgeway, eds. *Burn This House: the Making and Unmaking of Yugoslavia*. Durham: NC: Duke University Press, 1997.

United Nations Research Institute for Social Development. *States of Dismay: The Social Effects of Globalization*. London: Kegan Paul/Earthscan, 1995.

# Part II

# The Displaced and the Dispossessed

*The counterpart to stateless capital is stateless and homeless people.*

*THE END OF THE* Cold War was not so different from the end of previous wars in that the "consequences of the peace" included new categories of the deprived and the displaced. The war's end tended to shut down conflicts that had been provoked or perpetuated by superpower interests, but other conflicts were unleashed that had been suppressed by Pax Sovietica or Pax Americana or by common superpower concerns about letting Third World bushfires get out of hand. The cookie-cutter approach to the delineation of new states also generated conflict and refugees.

Apart from peoples displaced directly by the fall-out of the peace — by abrupt shifts, for example, in national boundaries — a much greater wave of refugees was being generated by shifts in trade patterns and investments and by the global monopoly of an economic model that treats people as just another, potentially disposable, factor of production.

Meanwhile, in the late twentieth-century, there were no states anywhere raising torches and issuing invitations to the "huddled masses yearning to breathe free." For a time the logic of the Cold War had dictated that the US and the West generally should shun those fleeing right-wing oppressors but harbor refugees from communist states in order to highlight the abuses and failures of such regimes. Liberation from Cold War logic has meant that anti-immigrant prejudice may be allowed to override in all cases.

Camps for Vietnamese boat-people in Hong Kong and elsewhere began to close in the early 1990s, as their hapless populations were forcibly repatriated. Even the exceptional open door for Cuban refugees in the US was closed in 1995. Ironically, fear of Haitian refugees on the part of some who would otherwise have opposed such action gave the Clinton Administration the margin of support necessary to depose Haitian military usurpers and reinstate the country's elected president in 1994.

The Strangelove logic of the Cold War had allowed the US to join China in supporting the extraordinarily brutal Khmer Rouge against the Vietnamese occupiers of Cambodia. The disintegration of Vietnam's great power ally meant that at last the US could step aside and allow the United Nations to attempt the repatriation of 300,000 Cambodians and the reintegration and resuscitation of that long-suffering nation. The immensity of literal and political minefields to be dealt with assured that such resuscitation would not be easy.

In other areas — Central America, Southern Africa, and Bosnia, for example — former refugees are being resettled in their homelands, in part because social peace and hope are being restored and in part because the temporary refuge they were offered is being terminated. Elsewhere, though — Rwanda and Burundi, Afghanistan, Liberia, Sierra Leone, Sri Lanka, Chechnya, Sudan, and the Horn of Africa — new refugees are being generated. In Rwanda alone almost a million people were slaughtered in 1994 in a version of "ethnic cleansing" that left another three million homeless. In 1998, a "family feud" between the leaders of Ethiopia and Eritrea (they are cousins) has sent tens of thousands fleeing in both directions across a border that until 1993 wasn't even there.

In 1996, according to the US Committee for Refugees, there remained some fifteen million persons around the world officially recognized as refugees.[1] And that figure was a trivial one compared to the numbers being displaced by failed or "reformed" economies, despoiled and polluted habitats, concentration of land and resource holdings, mechanization of agricultural and technological advancement in production and services, downsizing and out-sourcing, shrinkage of the public sector, and fraying of social safety nets. The United Nations has identified about forty-six million people as displaced and essentially refugees. This is in addition to more than 100 million categorized as homeless (not counting the approximately twenty-three million in Bangladesh and perhaps two million more in the Caribbean and Central America made homeless by flooding in 1998.) And so-called white slavery — trafficking in sexual bondage — is on the rise.

The contemporary global game of musical chairs owes much, of course, to population explosion; according to the UN Population Fund, while the pace of world population growth had decelerated since the 1960s, it still exceeded eighty million a year in the 1990s. Above all, though, it is the nature of capitalism in its post-Cold War incarnation that provides the explanatory link between the contract labor forces in East Asia — booming until the meltdown of 1997 — and the oil-drunk Middle East, the new waves of documented and undocumented Latin American migrants in the US, the indigenous peoples displaced in Borneo and Brazil by rainforest exploitation, the burgeoning populations of street children in Bombay and Bogota, and the homeless on the streets of America's cities. In most such countries, including European and European-settled ones, where conquest, the fallout of colonialism, and spurts of economic growth have created an ethnically distinct work force, citizenship has been somehow grandfathered — that is, based on lineage rather than place of birth or residence. In most states, indigenous peoples, like immigrant workers, have been excluded from the effective exercise of citizenship through such devices as literacy tests.

In the late nineteenth and early twentieth centuries, the Western Hemisphere became the escape valve for the Old World's "teeming masses," and in the middle of the twentieth century, the new Europe compensated for citizenship restrictions by extending many of the rights and benefits of citizenship to resident foreigners. In the 1990s, however, the globalization of the market and the redefining of competitiveness in terms of flexibility — i.e., reduction of labor costs — has forced workers in Bonn to compete with those in Bombay. It has left more workers competing for fewer jobs and generated a backlash against those who, for whatever reason, might be seen as not belonging.

Europe has begun to tighten its rules with respect to refuge, immigration, and guest labor, and to deal less generously with non-citizens. The French, for example, decided in 1993 that citizenship, even for those born in the country if they happen to be of immigrant parents, should be earned. The turnaround in the US has been even more abrupt.

Even as the US and Mexican economies became more closely intertwined in NAFTA, as money and goods moved ever more freely across the border, walls were growing longer and taller in a futile attempt to block the movement of people. At the end of 1997, the United States was putting the final touches on a fourteen-foot-high wall dividing Nogales, Arizona, and Nogales, Senora. The US already had sixty-two miles of steel walls and chain-link and barbed-wire fences along its border with Mexico. The new wall, prototype for more to come, is designed to resist penetration by climbers, by vehicle, by firearms, chisels, hammers, and welding torches; but it was meant to be "friendly looking." Mexicans appeared to be unimpressed.

Scapegoating has been most dramatic in California, where a majority of the people are now listed as some kind of minority. Proposition 187, a popular initiative passed in California in 1994, would have denied all public services, including school and routine health care, to illegal aliens. It has been struck down by the courts, but it served the political purpose of tapping into and channeling great frustration that might otherwise be directed at economic elites and political leaders. The US Congress, lashing out at the growing community of Hispanics, passed an English-only bill in August of 1996, curtailing the use of other languages for official purposes. And in that presidential election year, the Republican platform advocated the negation of the Fourteenth Amendment, the post-Civil War amendment making citizenship automatic to children born in the United States.

That is not to say that there has been no resistance. Even those who might appear least well-armed to take on a faceless juggernaut, like indigenous communities around the world, have organized locally and globally and have undertaken creative and sophisticated campaigns of resistance. And the backlash to a perceived onslaught of immigrants and multiculturalism has generated a backlash of its own.

The scapegoating of Hispanic immigrants — legal or not — in the US in the 1990s has served to a degree to unite a population previously divided by ideology, class, and country of origin. Organization and mobilization campaigns doubled the naturalization rates between 1994 and 1996, when two million immigrants became citizens. Both newly and previously naturalized citizens were registering to vote in record numbers in part because they feared losing eligibility for earned benefits. And whereas Republicans in California could count on about 40 percent of the Latino vote before Governor Pete Wilson promoted Proposition 187 in 1994, they received only about 18 percent, according to exit polls, in 1998.

Even so, this phase of immigrant scapegoating is not likely to pass in the near future because, unlike such phases in the past, it is not a response to a cyclical economic downturn. Rather, it is a response to a system that allows those who control the movement of capital ever greater control over labor markets as well. Parsimonious allotment of citizenship and its attendant rights in a globalized economy — one in which subsistence, family autonomy, and national autarchy are not possible, in which labor has no choice but to follow capital — becomes a means of restructuring and limiting participation even as formal democracy spreads. Kuwait and Saudi Arabia offer extreme examples of how citizenship as a privilege rather than a right can allow an isolated elite to preside over a permanently alien underclass. Most of the 117 people executed in Saudi Arabia in 1997 without access to lawyers were foreign workers from developing countries.[2]

Under the constraints in the twentieth century, and especially after World War II, of a marginally competitive global economic system — one that offered an alternative market or trading system — capital in many countries came to be harnessed, to some degree, to the service of the national community. But the collapse of the Soviet bloc market, along with such technological advances as electronic funds transfer, liberated capital from its social harness and allowed for the establishment of a creditor cartel.

Like a glutton or a drug addict, the system, now liberated from social control, has become dependent on ever-greater resource inputs to fuel ever-faster rates of growth and ever-greater profit margins. And publics around the world appear to have accepted the idea that they must be sacrificed, along with the planet's finite resources, to the infinite appetites of the beast.

Some countries extraordinarily blessed by nature and cursed by colonial and neo-colonial regimes, desperate in particular for foreign exchange, have found a new way to make a living tapping into the ethical tone of the times. Many Caribbean island states are now selling citizenship. In 1997, St. Kitts and Nevis was charging $250,000 as the minimum "real estate investment" in order to qualify for citizenship, up from $100,000 a year earlier. Citizenship in Dominica was a bargain at $50,000, but there was no property thrown in. Most of the passport shoppers came from countries, including Russia and the US, that permit dual citizenship. What many are buying is tax avoidance and/or financial secrecy.[3]

# Notes

1. The 1951 United Nations Convention Relating to the Status of Refugees and the corresponding 1967 Protocol defined "refugee" as: 1. A person "outside the country of his or her nationality" who 2. has a "well-founded fear" of persecution. This definition does not include people who are fleeing war, famine, natural disaster, or economic deprivation. The UNDP Human Development Report for 1997 says that at the end of 1995 there were sixteen million refugees as such, another twenty-six million internally displaced and another four million homeless, jobless and utterly hopeless — more than 80 percent of them women and children.
2. Amnesty International reported in 1997 that execution, torture, amputation, flogging, and arbitrary arrest and detention of political suspects are normal practice in Saudi Arabia.
3. The Vatican was not selling citizenship and had not returned to selling indulgences as such; but the Archdiocese of Los Angeles announced at the beginning of 1998 that Pope John Paul II was awarding knighthood in the Pontifical Order of St. Gregory to Bob Hope, Ricardo Montalban, Roy Disney, and Rupert Murdoch. Such knighthood is bestowed in recognition of "unblemished character"!

# Chapter 6

# Ethiopia's Costly Family Feud

*War is expensive but always affordable;*
*peace has to pay its own way.*

*There are no winners in wars of attrition,*
*just losers in disproportionate numbers.*

*IN TOWNS AND* villages around the northern highlands, men gathered around a few local TV sets, listening respectfully, even supportively, while the Prime Minister spoke of the transgressions of the enemy and the patriotic duty of mobilization for war. But what had drawn most of them out to brave the elements of that rainy season in mid-1998 in search of the nearest TV set was not news of war but the World Cup soccer playoffs.

War fever was not running high in Addis Ababa either. Herds of goats mowed grass in the better neighborhoods and followed longhorn cattle and donkeys loaded with firewood up and down the hilly streets that in the rainy season became ribbons of ruts and potholes. On the more nearly level stretches, ragamuffins played soccer with rocks or any relatively rounded object they could find. Men and women draped in sheer white cotton trudged past crumbling monuments, splashy new offices of banks and international organizations, fruit stands, store fronts bearing the names of now familiar non-governmental organizations, and huts of mud and wattle, tin and cardboard.

Things seemed normal in this village of two million inhabitants, as normal as one might expect in a capital that over the past two decades had suffered an abrupt swing from pompous monarchy to Marxist tyranny; severe famine; insurrectionary war; and rapid population growth. Beneath the broad open smiles was anxiety and mistrust. Like mountain people elsewhere — Afghanistan, Papua New Guinea, East Tennessee — they had struggled to hold on to their culture and their turf, and in the process they had learned to suspect the motives of foreigners and neighbors alike. But the struggle this time was different: it was fratricidal.

## A Test of Wills and Egos

Most wars are stupid, and this one was stupider than most. The rhetoric was about violated territory, but the reality had more to do with violated trust and violated egos. On both sides of the border it was suggested that the two prime ministers, former comrades-in-arms, should settle it with a fist fight and leave their war-weary peoples — in fact historically and culturally the same people — out of it.

A simmering border dispute had turned violent when Eritrean troops on May 6 moved onto what Ethiopians claimed was the wrong side of the border in the northwestern region. Eritreans followed by occupying several hundred square miles in some six patches along the 625-mile border and bombing the capital of Tigre province, Mekele, accidentally hitting a school. For its part, Ethiopia engaged Eritrean troops along the contested border and bombed the international airport in the Eritrean capital of Asmara. Eritrea countered with a threat to bomb Addis Ababa. An uneasy truce or at least a containment of hostilities took effect in mid-June, but armies continued to mobilize and mass on both sides of the border.

On the Ethiopian side, the threat to bomb Addis Ababa was not taken very seriously, but the threat of terrorist activity certainly was. The airport in Addis Ababa may not have achieved a high level of security, but it certainly exhibited a high level of anxiety and inconvenience. Vehicles dropping off and picking up passengers were stopped at some distance from the terminal, and passengers in early July encountered an obstacle course of security checks not only entering the airport but leaving it as well. Similarly exaggerated levels of security controls prevailed at government buildings, museums, schools, and hotels. The palatial new Sheraton — with three hundred rooms, Africa's largest hotel — was offering accommodation at about one-third of its standard rate, but appeared to be lodging no tourists and few businessmen. Public places were virtually empty.

Actual armed conflict came as something of a surprise even though the build-up to it had been under way for more than a year. It evolved with more of the ethos of a contested divorce than of an international war. After all, the leaders of the two countries, Meles Zenawi of Ethiopia and Issaias Afewerki of Eritrea, were of adjoining provinces of what had been the same country and their organizations had fought side by side in the struggle to throw off the oppression of the Dergue, the ghoulish regime of Colonel Mengistu Haile Mariam. But the comradeship in arms did not survive their coming to power.

## An Inopportune Separation

As has so commonly proved to be the case, the pooling of sacrifice for war turned out to be less damaging to relationships than the subsequent division of the spoils. In fact, Ethiopia was unprepared to lose Eritrea as a province, and Eritrea was not prepared to get along without Ethiopia. But both men wanted countries to lead. And to the Eritrean leaders the insurrection against the Dergue, which had ruled Ethiopia from 1975 to 1991, represented simply the continuation of a thirty-year war of secession. They were prepared to settle for nothing less than independence.

Eritrean secession, which was formalized in 1993, left Ethiopia landlocked and lacking what had been the country's only petroleum refining facility. But it left Eritrea in even greater hardship — a string of ports baking beside the Red Sea without a hinterland. The new country also found itself running short of foreign assistance and investment, since the new government of Eritrea was even more resistant than that of Ethiopia to the economic restructuring expected by major donors, private creditors, and the International Monetary Fund.

Initially the two countries responded to the obvious need to cooperate, trading freely and using the same currency. Eritrea earned a major portion of its foreign reserves through the export of Ethiopian coffee. It bought grain from Ethiopia and sold oil from its aging refinery to Ethiopia for the Ethiopian currency they shared, the birr. But in time minor irritations grew into major ones as leaders in each country began to see each other as taking advantage, and in 1997 Eritrea introduced its own currency.

This meant that Ethiopia had to pay in hard currency at international market prices for its oil, at which point it began to take its business elsewhere, to facilities just south of Eritrea in Djibouti. Eritrea found no such accommodation for its predicament; it now has to pay hard currency for the coffee it used to export and, worse yet, for tef, its staple grain. Lacking the arable land to feed themselves, Eritreans now spend ten times as much as their Ethiopian neighbors for their grain.

Diplomats and academicians in Ethiopia doubt that Eritrea has anything serious to gain — or Ethiopia much to lose — in the barren border area Eritrean troops now occupy. But Ethiopian acceptance of any territorial loss that would favor the Eritreans might be seen at home as indication of such weakness as to invite plotting against the government of Meles. Meles might use the provocation of Eritrean incursions as an excuse to seize the port city of Assab, but has stated publicly that he has no intention of doing so.

Ironically, the absence of obvious strategic objectives in this conflict is in a sense the bad news as it leaves would-be mediators with no handles to pick up. The negotiating team sent early on by the United States and Rwanda found Ethiopia responsive to their plan, since it called for Eritrea to withdraw from occupied territory, but not surprisingly Eritrea balked. The UN

Security Council called for mutual restraint and passed the buck to the Organization of African Unity (OAU), which gave no sign then of knowing what to do with it. The leader of Uganda, Yoweri Museveni, who wields considerable influence in East and Central Africa, finally became engaged in mediation efforts, but with misgivings about involvement in a "family affair."

## Keeping It in the Family

The fight is a family one quite literally in that Meles and Afewerki are cousins but more importantly in the sense that they have emerged from a common revolutionary struggle. The real problem derived from an ill-conceived victory. In the pursuit of independence for Eritrea, the Eritrean People's Liberation Front (EPLF) adopted the strategy of undermining the Dergue by promoting ethnic separatism elsewhere in Ethiopia. As their efforts showed promise, they gained allies in the country and beyond, and the movement spread. The Tigrean Liberation Front, sponsored by the Eritreans as a diversionary attempt to weaken the Dergue, surprised everyone, and perhaps itself, by actually overthrowing the Dergue and coming to power. At that point the Eritreans might have reconsidered their plan. But they chose not to. The Tigreans who now control Ethiopia come from the province that borders Eritrea, and are even more intermarried with Eritreans than are other Ethiopians — in fact Prime Minister Meles's mother is Eritrean.

Although ethnically similar or identical to people in Ethiopia, the Eritreans are culturally somewhat distinct, because of their years under Italian rule. They are generally better educated, more urbane and cosmopolitan than Ethiopians, and they had apparently concluded that their country cousins constituted a burden rather than a base. With his junior partner Meles in control of the new Ethiopia, Afewerki must have assumed that he would be giving the orders in Ethiopia as well as in Eritrea, allocating benefits and hardships between the two countries to Eritrea's advantage, which proved to be a serious miscalculation.

Each leader might feel he had the advantage in a military confrontation. The Eritrean leadership has a lifetime of experience in fighting a war; what they lack is experience managing a troubled economy in peacetime. The Ethiopian leadership, which was linked so long, and in an apparently subordinate relationship, to Eritrea — even Meles's palace guard was Eritrean — now appears to be expanding its political base. At least in the short term, studying war generally has the effect of promoting national unity, which was sorely needed in Ethiopia. And even though they are not enthusiastic for war most Ethiopians, traditionally uncomfortable at the airs of superiority they think the Eritreans give themselves and still peeved that the uppity Eritreans wanted to go their own way, seem convinced that the Eritreans are indeed the aggressors.

In the long run, however, both leaders are playing with fire — figuratively and literally. Meles's grip on his military establishment is tenuous. He was forced to release from prison air force pilots he had imprisoned for bombing Eritrea under orders of the Dergue — because after the onset of hostilities he needed forces experienced in bombing Eritrea. Afewerki is finding out that the coast needs the hinterland more than the hinterland needs the coast. And this standoff is worsening his already difficult relations with foreign donors and international organizations. Even if genuine peace should soon be restored, much of the damage in displacement of people and resources is irreparable. Several hundred people – mostly civilians – have been killed. Tens of thousands of Ethiopians have been expelled from Eritrea and Eritreans from Ethiopia, leaving both countries with broken families and broken lives, and a bitterness that will not soon be dissipated.[1]

After five months of uneasy truce, marked by continual reinforcement of troops and weapons along the contested border and punctuated by sporadic artillery exchanges, a renewed effort at mediation offered a glimmer of hope. A committee of the OAU, comprising the presidents of Burkina Faso, Djibouti, and Zimbabwe, persuaded Meles and Afewerki to meet with them on November 7 and 8, 1998, in Ouagadougou, in Burkina Faso.

Talks were held separately, as the feuding leaders still refused to meet face-to-face. Neither was willing to accept the committee's proposed measures of de-escalation, mainly Eritrean withdrawal from the newly occupied Badme region, to be replaced by international military observers and interim civilian administrators while a UN cartographic unit undertook demarcation of the border. But both leaders expressed willingness to reflect on the proposals made until the issue could be take-up in December by the OAU's central organ for conflict prevention, management, and resolution.

## When Eating Had Priority

With a per capita gross national product of about $100 annually, Ethiopia ranks 170th among the 175 countries in the UN Development Program's human development index. Eritrea, at 168, is only two rungs ahead. Ethiopia's per capita food production remains below the level it had achieved in the late 1970s. Food is still in short supply in the northern regions of the country, but a few years of peace had been helpful.

Gabril's thirty-year-old Datsun looks like most of the other cars in Gondar. As it bumps over corrugated roads, one marvels that its parts, few of them serving their original purpose, maintain even short-term attachment to each other. Home for Gabril's family of five consists of two small rooms with a dirt floor. But with a live-in servant girl, Gabril's family is among the more prosperous in Gondar, one of the larger towns to the north of Lake Tana, where the ruins of sixteenth and seventeenth century castles stand witness to the region's last era of prosperity. Gabril is cautiously supportive of Meles's tough talk about resisting Eritrean aggression, but seeing the military encampment outside Gondar swelling once again with recruits and refugees makes him uneasy. After a few years of peace, conditions had become much better in his neighborhood: people were eating two, even three, times a day and there were smiles on children's faces.

Lalibela, to the East, where twelfth-century Christians had carved imposing churches out of solid rock, had been a center of resistance to the Dergue. The devastation brought by the conflict, compounded in the mid-1980s by a terrible drought, gave rise to famine. Safui, who was a child at the time, remembers that his parents had to sell their house to buy food. Diseases such as cholera swept through the weakened population. So many people were dying that they had to be buried in mass graves.

Things began to get better in the 1990s, with development assistance from the Dutch and Finnish governments and from nongovernmental organizations such as Plan International. Six years ago electricity became available to some establishments for a few hours a day and since last year it has been available all day. There is even running water now for a few hours a day, brought by a pipeline the villagers laid themselves with Finnish technical assistance; but the spring is too far away and lacks sufficient volume. In hopes of drawing tourists to their ancient churches, Lalibela is building an airport and connecting it to the town with an all-weather road.

In the 1990s, after more than a decade of neglect and decay, both Ethiopia and Eritrea were beginning to attend to the basic elements of physical and social infrastructure. Both countries are overwhelmingly dependent on subsistence agriculture, but both are badly deforested and eroded and lacking in modern technology. In a sense Ethiopia is Africa's water tower, its mountains providing the point of origin for several rivers, but only 12 percent of its own land is under cultivation and hardly any is irrigated. The French government has launched a major effort to introduce irrigation while the government of Finland has expanded its support for self-help efforts to supply running water to about two hundred villages. Currently piped water reaches perhaps 3 percent of the population in rural areas.

Health and education are priorities for many of the international development agencies that account for 22 percent of Ethiopia's budget. Only about a third of the population is literate. Although half of the country's sixty million people are under age fifteen, fewer than a third of the school-age population is actually in school. The biggest health problem is said to be malnutrition, which increases susceptibility to all kinds of diseases. Although the incidence of HIV and AIDS infection is lower than in some neighboring countries, it is rising steadily and currently stands at 7.4 percent of the population. Life expectancy for the population as a whole is about forty-seven years.

In the 1998–99 budget, passed on July 7, the Ethiopian parliament appropriated for military expenditures three times the amount appropriated for social expenditures and four times the sum budgeted for economic development. In the accounting system of international politics, war is always affordable; peace has to pay its own way. Whether Eritrea and Ethiopia should be one state or one market or two, they are clearly in need of each other and everything else as well — except war.

## Notes

1. The Ethiopian government claims that in the six months following the outbreak of hostilities in May, 30,246 Ethiopian nationals were deported from Eritrea. The Eritrean government claims that thirty-five thousand Eritreans had been deported from Ethiopia.

Chapter 7

# A World of Refugees: The Uprooted of Indochina

*Like high-altitude bombers, ultimate decision makers in the Global Village rarely need be confronted by the consequences of their actions or inactions.*

*The easiest way to solve a problem is to redefine it.*

*DURING THE COLD WAR*, the prospect of strategic advantage served as incentive to some level of attentiveness to the needs of some refugees. Cambodians in Thai border camps, for example, provided a captive constituency for the "coalition" of guerrilla forces — mainly Khmer Rouge — fighting the Hun Sen government and kept open supply lines for the guerrillas. Absent such strategic imperatives, would-be receiving countries are now less inclined to receive. Neither the Thais nor their ASEAN allies nor the morally indignant West has offered any manner of effective protection to Burmese or Timorese refugees — much less Chinese dissidents — fleeing abusive governments.

In the relatively prosperous West, even where demand for low-wage labor remains strong, and where investors insist on a labor market surplus in order to maintain employment "flexibility," immigrants, legal or otherwise, find conditions in their adoptive lands ever more precarious. In each country, prejudice and discrimination fall unevenly on certain ethnic groups. Hispanics in the US, Pakistanis in the UK, Turks in Germany, North Africans in France, Albanians in Italy, and Gypsies throughout East and Central Europe found themselves in the 1990s facing ever more legal and social constraints, economic hardships, and acts of violence and intimidation.

## Vietnamese "Refuge" in Hong Kong

On the slopes of once-green mountains that drop into Hong Kong Bay, the Banyan tree spreads its roots and digs them right through concrete walls. Such is life in the commercial hub of the twenty-first century: tough, resilient, transcendent. Such is life, in particular, in the Whitehead Detention Camp, which by the early 1990s had become home, so to speak, to some twenty-four thousand Vietnamese boat-people.

Mai stood all of 4'9". Childlike in appearance and demeanor, she was actually twenty years old. What frustrated her most about the camp, she said in confident English, is that like the country she left behind, the camp stifled creativity; it offered no space for intellectual growth. She did not mention among the hardships the barbed wire, or the stifling heat, or sharing a single bunk with her younger sister. Only when pressed did she admit that she missed birds and flowers, cats and dogs.

### An Offense against Nature

There was no ambiguity about the nature of this camp — no pretense of relief or charity or even re-education, like the "reeducation" camps in Vietnam or the "seminars" for royalists and other losers in Laos. It was straightforwardly a detention camp, run by the colony's corrections department. Moreover, it was a maximum security facility. A US congressman who visited in the early 1990s stopped at the outer gate and would go no further. He was overcome, he said, because it reminded him so much of Auschwitz.

A double row of fencing, with barbed wire on top and in between, interspersed with spikes, marked the perimeter. Additional double rows of fencing complete with barbed wire and spikes separated the ten internal camps from each other and from administrative operations. Since a few determined souls had overcome that incredible obstacle course to make a getaway, the original fencing was being replaced in some areas by a kind of mesh with razor-sharp edges.

Inmates were confined permanently to their individual camps, where several thousand lived three-deep in closely spaced bunks in almost windowless quonset-like huts of corrugated tin, eight or ten of them spaced a few feet apart on a concrete base. Layout and construction were so ill-conceived from any social, physiological, and/or aesthetic perspective that one was forced to wonder if maximizing discomfort was the intent.

There was not a single tree to filter the rays of the relentless sun. There was no grass, no dirt, nothing green at all and no animal life apart from roaches and rats. There were no streams or wading pools except those left carelessly by rain. The only available water came from a community spigot; and yet just a few yards from the mean fences stretched a glorious beach.

The camp, in fact, squatted like an intentional offense against nature in an otherwise green-carpeted inlet of one of Hong Kong's many beautiful bays.

## A Catch-22 for Care-givers

The few TV sets, soccer balls, and other sources of distraction in the camp had to be supplied by charity or relief organizations. Under the umbrella of the United Nations High Commission for Refugees (UNHCR), such organizations, both local and transnational, offered a modicum of health care, psychological counseling, adult education, and other social services, but their activities were restricted and closely monitored by correction authorities. (Until 1990 even the teaching of English was forbidden. Authorities finally gave in after it became clear that prohibition was futile. Ever larger numbers were hiding books under their pillows and studying English by flashlight at night.)

Relief workers and organizations were not to acquire a liaison function between prisoners and wardens, much less to represent individually or collectively the interests of inmates. The offenses most likely to cause an organization to be banned from the camp were talking to journalists and allowing photographs to be taken. They knew all too well that in this case, even more than most, a picture would be worth a thousand words. The UNHCR once took a stand on behalf of the rights of inmates to post slogans demanding freedom, and a few of the Tiananmen-inspired statues of liberty, systematically pulled down earlier by authorities, had been erected again; but such expression was tolerated only so long as there were no media to play it up and transmit it.

The Catch-22 for those who cared enough to offer some services or amenities to the refugees was that they served only at the sufferance of correction authorities and they were unavoidably co-opted into the policing system. The UNHCR was expected to keep the organizations under its umbrella on a short leash. Likewise, administrators of relief organizations were obliged to rein in their volunteers. Even the volunteers had to be concerned about the limits beyond which action or free expression on the part of refugee clients would result in the termination of programs and the banning of agencies. Sooner or later everyone who worked directly with the refugees faced the dilemma of whether to act as a censor, or to risk reprisals ultimately damaging to the people they were trying to help.

Even more than confining the boat-people, the Hong Kong government's extreme security measures seemed designed to keep truth from escaping. Highly sensitive to international opinion, the limited home-rule government saw itself as unfairly maligned. It complained that it was already spending far more than the Colony could afford or should be expected to on these noncitizens. Guards and barbed wire are no doubt costly; and local opinion polls in the early 1990s indicated that the government was under popular pressure to do less, rather than more, for the most recent wave of refugees.

## The Exhaustion of Empathy

The first wave of Vietnamese refugees to pass through Hong Kong, seeking asylum in the mid-1970s, were largely those who had served the South Vietnamese government or assisted in the US war effort. Most of them were ultimately settled in the United States. The second wave, beginning in the late 1970s following Chinese-Vietnamese border clashes, consisted mainly of ethnic Chinese. They were the first of the Vietnamese refugees to become known as boat-people. Their plight acquired a high profile in the West, in part because it had the strategic merit of drawing attention to the failings and abuses of the Vietnamese government. Eventually most of these boat-people were absorbed by Hong Kong and other ethnic Chinese communities. Some seven thousand of them, granted refugee status but awaiting resettlement, lived in camps that in the early 1990s were open so that the refugees could take jobs in Hong Kong if they could find them.

The most recent wave, however, beginning in the late 1980s, had come from the northern part of Vietnam. Whatever else they may have been fleeing, these Vietnamese were certainly fleeing economic deprivation — a condition the West finally began to help remedy in the mid-1990s simply by lifting economic sanctions against Vietnam. Ethnic difference, among other things, has meant less empathy from Hong Kong residents, and the end of the Cold War has meant the end also of the propaganda advantage for British, US, or other Western governments in publicizing the desperation of the Vietnamese. In fact, the sheer volume of this latest wave led the government of Hong Kong to a kind of panic and to the conclusion that it must be stopped once and for all. On one occasion in the late 1980s, it resorted to forcible repatriation, but open protests from the US and elsewhere were such that that remedy was not repeated until the 1990s, when the Cold War was definitely over. The strategy devised subsequently was the fabrication of a new category of homelessness, a status somewhere between refugee and illegal alien: asylum-seeker.

After three years at Whitehead, Mai remained an "asylum-seeker." She dealt with life in the camp by deeming it unreal. She could smile serenely through this nightmare because she was still clinging to hope. She was among the relatively fortunate in that her application for "refugee" status had not yet been reviewed. When I visited in 1991, about half of the residents of Whitehead were less fortunate. Their applications had been screened and, in 90 percent of the cases, rejected. As long as Hong Kong refrained from resorting to forcible repatriation, their options were to return willingly or to remain incarcerated.

The distinction between political refugees (fleeing persecution and entitled by international law to asylum) and economic ones is not unimportant; but it lends itself all too readily to becoming an excuse or cover for official indifference toward human suffering. Such callousness is made easier by the fact that blame can be — in fact, must be — spread across nations, peoples, and classes and filtered through layers of bureaucracy. Like high-altitude bombers, ultimate decision-makers rarely need be confronted by the consequences of their actions or inaction.

The worst fears of some of the boat-people were realized in late 1991, when the British and Vietnamese governments reached agreement that was to initiate forcible repatriation once again. US official outrage was now muted. At the time of formal handover from British to mainland Chinese authority in July 1997, eleven thousand Vietnamese boat-people remained incarcerated in Hong Kong.

## New Life in Cambodia's Killing Fields

Through the pulsing, psychedelic lighting, one could read "Disco, Lambada, Rock and Roll" over the bandstand. In fact, the band also featured a reasonable facsimile of the Nashville sound — Country and Eastern, you might say. But it was the popularity of "The Tennessee Waltz" that gave away the fact that my husband and I were in Southeast Asia. This was the New Boëungkôk (Bangkok) Restaurant in swinging downtown Phnom Penh. On the edge of the Killing Fields, the beat goes on.

The extent to which women outnumbered men at this city's most popular nightspot might have been explained, like so many other contemporary Cambodian anomalies, by the massacres of Pol Pot. Our friend Thoen, who was thirty-five years old, said the male-female ratio of his generation had been left at about 30 to 70. Perhaps explanation for the disparity in this case was less extraordinary; women appeared to be available for purchase, along with beer, drugs, and surplus arms. It was surprising how many things were available in this city of more than one million that was so recently a ghost town.

A sign in Khmer on the wall of one of the restaurants we frequented advertised black cobra. All of the restaurants in the city — apart from that of the crisp new, world-class Cambodiana Hotel, where UN technocrats and Japanese businessmen stayed — had the same printed menu, which had no particular relationship to what was available. But apart from pockets of flood or drought here and there around the country (Phnom Penh itself regularly suffers major flooding in early September), there was no real shortage of food. According to Grant Curtis, director of the recently opened office of the United Nations Development Program (UNDP), Cambodia's most glaring deficiencies, as it braced in 1991 for an onslaught of diplomats, developers, investors, and deal-seekers, were clean water, power, and trained service-delivery personnel.

## Rebuilding from Scratch

Pol Pot's murderous campaign against city-dwellers, the foreign-influenced, and the educated in general devastated the country's human resources infrastructure. It was left in 1979 with some five thousand teachers and forty-five medical professionals for the whole country. That was the situation encountered by the Hun Sen government, established when Vietnamese troops routed the Khmer Rouge forces, driving them into mountain strongholds on both sides of the Thai-Cambodian border. (The Hun Sen government continued to be supported militarily by Vietnam until Vietnam was itself abandoned by its benefactor, the Soviet Union.) Thus, surviving Cambodians who had not escaped into exile or who were able to return from exile had to undertake the task of rebuilding from almost unparalleled devastation — without an educated middle class, experienced in administration and service delivery, and without benefit of international assistance. The Vice Minister of Education told us that his ministry's mandate had been one quite literally of zero-based planning, that is, starting with nothing.

Far from the bureaucratic hassles one might have expected from a communist state, there were scarcely enough bureaucrats in the Cambodian capital to carry out the normal functions of any government. When we arrived at the airport, there were no customs agents (they had taken off early that day) and it was only by special request that we got our passports stamped. Whereas we had once spent one entire day in Czechoslovakia some years earlier getting a one-day visa extension, a Cambodian official gave us a ten-day extension simply by writing in a "1" in front of the "9" on the original visa.

Though the people were back by 1991, there were still ways in which it seemed that Phnom Penh had not yet been fully reclaimed. (After a couple of weeks of being perennially stuck and slowly asphyxiated in Bangkok traffic jams, such urban underdevelopment was sometimes refreshing.) Phnom Penh at night had its special charms. Where else in a city of more than a million could one look up to a black velvet sky studded with diamonds. There were almost no city lights to compete with the brilliance of the stars and no pollution to shroud their dazzling performance. Cars were scarce enough to command right-of-way right down the middle of the street. Whereas in Ho Chi Minh City (which we perceived as desperately poor and exceedingly underdeveloped until we arrived in Phnom Penh) transportation was largely by motorscooter, in Phnom Penh it was almost entirely by bicycle. When we asked about air conditioning at a Phnom Penh hotel, we were told with good-humored impatience, "This is not Vietnam, you know."

## Treating the National Trauma

Cambodia still suffers from post-traumatic stress syndrome. The answer to every question we asked began with, "You have to understand what happened to us when the Khmer Rouge took over." Every survivor had his own story of terror and loss; and the nightmare was not necessarily over. The Khmer Rouge continued to hold territory in 1991 in an irregular finger-like pattern, following the crests of mountain chains from the Thai border to the interior of the country, including areas a mere ninety miles from the capital; and both sides frequently reported cease-fire violations. Our driver was called away suddenly for the funeral of his brother — his last surviving relative — who had been killed in a truce-line skirmish a few miles from the great temple of Angkor Wat, near Siem Reap (where we were in fact headed the following day). Thus the prospects of the settlement that began to take shape in June in the Thai beach resort of Pattaya and that was finalized under United Nations tutelage in Paris in October evoked equally profound hope and fear — hope, because Cambodians were tired of dying, and fear because it remained unclear what role the Khmer Rouge would play in the configuration of a future government.

Along with Hun Sen and the Khmer Rouge, the all-party settlement included Prince Norodom Sihanouk. The Nixon Administration, not content with a neutralist Cambodia in the late 1960s, had played "double or nothing" with a weak hand, conspiring to have Sihanouk overthrown. But in the late 1970s and the 1980s the US and China had used Sihanouk as cover for backing the Khmer Rouge against the Soviet-backed Hun Sen government.

By 1997, the Khmer Rouge forces had been splintered and weakened. Pol Pot himself was tried and sentenced to house arrest in the shrunken redoubt of the Khmer Rouge until his death in 1998. Meanwhile the strange bedfellow coalition government, featuring Sihanouk's son, Prince Ranariddh, and Hun Sen as co-Premiers that had emerged from the 1993 elections had broken down as Hun Sen moved toward autocratic rule. Attacks by his forces not only against remaining Khmer Rouge strongholds but also against military and civilian supporters of Ranariddh were creating a new generation of refugees.

To no one's surprise, new elections on July 26, 1998, left control in the hands of the Hun Sen government and its Cambodian People's Party. The assessment of international election monitors was mixed, but opposition parties charged fraud. Amnesty International reported that in areas where opposition parties were challenging election results, villagers were receiving death threats and were fleeing their homes.[1]

## Resettlement or Reintegration

Whatever the shape of the government to emerge at the end of the 1990s, it will be vexed by the vestiges of war, including the ongoing process of resettlement of the approximately 350,000 refugees who had been virtual hostages — some for more than a dozen years — in those camps just across the border in Thailand. The international agencies that were to assume much of the responsibility for the effort were by no means prepared.

One of the most immediate obstacles to orderly resettlement was a legacy of decades of conflict. The rural areas to be reclaimed are studded with land mines. And these are for the most part modern, high-tech mines, not subject to detection by traditional means. A problem foreseen for the longer term is that displaced peasants, having lived for so long in camps that were essentially urban, would be hard to keep down on the farm. They were likely to turn up all too soon in a city even less prepared to absorb labor than it was before it was forcibly evacuated in the mid-1970s.

UN Development Program Director Grant Curtis had been concerned that the needs of the eight million Cambodians already in the country in the early 1990s not be neglected while development agencies focused on the needs of the returning refugees. It was important that new programs envision "reintegration" rather than simple resettlement. All Cambodians have suffered upheaval and unspeakable hardship; in a way all of them are refugees.

## Notes

1. *Amnesty Action*, AIUSA, Vol. XXI, No. 4, Fall 1998, p. 4.

## Chapter 8

# Trafficking in Labor: Southeast Asia and the Modern Muslim World

*Exploited outlanders, pouring into the metropolis*
*as refugees, immigrants, or guest workers, eventually take over.*

## Brunei's Modernized Feudalism

After more than five years of graduate study in Great Britain, Asliza was anxious to return to her native Brunei. But the country she returned to was not the same one she had left. She didn't mind covering her head with the traditional *tudong*, but she had trouble covering her mouth. Speech was not free, not even for men, much less for women. When Asliza went away to study in the late 1980s, Brunei was a rapidly modernizing, albeit officially Muslim, state. The facilities that mattered most to the people who matter most, such as those governing palace security, were as modern as limitless riches could buy. But socially, in the early 1990s, the country reversed its course and retreated more deeply into the Middle Ages.

Brunei is either the world's richest country, per capita, or a very poor country ruled by the world's richest autocrat (with some thirty-eight billion dollars in assets), depending on how one conceives the relationship between the Sultan and his subjects. The Sultan's own conception is clear enough. Virtually all public works are described as gifts from the Sultan. There is no clear distinction between assets of the state and of the royal family. The Sultan claims personal ownership of 90 percent of the land, including, of course, the immensely productive oil fields.

Now a modest 2,226-square-mile enclave in Malaysian territory, the Sultanate of Brunei claimed the entire island of Borneo in the sixteenth century. Pushed by armed resistance back to the top of the island, the royal family sought British protection in 1888. The British investment proved to be a sound one when petroleum was discovered in 1929. The protectorate soon became the third-largest oil producer in the Commonwealth.

In 1959, the British administration of Brunei was detached from that of (now Malaysian) Sarawak; the Sultanate acquired greater executive authority and drew up its first written constitution. Elections were held in 1962, but the royal family was not pleased with the results and negated the process. The popular uprising that ensued so weakened the Sultan that he vacated the office in favor of his son, who was inaugurated in 1967.

## Royal Prerogatives

A State of Emergency has been in effect since the 1960s. Prisoners are still being held for involvement in the uprising of 1962, and people continue to be arrested and imprisoned from time to time for political offenses. Even now speech is carefully guarded. Criticism of the monarchy and the royal family is strictly prohibited. All offices and shops display portraits of the Sultan and his two official wives — the first, now middle-aged and of noble descent, the second, a younger woman who had been a stewardess on Royal Brunei Airlines. It seemed to me that in those ubiquitous portraits, the first wife was scowling at the second. It is generally understood that the Sultan also has a great many kept mistresses.

I cannot speak for the palace of the first wife — with 1,700 rooms, the world's largest. But along with a few hundred other honored guests, I was able to have tea with wife number two in her not-so-shabby digs. The palace of the second wife is a maze of marbled and gilded halls and pavilions. In a single parlor we observed the paintings of a half dozen European masters. Brothers and sisters, aunts, uncles, and cousins — even distant relatives — have their own palaces. (The most important administrative posts are also held by members of the royal family.)

When I visited in 1995, new monuments, archways, and reviewing stands were going up around the capital city for the celebration of the Sultan's forty-ninth birthday. It was to be a grand bash, though nothing on the order of the Silver Jubilee spectacle of 1992, or the 1996 wedding of the Sultan's daughter, before five thousand guests.

## Social Incongruity

The *tudong,* as the scarves worn by Muslim women are called, came back in 1992, about the same time that cellular phones started arriving in large numbers, and they are often seen together. Women are by no means secluded from the modern world, or even from modern responsible professions. But within modern institutions and professions they are expected to stay in their place. It is stunning to see gatherings of several hundred professionals in which the men all sit on one side of the room and the *tudong*-topped women on the other.

The main organization representing women's interests is the organization of government ministers' wives. Most of the leaders and active members are effective and respected professionals in their own right, and their concerns are hardly different from those of women's movements elsewhere. But they can be credentialed, or legitimized as spokeswomen, only through the positions of their husbands.

Other kinds of social conservatism are of recent derivation and are by no means universally observed. The liquor ban was instituted only in 1991. It did not really dry up the country, because those who wanted to drink stocked up well before the ban. Moreover, black market supplies are abundant and still cheaper than taxed products in neighboring states. And nearby Labuan, the Malaysian money laundering island, also serves as a party town and supply depot for Brunei.

But prohibition, we were told, had ruined public social life; it drove socializing back to private clubs and private home — or palaces. The strict new laws do not apply to the royal family. Pilots of low-flying planes reported what one might call major orgies, or well-attended non-costume parties, in the courtyard of one of the most imposing palaces.[1]

Apart from the likelihood of punishment for nonconformity, why do the people accept such conspicuous consumption and ostentatious law-flaunting by the monarchy? Many accept because they find that the benefits of citizenship outweigh the costs.

## The Citizenship Elite and Imported Labor

For a tuition-free institution, the state-run University of Brunei has an unusual problem: it does not have enough students to populate its resplendent new campus. Education at all levels is free, to men and women alike, but only to citizens. For citizens, health care is also free, housing is subsidized, and there are no taxes. Nor are jobs hard to come by; half of the citizens of the Sultanate work for the government.

But citizenship itself is a privilege, not a right, and essentially one that can be acquired only through inheritance. It is inherited through the father; a woman who marries a non-citizen loses citizenship for herself and her children. There is no right to citizenship based on being born there or on length of stay in the national territory. Naturalization comes about only through a Malay "literacy" test that is rarely passed. Like literacy tests elsewhere, it is essentially a racial or ethnic screening device.

The permanent or long-term population of the country is only about 70 percent Malay or para-Malay. Some 15 to 20 percent is ethnic Chinese, urban business people whose local roots may go back several generations. Another 10 to 15 percent is non-Malay indigenous. Many of them were driven from the rainforest when the Sultan set aside huge tracts as nature preserves. Indigenous peoples were not considered to be a part of that nature and so were prohibited from pursuing the hunting, fishing, gathering, and subsistence farming that had constituted their way of life.[2]

The citizenship difference is easy to spot. There are model water-villages, subsidized housing for citizens, that are spacious and endowed with all the modern amenities — running water, electricity, several bedrooms, each equipped with television, telephones and ghetto-blasters, luxurious furnishings, and royal family photos. The model villages, though, are surrounded by acres of squalid non-subsidized water villages, flimsy and crowded, lacking the most basic requirements even for safety and sanitation.

When the economy of Brunei booms, citizens find themselves more and more likely to constitute a minority of the population in the country at any given time, because at least a third of the labor force — the manual, or less-skilled labor force — is imported. Labor is recruited from Malaysia, Indonesia, Thailand, Burma, and the Philippines — all of the neighboring countries except China. (There has always been concern about expansion of the Chinese sphere of influence). There is no minimum wage for alien contract labor. Payment is whatever the labor contractor can negotiate. Contracts are for periods of up to two years, but a worker can be deported at any time if his behavior is deemed to be troublesome.

## Malaysia's Tower of Babel

Malaysia is a federation of historic sultanates, overlaid with a more modern parliamentary system. The interethnic tensions that had long bedeviled this mainly Malay, Chinese, and Indian population have been eased since the mid-1980s by annual economic growth that until the meltdown of 1997 was running at a clip of 6 to 8 percent.[3] The big issue now is foreign labor, contracted to fuel the boom. Prejudice and discrimination have been redirected toward Filipino, Thai, and Indonesian (especially Timorese) construction workers, even though it is hard to see what citizens might begrudge them. There is no citizenship for newborns, no services for the families of the contracted workers, and no floor under their wages. Having learned nothing from the futility of Chinese efforts to hold off the Mongolian hordes, Malaysia was building a great wall to keep out uninvited Thais.

Kuala Lumpur is in many ways a mess. Its traffic jams are awful. Its stunningly rapid growth seems to have been utterly unplanned. But architecturally it is a fairyland — a laboratory for every new idea in high-rise construction. The most fascinating project underway when I visited in 1995 was a set of towers — twins, one going up under Korean contract, the other under Japanese. The project, costing more than a billion dollars, was to serve as office space as well as a civic center. Completed by early 1996, the Petronas towers, with 174 floors, are for the time being the tallest buildings in the world.

When I first visited — and stayed at a hotel that seemed to be right under the massive structures — all was going well, according to our friend Ian, an Australian engineer serving as a construction supervisor. Work was underway twenty-four hours a day, and only three workers had fallen off. (Those on the Korean tower, we were told, refused to wear their safety lines.) Returning two months later, I found that all work had stopped on the Japanese tower. The Japanese had not owned up to having a major problem, but since the stoppage was costing more than a million dollars a day, the press was suspicious.

In fact, Australian surveyors examining the bridge that was to pass between the two towers compared notes and found discrepancies. It appeared that the Japanese tower was sinking and leaning. Investigators were uncertain as to how the mistakes and miscalculations had come about, but our friend Ian had a theory. He suspected that with Japanese and Korean managers, Australian contractors and surveyors, Malayan foremen and Indonesian laborers, earning about 12 ringgit (US$15) per day, each speaking his own version of English, there was ample room for a communications failure.

## The Kuwaiti Citizenship Elite

In the extravagance of its pageantry, the presumptions of its rulers, and the rigidity of gender relations, Brunei may seem a relic of the distant past. But its social relations in general are very modern — in fact, the wave of the future if current global trends hold.

There are a number of countries, particularly in the oil-producing regions of the Middle East, where great wealth is shared by an ever more narrowly drawn citizenship elite. This social profile was set in relief in 1990 when Iraq's invasion of Kuwait sent much of its labor force packing, wreaking havoc on the economies of labor-exporting countries like India, Pakistan, Syria, and Jordan. Laborers who stayed — e.g., Palestinians with no country to return to — suddenly became not only illegal aliens, but enemy aliens as well.

Tens of thousands of foreign workers from countries whose leaders had supported Iraq were deported during and after Operation Desert Storm. But by 1996 Kuwait was again aswarm with foreign workers, particularly from Egypt, Pakistan, and the Philippines. According to Kuwaiti government statistics, 1.3 million of the country's 2 million inhabitants in 1996 were non-Kuwaiti, and only 176,000 of the 1.1 million members of the labor force were Kuwaiti citizens.

Of the fortunate few who enjoy citizenship, 93 percent work for the government. Kuwaiti citizens are guaranteed shorter working hours and a minimum wage of more than twice what foreigners receive. The citizenship elite pays no taxes but receives extensive benefits, including free medical care, education at all levels, and generously subsidized utilities. But all citizens are not created equal. Women do not have the right to vote, and even male voters must be able to trace Kuwaiti ancestry back at least a generation.

Moreover, Kuwaiti's non-citizens do not necessarily have citizenship elsewhere. In addition to the deportable foreign workers, there is a category of non-citizens known as the *bidoon,* or stateless. They are generally of Iraqi or Iranian origin, though their families have lived in Kuwait for generations. Their numbers are down from some 220,000 before the war to about 117,000 in 1996, but they still outnumber the actual eligible voters.

## A Buyer's Market for Labor

Such cases as Brunei and Kuwait are exceptional, but only in the extremes they represent, not in the logic or the consequences of their policies. All over the world rules governing citizenship are being tightened and doors are being closed on refugees and immigrants, partly because with shrinking social service budgets, taxpayers and governments are anxious to decrease demand for such services.[4] But competitiveness as labor cost reduction demands a labor surplus. Increasingly that demand is being met by foreign contract labor. In fact, the recent boom must be explained in part by the availability of cheap and docile labor.

In 1980, Japan, South Korea, Malaysia, Singapore, Hong Kong, Thailand, and Taiwan altogether were employing only about a million foreign workers. By 1997, that number had grown to more than 6.5 million. Just as labor contracting in the domestic sphere removes legal liability, messy transactions, and even personal guilt from growers and manufacturers, employed internationally it leaves importing countries free of responsibility for the unmet needs of underpaid workers and free even of awareness of those needs.

When economies "head South," so must labor forces. Following upon the East Asian financial meltdown of 1997, Malaysia was preparing to deport about a million foreign workers, many of them to Thailand, where one or two million jobs were being lost, and to Indonesia, where unemployment was expected to rise some six million in 1998. The Thais would, in turn, expel some 250,000 workers, mostly Burmese. Indonesia would expel Filipinos, but for the most part, Indonesians could be expected to turn their wrath once again on ethnic Chinese merchants. The International Labour Organization estimated in September 1998 that in the year more or less since the onset of the East Asian crisis, ten million people had lost their jobs. Downward pressure on wages and labor conditions is not limited by a need for workers to double as consumers, or even by a need for a particular national labor force to reproduce itself; recruiting across a broad multinational or multi-state region makes the labor market always a buyer's market.

## Notes

1. In 1997, a former Miss USA filed a lawsuit in a Los Angeles court against the Sultan, his brother, and a Los Angeles talent agency on grounds that she was held against her will in a royal palace in Brunei and expected to serve as a sexual toy. The Sultan has been granted immunity by the State Department, but his brother has not.
2. It has been found in Borneo's and other rainforests elsewhere, that the first requirement for large-scale exploitation, e.g., logging or dam construction, is getting rid of the indigenous people.
3. The growth trajectory experienced a setback in late 1997 when global money market speculation and capital flight sent Southeast Asian currencies into a deep plunge.
4. Religious affinity has been responsible for some exceptions to the cold shoulder to refugees. Malaysia's provinces of Sabah and Sarawak have made room for refugees from Bosnia and Mindanao.

## Part II: The Displaced and the Dispossessed Suggested Readings

Appleyard, R.T. *International Migration: Challenges for the Nineties.* Geneva: Imprimerie Genevoise, 1991.

Black, R. and V. Robinson, eds. *Geography and Refugees: Patterns and Processes of Change.* London: Belhaven Press, 1993.

Chaliand, Gerard. *A People Without a Country: The Kurds and Kurdistan.* Brooklyn, NY: Olive Branch Press, 1996.

Deacon, Bob, with Michelle Hulse and Paul Stubbs. *Global Social Policy: International Organizations and the Future of Welfare.* London: Sage Publications, 1993.

Doughty, Dick and Mohammed El Aydi. *Gaza, Legacy of Occupation: A Photographer's Journal.* West Hartford, CT: Kumarian Press, 1995.

Harris, Nigel. *The New Untouchables: Immigration and the New World Worker.* New York: I.B. Tauris, 1995.

Helsinki Watch. *The Kurds of Turkey: Killings, Disappearances, and Torture.* New York: Human Rights Watch, March 1993.

Isbister, John. *The Immigration Debate: Remaking America.* West Hartford, CT: Kumarian Press, 1996.

Kaplan, Robert. "The Coming Anarchy." *The Atlantic Monthly* 273(2), 46, 1994.

Martinez, Elizabeth. "It's a Terrorist War on Immigrants." *Z Magazine* 10, No. 7/8, July–Aug. 97, pp. 29–36.

Rifkin, Jeremy. *The End of Work: The Decline of the Global Labor Force and the Dawn of the Post-Market Era.* New York: G.P. Putnam's Sons, 1995.

Rinehart, James. *The Tyranny of Work: Alienation and the Labor Process, 3rd ed.* New York: Harcourt Brace, 1995.

Shiva, Vandana. "Homeless in the Global Village." *Earth Ethics* 5, No. 4, (1994): 3

United Nations High Commission for Refugees. *The State of the World's Refugees in 1997.* Oxford: Oxford University Press, 1998.

# Part III

# Second-Coming Capitalism and Comparative Disadvantage

*It's a good bet that those who argue for short-term sacrifice for long-term gain are taking their cut in the short term.*

*Down-sizing and out-sourcing mean that your job has gone to China.*

*IN 1970, PRESIDENT* Emilio Garastazú Médici, the least charming of the generals who ruled Brazil for two decades, commented that "The economy is doing fine, but the people are not."[1] Most commentators at the time had the grace to be amused. Who would have thought that two decades hence the abstraction of "the economy" would have become so complete that it could be generally accepted that sacrifice on the part of already wretched populations could be necessary for restoring the health of their economies? Where eyebrows are raised by such semantic construction, believers assure skeptics that while it seems that only the high-rollers are profiting, trickle-down will result in generalized prosperity in the long run. No evidence is required because, as the late British economist John Maynard Keynes observed, "In the long run, we are all dead."

The long run is in fact a concept antithetical to the economic system of the global village. I have called the system Second-Coming Capitalism partly in reference to its apocalyptic approach to resource management (There may be no tomorrow; get yours now).

Second-Coming Capitalism refers also to the return of a cruder, Spencerian, or Social Darwinist kind of capitalism that had been superseded, especially after World War II, by a socially more responsible, government-regulated, mixed economy with all-inclusive service and social welfare provisions. Moreover, fortified by technological breakthroughs, global reach, and concentration of economic power, that cruder version of capitalism has returned in more virulent form, like bacteria that had developed resistance to antibiotics.

## Sustainability and Development

Second-Coming Capitalism, combining twenty-first-century technology and nineteenth-century social relations, is the essence of disequilibrium. Feudalism had its drawbacks, but the system had the merit of sustainability. When a particular set of families worked generation after generation on the same estate or hacienda, the landowner had a material interest in their survival and, to a degree, even in their health and well-being. The serfs, in turn, had a material interest in the prosperity of the estate, and both lords and serfs had an ongoing interest in the regenerative capacity of the land.

At the other end of the development spectrum, a democratic, social-welfare state also had a built-in symbiosis. Owners and managers servicing a domestic market were obliged to pay their employees enough that those employees might double as consumers.[2] Wage-and-salary workers, in turn, had a material interest in keeping local or national business profitable, because the reinvestment of profits maintained jobs; and the taxes they paid, along with those paid by employees, sustained the services — education and health, street lights, sewage systems — on which all depended for a comfortable standard of living or, at least, for personal and family security. Where workers could count on jobs and producers could count on markets, there was a presumption of continuity of community and thus incentive to preserve its habitat.

The breakdown of feudal systems, and at the same time the breakup of more nearly egalitarian, self-sustaining, rural kinship communities and their replacement with crude, unmediated capitalism led to sweatshops, child labor, homelessness, and lawlessness and other aspects of Dickensian urban blight as well as rural desperation resulting in banditry, land-grabs, and migration on a massive scale.

Such social instability inspired new change strategies and new forms of collective action, including rural and urban insurgency, demonstrations and riots, and organization along newly recognized lines of identity and interest — labor, women, students — and finally, the construction of new coalitions of middle and lower classes represented by broadly based political parties or movements. Instability, therefore, ultimately gave way in much of the "East" to what was ambitiously or hysterically labeled Communism and in much of the West to the so-called social welfare state. To the extent that decolonizing Third World countries escaped unmitigated anarchy or tyranny, most settled in on some variation of Eastern or Western systems or some cross between them.

In politics, there are no happily-ever-afters, and emergent systems based on social compromise, or "contract," were soon to be challenged. The ideal of contract was salvaged in Western Europe, at unspeakable cost, emerging bloodied but unbowed from World War II. But efforts to negate the social contract, repressing and dissolving social organization on behalf of those whose capital gains were based on the exploitation of unprotected resources, including labor, were more successful around Europe's southern fringes and, more recently, in Brazil and in South America's Southern Cone.

For a time, in the most developed of the Western Hemisphere states, the competition between national and foreign industrialists had made possible a nationalist coalition, uniting labor and elements of the middle class with business interests in need of a national market and of government support against foreign interests. All coalitions that for a time serve the interests of the unpowerful are unlikely ones — strange bedfellows. Were that not so, stark inequality would not be an issue. And all develop contradictions or self-destructive tendencies and in time break down. In this case, the nationalist coalitions broke down for both economic and political reasons, leaving both markets and polities unprotected.

Public protection of domestic industry, which occurred at some phase in the development of all industrialized states, had the disadvantage of sustaining many monopolistic and inefficient industries, but its absence does not necessarily mean the absence of monopoly and inefficiency. For late developing states it has generally meant that the state is compelled instead to subsidize or favor monopolistic or oligopolistic and inefficient foreign-owned industries.

Efficiency, moreover, is a value-laden term. Economic nationalism defines efficiency in social or collective terms, while its nemesis, neoliberalism, defines efficiency from the perspective of the individual or corporate profit-seeker. A nationalistic, or social, perspective also called for accumulation or growth in profits based on expanding effective demand (more jobs, higher wages) within the national market, rather than "supply-side" cost reduction through down-sizing, or job shrinkage, and wage suppression, made feasible by the globalization of the market. At any rate, changing circumstances and perceptions, along with Cold War rhetoric and covert intervention, splintered the nationalistic alliance and generated a wave of counterrevolution. Economic aspects of these counterrevolutions offered a preview of the neoliberal new world order that was to follow the implosion of the Soviet Bloc.

The demise of the Soviet bloc — the alternative market — meant the end of the most important aspect of economic competition at the global level — competitive means of structuring and even of interpreting economic transactions. The end of the Communist menace, with respect to which the democratic welfare state might be posed as a compromise, a moderate course — an alternative for the less affluent or less greedy — left the welfare state as the exposed extreme to be targeted.

But it was no longer necessary to take on the welfare state through the means common during the Cold War — military assault or paramilitary/ intelligence subversion — because the function of economic decision making had been lifted from the national arena and transplanted to a global one. In the absence of competing economic systems, and thus competing credit markets, it became possible to establish a centrally planned economy at the global level with rules enforceable through credit conditionality. In such a system the biggest businesses compete less for the loyalty of consumers than for rank in investment portfolios and in parliamentary lobbies.

Like municipal governments able to decide where to put the stop lights, national governments were left with a full docket of trivial decisions but no autonomous means of reallocating resources on a major scale or even of meeting broadly shared public needs. In general, they have responded by reallocating responsibilities (but not resources) to regional or local governments, or to the non-profit sector. Meanwhile, for the maintenance of their own positions, national governments have become beholden to business and financial interests operating at the global level, and only indirectly to their own populations. In other words, in order to compete for the support of their own citizens, they must first compete successfully for the support of those financial interests whose contributions underwrite political campaigns and whose credit and investment decisions can sustain or sink an economy.

Much of what used to be the budgetary authority and regulatory power of government has already in practice fallen under the jurisdiction of the International Monetary Fund, the General Agreement on Tariffs and Trade, and, in the 1990s, the World Trade Organization. The Multilateral Agreement on Investment (MAI), nearing completion in early 1998, appears to wrest from government the last pretense of a bargaining position vis-à-vis multinational capital. The MAI proposes to eliminate all restrictions and conditions on the movement of capital across national frontiers and all instances of preferential treatment of national over foreign capital. The agreement gives multinational banks and corporations the power to sue governments for past and potential profit loss due to restrictions.

The twenty-nine member states of the Organization of Economic Cooperation and Development (OECD) met in Paris in late February, 1998, to put the final touches on the agreement. At that meeting, Renato Ruggerio, director-general of the World Trade Organization, commented that "We are writing the constitution of a single global economy."[3] If the treaty is indeed signed by the club of First World governments, Third World governments will be offered the opportunity to follow suit. It will be an offer they cannot refuse, because refusal would surely mean being frozen out of capital markets — denied the credit and investment that are now the glucose of the global economy.

## Sectors Out of Sync

The initiative for drawing the line between public and private domains, for determining which resources, which services, which responsibilities, and, above all, which decisions should rest with public, elected officials as opposed to private, profit-seeking interests has been seized by the private sector. The public sector is thus in danger of becoming little more than a residual category, a security guard and a tax collector, in effect, for corporate and banking interests that have no nationality.

It has been common to assume that the social service functions that have been stripped from governments can be, and indeed should be, assumed by the non-governmental, non-profit sector. But that constitutes a special tax on the caring, a relatively narrow tax base. Moreover, the non-profit sector is not a substitute for government. To flourish and to serve the public interest, that sector requires the support and protection of a strong government.

Other functions that have escaped outright privatization have been removed from general operating budgets to be supported by state lotteries and other gaming options (a special tax on the stupid — a broader tax base, apparently, than the caring.) Typically, the legalization of gambling is sold to the public as a means of supporting some essential service, like basic education, that taxpayers have come to see as a burden. But it would be naïve to assume that at a time when initiative lies with the private sector, an operation so lucrative as gambling would long be left in the public domain.

A far more lucrative form of gaming already in private hands — the Stock Market — is reaching out to absorb not only private pensions but the public entitlement program that had become the linchpin of the modern social welfare state: social security. The stakes in this game are enormous — not only the retirement livelihood of countless millions, the budgets of their children and grandchildren and the economies of their communities, but also a major revenue source for already beggared governments. The house advantage in this casino does not go to the "little house on the prairie." It should be remembered that a sharp decline in the stock market may be attributed to "profit-taking."

## Public Corruption and Corporate Cannibalism

The state of play in the struggle between public and private sectors determines not only which of the sectors is dominant, but also the nature of both sectors and to a degree the nature of the non-governmental, non-profit sector as well. The experience of more or less modernized economies in the post-industrial revolution period suggests that only with an economy mixed and monitored to serve public as well as private interests can each of the two sectors maintain a measure of independence from the other.

We have seen in Part I the kind of stalemate that develops when market monopoly falls to government and the same collectivity of people as workers cheat themselves as consumers. A saying common among Soviets was, "We pretend to work and the government pretends to pay us."

We have also seen the other extreme, in which governments, regardless of ritual and selection procedure, become utterly dependent on a limited number of private patrons. Perhaps the connections are harder to trace in the more highly technified, bureaucratized, and globalized marketplace. We should recognize, however, that one of the manifestations at either extreme is corruption on a massive scale of both government and business. Just as the counterpart of genuinely democratic, accountable and responsible, competent and fiscally viable government is a business community that deals fairly with employees and consumers and neighbors, the counterpart of a predatory private sector, ready always to take the money and run, is irresponsible, fiscally unviable and readily corruptible government. Under such circumstances, governments do not necessarily shrink. They may even grow in terms of money collected and spent and in coercive power. But they shrink from commitment to the public interest.

## Privatization and Profit

A standard sequence of events in privatization has been that the government sells an enterprise or most of its shares at give-away prices to "insiders," often the same high-level bureaucrats who were running it for the government. The new owners drain its capital and strip its assets, forcing it into bankruptcy. Especially if it still has a number of employees, the government is then forced to bail it out with public funds, investing enough to make it attractive to foreign investors.

With loans underwritten by their own host government and/or international financial institutions, multinational corporations then purchase the enterprise, again at give-away prices for a number of reasons, including the likelihood that the seller's currency has been deeply devalued. The multinational corporation then lays off supposedly "redundant" workers and "allows" prices to rise to free-market levels — that is to say, as high as the market will bear, which may be very high indeed if, as is so often the case, the "product" is an essential and essentially-monopolized service or utility.

The process is not limited to hopelessly weak, defeated, and dependent Third World governments. British Rail was sold off by the Thatcher government in November 1995 to three companies for £7.8 billion, a price widely viewed in Britain at the time as scandalously low. One of those companies, comprised of former British Rail managers, was sold six months later for a profit of £80 million. Meanwhile, Britain's rail service had become the most expensive in the European Community. MP Glenda Jackson, then a Labour Party transport spokeswoman, said, "This is absolutely scandalous. Since Porterbrook was privatized not a single new train has been built or even ordered and yet here are the managers turned into overnight millionaires. Yet again the taxpayers suffer while the fat cat controllers lick the cream."[4]

A few decades ago in the capitalist West, most businesses were family owned and operated. It made no sense to lay waste to the land or to strip assets because those businesses, including their work forces, their clienteles, and their reputations were to be passed down from generation to generation. Not so in today's fast-forward marketplace. The new class of corporate managers is as mobile as its money, and loyalty to the corporation is as quaint as loyalty to place. CEO reputations are based less on what they are able to do for their companies than what they are able to do for themselves.

Globalization, even more than its colonialist antecedent, represents a severance of symbiosis among capital, labor, and markets, and even among generations and layers of management within individual companies. Objectives are narrowed to profit margins and stock values in time horizons limited by quarterly reports. Sustainability of individual communities and countries and ecosystems is sacrificed to the sustainability of growth in profit margins for the corporate players left standing after the merger and pillage shakeouts.[5] But there are limits also to the sustainability of Second-Coming Capitalism as a system — though those limits may indeed lie in the long term, to which we will return in the final chapter.

## Victims of the Peace

In this post-Cold War era of overfed stock markets and underfed governments, we have seen steadily growing income and asset gaps, both between and within states. This gap owes a great debt to debt and its prescribed cures — on the one hand, export promotion in the pursuit of comparative advantage (for investors), and on the other structural adjustment, including the socialization of costs and the stripping away of social infrastructure.

In the late 1980s and into the 1990s, Caribbean states as a whole were paying out in debt service far more than they were receiving in new loans or other capital transfers. Moreover, even as lending slowed, debts and debt service ratios more than doubled. The Cuban case was exceptional in that Cuba's crisis owed less to its own debt than to the transformation of its major creditor state into a state of desperation.

Foreign debt should be understood not merely as a set of transactions, but rather as a set of relationships — above all, power relationships. Beyond certain levels of exposure, creditors become able to make demands that may be only marginally related to debt service. In fact, public credit — that is, credit from international or bilateral donors — has increasingly been used to leverage policy changes, like privatization and currency devaluation, enhancing prospects for private investors. In Russia and other newly independent states of the former Soviet Union, the push to privatization and the targeting of aid and investment from the West to cooperative leaders has transformed the former communist party elite into a new capitalist elite.

In the aftermath of World War II, the victorious allies made a point of punishing "war criminals," the leaders of the defeated states, but promoted relief and recovery for ordinary citizens. Not so this time around. Western favors have been lavished on the leaders of the vanquished evil empire (in exchange, of course, for access to resources and markets and privatization deals); it is the long-suffering private citizens who are being punished all over again. Of course, the stripping of the value of a currency is more subtle and impersonal than the plunder of a homestead or the looting of the land, but it is no less devastating to the victims.

The uncertain fate of Cuba demonstrates both the nature and the impact of the transition to a new world order. What has become known there as the "special period" is not so different from what the new order, with its monolithic controls over credit, trade, and aid has done to most of the rest of the Third World, except that it came so suddenly to Cuba and that, like the relative prosperity of the eighties, the scarcity of the nineties is more broadly shared. A lifting of the US embargo, a counterproductive vestige of the old world order, might give Cuba some momentary relief; but the island state would still have to come to terms with a global economic system hostile not only to socialism but even to what has been the Western-style social democratic welfare state.

# Notes

1. For elaboration on the Brazilian military's "economic miracle," see "Security for Whom?" Part IV in J.K. Black, *United States Penetration of Brazil* (Philadelphia: University of Pennsylvania Press, 1997).

2. In the US, this line of thought came to be known as Fordism, since pioneer manufacturer Henry Ford had said that he intended to pay his workers enough for them to be able to buy the cars they were making.
3. David Rowan, "Meet the New World Government," *The Manchester Guardian Weekly*, Vol. 158, No. 8, Feb. 22, 1998, p. 14. The prospects of the MAI suffered a setback in late 1998 as the resistance of the Socialist government of France was reinforced by the election of the Social Democrats, replacing the Christian Democrats, in Germany. Subsequently Britain's Labour government also expressed reservations about the MAI.
4. Jonathan Prynn, "Former British Rail Managers Share £80 Million Profit," *The Times* (London) Aug. 1, 1996, Section 2, p. 1.
5. In 1997, the world's 359 largest corporations accounted for some 40 percent of global trade.

Chapter 9

# Previews of the New World Order: Colonialism and the Caribbean Basin Initiative

*When belts must be tightened, it is always around the narrowest waists.*

"*IF THINGS DON'T* improve soon, I may have to ask you to stop helping me." That "potshot" from epigrammatist Ashleigh Brilliant might well be a message from Caribbean leaders to the international financial institutions and other major purveyors of foreign aid.

The Caribbean region is rich in historical intrigue, in cultural diversity and in the beauties and bounties of nature, but its people are poor — again. Much has changed in the world and in the Caribbean since those islands, at the expense of their own natural and social ecologies, first enriched European colonizers. Most of the islands are now independent states, and most had seen very considerable improvement in standards of living in the 1960s and 1970s. Tourism, tax sheltering, and export processing compete now with export agriculture as the region's economic mainstays. But the peoples of the Caribbean probably have more in common now, in the 1990s, than at any time since pirates were raping and plundering — and that is not the good news.

A World Bank economist noted that a Caribbean island like Montserrat[1] could become another Monte Carlo if governments could only be persuaded to sell their land to rich Americans for retirement homes.[2] A sure way to improve economic performance as measured in per capita GNP growth is to replace native poor people with rich foreigners. In fact, at least a fourth of the persons born in the Caribbean now live elsewhere, mainly in Europe and the US. Would-be workers in the Caribbean far outnumber available jobs, and the remittances of émigrés have become a crucial source of foreign exchange reserves.

## The Caribbean Basin Initiative and the Lost Decade

For the Caribbean, as for Latin America in general — indeed for most of the Third World and for considerable chunks of the First — the 1980s proved to be a lost decade. The only things going up were prices, taxes, interest rates, unemployment, disease, pollution, and crime. Everything else was going down: production and productivity, incomes, investment, export earnings, and services.

Obviously, the fate of the Caribbean in the 1980s cannot be attributed wholly to the consequences of the Caribbean Basin Initiative (CBI), but that initiative was certainly one of several important causal factors. Announced in 1981 and embodied in the US's Caribbean Economic Recovery Act of 1983, the CBI had an initial aid component of $350 million in economic support funds, of which the primary beneficiary was the government of El Salvador. The initiative thus became one of many subterfuges for pursuing the Reagan Administration's military agenda in Central America.

The CBI, however, was multipurpose. Goals included the promotion of Caribbean exports to the United States through the selective elimination of duties and the promotion of US investment in Caribbean Basin export industries. To that end, aid and trade were used as leverage to prompt policy changes attractive to investors. In other words, the objective was to enable US investors to take advantage of the region's resources, including abundant cheap labor, without prejudice to their shares of the US market.

Even though most of the leading products that were designated duty-free through the CBI were produced by US-based companies, most of the twenty-seven states deemed potentially eligible for participation in the program rushed to eliminate restrictions or taxes on US corporate activity that the US government deemed excessive and to deny preferential treatment to imports that might compete with US products. CBI eligibility rested not only on meeting requirements that were obvious, even if crude, like access for US companies to markets and resources and abandonment of any protection or advantage for local industries; eligibility rested also on agreement to vaguely worded passages that allowed for arbitrariness in the extreme on the part of US policymakers.

Meanwhile regional financial institutions were also under pressure to cater to US economic and political objectives. Before its invasion of Grenada in 1983, the Reagan Administration threatened the Caribbean Development Bank with a funding cut-off if it made loans to that country.[3]

Real incomes for the Caribbean as a whole were lower in 1988 than in 1980. During the decade in which the Caribbean Basin Initiative was to enhance the area's trade prospects, what had been for the Caribbean a trade surplus with the US became a deficit — that despite the fact that exports had increased substantially. While fifteen of the Caribbean countries exported more in 1986 than in 1980, all but five of them earned less, as a consequence of weakening commodity prices.

In Trinidad and Tobago, incomes dropped by 50 percent between 1983 and 1988, and unemployment doubled. In the Dominican Republic the "structural adjustments" of 1982–84 dropped the real minimum wage by more than 40 percent and reduced spending on health care, education, housing, transportation, potable water, and other municipal services by about one-third. Jamaica's adjustment effort began in 1977, and by the mid- 1980s social service spending had been cut by 41 percent. The figures cited above represent the outcomes not of policy failures but of policy decisions.

What the Caribbean had lost as a consequence of its new special relationship with the US in the realms of trade and investment was not to be compensated through increases in direct foreign assistance. On the contrary, US aid to the Caribbean fell nearly 90 percent between 1985 and 1995, from $226 million to $26 million, and USAID's regional office in Barbados was closed.

Ironically, the program designed ostensibly, in large part, to forestall the deepening of relations between Cuba and its Caribbean neighbors has left them more in need of Cuban assistance. And in 1998 such assistance was, in fact, forthcoming. While Cuba remained short of foreign exchange, the country had a surfeit of highly trained professionals. More than two hundred Cuban doctors, teachers, engineers, and other professionals and technicians were providing assistance to other Caribbean countries, and more than two hundred students from elsewhere in the Caribbean were studying in Cuban universities.

## Debt Peonage and Structural Adjustment

Recent trends in the distribution of wealth and opportunity in the Caribbean, as elsewhere, owe a great debt to debt and to its prescribed cure, structural adjustment. At the beginning of the 1990s, Caribbean debt stood at about $21 billion, for a population of some twenty-five million. The debt represented 79 percent of total GNP for the region.

Foreign debt, like a feudal or colonial relationship, may become a semi-permanent money or value extraction system. By the late 1980s Caribbean states, harnessed to debt service, were on the losing end of capital flows. The International Monetary Fund alone was coming out almost a billion dollars ahead for the last half of the decade. Moreover, even as lending slowed in the 1980s, debts grew by 125 percent and debt service ratios (the proportion of annual export earnings devoted to debt service) doubled.[4]

How did such debt peonage come about? Some part of it must be attributed to consumerism. Advertising campaigns have been highly successful in generating demand for foreign goods, resulting in ever-increasing drains on foreign reserves for imports. Along with other Latin American and Third

World states, some of the Caribbean countries attempted in the 1960s and 1970s to slow that drain and to deal as well with the deteriorating terms of trade for primary products by manufacturing on their own some of the products previously imported. But, in general, this flirtation with import substitution industrialization leaned too heavily on capital-intensive Western technology and generated even greater indebtedness.

The energy crises of 1973–74 and 1979–80 dealt a particularly severe blow to the energy-shy Caribbean and resulted in a dramatic increase in indebtedness. Of course, the flip side of that coin was that creditors awash in petrodollars were most anxious to unload them into loan portfolios, so even oil exporters or refiners, urged on by creditors, deepened their debt exposure. Debt exposure was also magnified artificially (artificially in that nothing of value was obtained in exchange) by floating hard currency interest rates, rates that floated into the stratosphere in the early 1980s.

Finally, beyond certain levels of exposure the debt treadmill itself takes over. New loans become necessary simply to maintain service of previously incurred obligations. At that point debt peonage becomes an all-encompassing relationship, allowing creditors to make demands that may be only marginally related to the debt.

Given the unfairness, the hypocrisy, even the absurdity of a debt that creditors and debtors alike know very well is ultimately unpayable, a debt that by the nature of the system can only grow rather than shrink, why do debtor governments continue to pay? The answer is simple: No credit, no imports. In the post-Cold War world there is no alternate trade bloc, no barter option; and autarchy has been universally deemed to be unfeasible or undesirable. Castro's Cuba is busily soliciting foreign investment and otherwise seeking increased integration into the global economy. Even Nicaragua's revolutionary government in the 1980s saw no alternative to servicing debts incurred by Somoza for the purposes of feathering his own nest and bombing his own cities.

Another reason why debtor governments continue to play the game despite a deck heavily stacked against them is because those who make the mess are not obliged to clean it up. There are at least two dimensions to that kind of transference. One has to do with long-term versus short-term accountability. Benefits accrue to the government that takes out the loan and has use of the capital. Burdens fall to some future government, and perhaps even future generations.

The other dimension is one of class. When the party incurring debt is a state and the collateral is, in effect, a work force, it stands to reason that those who repay, or service, the debt will be those who have no choice — and those who incidentally had no access to the money. If the state-holding classes who actually borrowed and spent the money had to repay it themselves — with interest — the game would surely grind to a halt.

The mechanism, or policy package, for ensuring that when belts are to be tightened it will be around the narrowest waists has come to be known as structural adjustment. Even those Caribbean mini-states, like Barbados, that had been quite prosperous and enjoying economic growth until the 1980s were falling prey to credit conditionality in the early 1990s. In September of 1991, Barbados found itself with foreign reserves expected to last no more than one and a half weeks. At that point the government entered into a Faustian bargain with the IMF. At the beginning of 1993, Prime Minister Erskine Sandford laid out in the parliament the additional steps that were to be taken to reduce effective demand, attract foreign capital, and otherwise follow through on the structural adjustment plan. These included: a decrease in direct taxes and an increase in indirect ones, including the introduction of a value added tax; an "incomes policy" to depress wages (The World Bank had complained that relatively high wages were discouraging tourism); a personnel pruning of 8 percent from the public service; privatizing of government enterprises; a cut-back of services and subsidies affecting the general public, such as transportation, and an increase in services and subsidies to industrialists and other prospective investors. And this plan, mind you, was drawn up by the broadly based Democratic Labor Party. How, you might ask, did it come to this?

## Comparative Vulnerability

The same forces that for the money-movers dictate comparative advantage leave the rest of us with comparative disadvantage — that is, the inability to produce what we would consume or to consume what we produce. Now, as in the heyday of European colonialism, comparative advantage dictates that fertile land in the Caribbean, as elsewhere, should be used for the production of export crops. But export earnings are rarely redistributed effectively to the population at large, while higher prices for imported food are. Caribbean states are importing an ever-increasing portion of their food; by the end of the 1980s according to figures compiled by the Caribbean Community (CARICOM) in 1988, about half of the area's population was undernourished.

Such vulnerability is by no means confined to the Third World. Ownership and management of agribusiness, manufacturing and retail operations alike become increasingly centralized and money becomes ever more mobile. Capital — production facilities or more liquid portfolio investments — settles and resettles where wages and taxes are lower. Like Sherman moving through the South, these money-movers leave in their wake a swath of devastated communities.

Thus Caribbean governments, like other governments of Latin America, Africa, and Asia, and even state and local governments in the United States, offer up whatever they can. Until public outcry applied the brakes in 1988, the government of Guyana was proceeding with plans to take in toxic waste from the United States in exchange for much-needed dollars.

With "free trade," the goods produced where wages are very low can be sold where they are much higher. But such a system of export orientation has built-in contradictions. In the global village, deterioration in terms of exchange for labor in the Third World means deterioration in the First as well. As wages drop in one region after another, the most acute shortage at some future point may be of consumers.

Meanwhile, the centrifugal forces that contributed to the dissolution of the Russian Empire have been felt also in the Caribbean. It is precisely as independence, for any people, becomes a pipe dream that it is most avidly sought and even, in a formal sense, achievable. "Independence" notwithstanding, governments are vulnerable at all times to seeing credit frozen, capital stripped, and currencies trashed. And those governments having what appears to be a genuine popular mandate are required, in effect to pay insurance premiums higher than would be demanded of more reliable elitist governments. They are expected to be solicitous of and subservient to multinational finance capital not only in deed but in word as well. Admitting that it had no options in economic policy would subject a government, or party aspiring to govern, to punishment just as surely as would acting as if it had options.

## The Undermining of Political Institutions

A party such as the Dominican Republic's Dominican Revolutionary Party (PRD), popular and reformist in its origins, would ordinarily be a source of anxiety for economic elites and a target for military repression — as indeed it was throughout most of its history and as recently as 1978. Because of that history, in fact, it was a much-subdued PRD that assumed the presidency in 1978. Even so, the most modest of its promised welfare advances were thwarted by the austerity measures imposed by the IMF, while the military lurked in the background. Seeing themselves under constant threat — feeling the pull of the short leash — PRD executives, President Salvador Jorge Blanco in particular, made concessions to the armed forces, to creditors, and to other foreign and domestic elite interests that would have embarrassed even the most conservative of the country's leaders. The political breakthrough that the PRD victory might have represented has yet to be realized. Through the 1980s and 1990s, parties and governments continued to lack credibility and maneuverability vis-a-vis economic interests. In 1997, according to the UNDP's human poverty index, 30 percent of the Dominican people lived in absolute poverty.

Even so, the Dominican Republic looked like a promised land from the perspective of the other end of the island, where Haitians in 1998 earned an average wage of US$250 a year and unemployment was estimated at 80 percent. Now that both countries are ruled by elected leaders, the Dominican state sugar corporation no longer buys cane-cutters from the Haitian government, but some twenty thousand Haitians entering legally and many thousands more entering illegally still work under conditions scarcely distinguishable from slavery. The misery that has been the lot of Haiti since it gained independence from France, becoming the modern world's first nation born of a slave revolt, has been deepened by years of popular struggle against a predatory military regime and, more recently, by the austerity measures imposed as a condition of IMF loans.

In 1988, Trinidad and Tobago, with unemployment already standing at 23 percent by official underestimation, bowed to IMF demands and adopted a new, more stringent, austerity program. Social unrest built to a crescendo that was expressed in 1990 in rioting and looting, catalyzed by an episode in which a number of government officials were taken hostage. The country's per capita economic growth rate from 1980 to 1995 averaged a negative 1.5 percent.

In Venezuela, characterized for more than three decades by high per capita income and stable civilian rule, the debt crisis of the late 1980s — in immediate terms a foreign reserves short-fall and IMF conditions for a stand-by loan — forced incoming president Carlos Andrés Pérez, of the Social Democratic Party, Acción Democrática, to adopt extreme austerity measures in 1989. The upshot was rioting and police countermeasures that resulted in some three hundred deaths by official count, a thousand or more by unofficial. The instability and discontent that followed generated a climate propitious for military conspiracy. Coup attempts in February of 1992 and again in November of that year were unsuccessful, but not, perhaps, by much. The apparent level of popular support for the conspirators left civilian leaders of both major parties shaken; and the economic shocks launched a period of economic decline and political instability that lasted into the late 1990s. The party system, as the country headed into presidential elections in December of 1998, was in shambles; and the candidate elected by a wide margin was Lt. Colonel Hugo Chávez, a populist in policy terms and a leader in the abortive coup attempt of early 1992.

## For Most, a Lose-Lose Strategy

The Caribbean Basin Initiative might be seen as a trial run, or preview, of what American and other leaders in the employ of the creditor cartel had in mind for a larger arena. With the end of the Cold War and the unchallenged victory of that cartel, the CBI model has come to dominate the global village. And the consequences for most of that village have been in the same direction, if not necessarily of the same magnitude, as those felt in the Caribbean.

Little wonder that many Caribbean leaders have been skeptical of US protestations of common economic interests. The fact is, however, that the policies that have so devastated the Caribbean have in no way redounded to the benefit of ordinary Americans. The same policies that have stripped the Caribbean and other Third World states of internally generated capital, obliterated social services, suppressed local markets, and kept labor cheap have served to draw US capital — and jobs — abroad.

The ordinary people — the middle and working or would-be-working classes — of the Americas, as opposed to the high-rollers who place their bets in a global game, occupy the same hemisphere. Now more than ever, as economic communities are roped off in Europe and Asia, Americans of North and South are destined to share either prosperity or destitution.

## Notes

1. Mother Nature's retort came in 1997 in a series of explosions of volcanic fury that virtually depopulated the island.
2. Cited in Kathy McAfee, *Storm Signals: Structural Adjustment and Development Alternatives in the Caribbean* (London: Zed Books, and Boston: Oxfam America, 1991), p. 3.
3. Robert Pastor, "The United States and Grenada: Who Pushed First and Why?" in Jorge Heine, ed. *A Revolution Aborted: The Lessons of Grenada* (Pittsburgh: Pittsburgh University Press, 1990), p. 209.
4. McAfee, *op. cit.*, 2; See also Ramish F. Ramsaran, "Domestic Policy, the External Environment, and Economic Crisis in the Caribbean," in Anthony Payne and Paul Sutton, eds., *Modern Caribbean Politics* (Baltimore and London: John Hopkins University Press, 1993).
5. The author was in the visitor's gallery when Prime Minister Sandiford presented the plan to the Bajan parliament on January 14, 1993.
6. In the US, the most immediate threat is that of a stock market crash.
7. For elaboration on the political costs of adjustment policies, see Jan K. Black, *The Dominican Republic: Politics and Development in an Unsovereign State* (Boston: Allen and Unwin, 1986).
8. Conversations in Trinidad and Tobago and in Curaçao and Aruba in January 1993.
9. Conversations with Venezuelan political leaders, including COPEI leader Enrique Pérez Olivares, former Minister of Education and Mayor of Caracas, January 18, 1993, and with Lt. Col. Hugo Chávez in May, 1998.

Chapter 10

# Privatizing Privilege: Russia and Central Asia

*The economic model of the global village constitutes a synthesis of East and West: privatization of gains and socialization of losses.*

*Real democracy is most likely to be found where the money isn't; money attracts the wrong kind of people.*

*"HOW ARE THINGS?"* we asked Anatoly when he met us at Moscow's Sheremetyevo International Airport. "Terrible," he said, "but not so bad." That seemed to sum things up pretty well. The economy was still in awful trouble in 1994, but had seen some improvement, at least, over the previous year. And some things were clearly a lot better than they had been on my earlier visits.

This was my third decennial visit to Moscow. At the time of my first visit, in 1974, there was a seasonal thaw in the Cold War and Muscovites were enjoying something on the order of a political decompression. My friends, who were not dissidents in any activist sense, but who like so many Russians had lost family members to Stalinist purges, were animated and optimistic, feeling freer than usual to speak their minds and to be seen with Americans. Economically, however, times were hard. People seemed well enough fed and clothed, but scarcity was readily apparent in empty shelves and skimpy displays in shop windows.

When I visited again in 1984, the situation appeared to have been reversed. Shelves were abundantly stocked, but on the streets and in the metros bodies were rigid and faces frozen. Friends were more guarded in their speech, and even the most hospitable were concerned about being seen to entertain foreigners.

In 1994, Russians still had their wonderfully wry sense of humor and their protective stoicism, and St. Basil's Cathedral in Red Square still laughed out loud when bathed in the warm late afternoon sun. But everything else was different.

# Restructuring Russia

## What's New?

Advertisements — omnipresent, larger-than-life billboards touting banks and cigarettes and Pepsi Cola. And microenterprise — kiosks offering fruit and flowers, baked goods and drinks, along with sidewalk "dufflebag" salespeople. It is hard to know how to feel about such changes. On the grayest and squarest of Stalinist streets, the ads seem a dose of vitality. But where whimsical remnants of more imaginative architecture have survived, the ads are at best a discordant note — a kind of aesthetic pollution.

As to the street merchants, again reaction must be mixed. Some seem to represent the seeds of a new small-business entrepreneurship, while others suggest desperation — the selling off of whatever was removable around the house. Just beneath the Kremlin Wall, in front of the kiosks selling lottery tickets and Philip Morris cigarettes, a half-dozen women stood in a row, each selling not a stand-full, but a handful, of food items — bananas, eggs, bread. They were reasonably well-dressed and seemingly self-conscious, the newly poor perhaps.

Other newcomers to Moscow's streets, also products of contemporary capitalism, are traffic jams, beggars, and muggers. The blue jeans Russian teenagers used to try desperately (and clandestinely, of course) to buy from American and European tourists are now standard uniform, along with jogging suits, and teenagers now sport ghetto blasters, headsets, and the occasional skateboard. Along those streets we also saw mini-skirts and mini-markets, Mercedes dealerships, and, on most sidewalks and buildings, another ten years of deterioration.

Service in hotels, restaurants, and shops was mixed this time — in some cases extraordinarily gracious, unlike the range from sullen or amused indifference to outright hostility that had been the norm in decades past. That is not to suggest that Russians in general are xenophobic or lacking in courtesy or compassion. It is just that "service" was a special case, based on a curious disincentive system. With little hope of earning more and little fear of being fired, workers had more to gain in denying service, thus preserving their own time and energy, illusion of control, and perhaps some goods to pilfer, or in extracting a petty bribe, than in offering the service.

## Who's Who? Money and Status

Since my husband and I were guests of an institute of the National Academy of Sciences, I thought it peculiar that the Institute driver who took us to the airport was openly rude to us and to the Russian professor who accompanied us. I understood, though, when I learned that the driver earns more than the Institute's director.

Getting in sync with international capitalism has meant a massive rearrangement of status, as a person's worth comes to be measured by his or her material assets or earning capacity. And earning capacity is largely a function of access to hard currency. The case of drivers is said to be a special one, since much of the service is operated by gangsters; but any occupational group whose skills or services are in demand by foreign investors and advisers is at a distinct advantage.

For most of Russia's educators, the freefall in income has meant a slide in status as well. Research institutes are closing and university salaries advance glacially while inflation is a raging torrent. Distinguished social scientists and administrators are forced now to hire themselves out as translators or language teachers for newly established foreign companies or private schools. A friend of mine who is a very senior professor at the University of Moscow had seen a five-fold increase in her salary since 1990. But price increases since then had ranged from fifty- to one hundred-fold.

The decline was the steepest for pensioners. It was estimated that about a third of the population over fifty, some eleven million people, were living below the poverty line. In fact, the average pension was well below what authorities considered the minimum required to survive in Moscow. Russia's mortality rate was unprecedented in the twentieth century in peacetime and in the absence of major famines or epidemics. The rate had increased between 1990 and 1994 by 40 percent, from 11.2 to 15.7 deaths per one thousand people. Male life expectancy fell from 63.8 years to 57.7 years, and female life expectancy from 74.3 to 71.3 years. The deaths were attributed largely to stress-related cardiovascular disease, accidents, often alcohol-related, suicide, and homicide.[1]

## Anarchy in High Places

At least for foreigners, Moscow had become one of the most expensive cities in the world — and one of the most crime-ridden. The two problems are not unrelated. Prices reflect the costs of "security," and generalized insecurity reflects the costs of stratospheric prices.

For the better part of seventy years, the security of the Soviet state meant the insecurity of its most spirited people. Those who made a point of befriending foreigners, particularly Americans, were keenly aware of placing themselves at risk. Once again the security issue looms very large among

Muscovites as well as provincials of the defunct Soviet system. Its source now, however, is not authority, but rather the lack of it. The breakdown of state authority has left in its stead the anarchy of competing authorities. This is evident in stalemates and zigzags in most policy areas.

Anarchy in high places was evident also in the existence of rival mafias (US government estimates run to more than four thousand) that in the manner of Chicago's mobsters of the 1920s pay off the police, run their protection rackets more or less openly, and flaunt their new wealth. (Former KGB members are believed to figure prominently among mafia leaders.) Among the vehicles that jam Moscow's once empty boulevards are an extraordinary number of Mercedes, BMWs, and stretch limousines. In Moscow, a young Russian friend had started a very promising computer business, but he refused to pay mafia protection fees, so forty of his seventy employees had to be assigned to security.

Such organized violence on a major scale seems to encourage also a less organized kind, a tendency reinforced by weak government and economic desperation. US networks reported in 1994 that the homicide rate in Russia was twice that of the US and rising. Whether or not that is true — figures are not highly reliable — Muscovites, to whom street crime was virtually unknown until the 1990s, are acutely aware that each year several thousand people in their midst are falling afoul of mafias or muggers.

## Nationalism Under Assault

One of the most popular attractions in Moscow in 1994 was an exhibition by neo-nationalist painter I. Glazunov. Like Solzhenitsyn, who was at that time making his way across the vast stretches of Siberia and broadcasting back his observations, Glazunov had suggested in his earlier muralesque paintings that the rich fabric of Russian culture and tradition would overwhelm the brittle and alien deviation represented by official communism. Glazunov's recent work, however, expresses chagrin that Russian culture itself is being submerged by a tidal wave of Western consumerism and banality.

Certainly an evening with the gilded youth at the Hotel Rossiya's classy restaurant and night club would offer no clue apart from language as to where one was. The ambiance was world youth culture as homogenized by MTV, with international prices to match. Elsewhere in Moscow at hotels and restaurants, imports — more expensive, of course, and not necessarily better — have replaced Russian beer, wine, and champagne. Even Russia's full-bodied vodkas, like Stolichnaya, are being pushed aside in the market by lighter-fluid-flavored imports like Smirnoff.

More disturbing to thoughtful Russians is the marginalization of domestic alternatives in the marketplace of ideas, particularly ideas relating to economic and political restructuring. None of the Russians with whom I spoke was sympathetic with the chauvinistic version of nationalism represented now by Vladimir Zhirinovsky, but most were disturbed by the sense that Russia was being swept along by an alien tide, with no nationally generated interpretation of what its destiny might be or should be.

Dr. Andrei Grachev, former adviser to Soviet leader Mikhail Gorbachev, commented in 1997 that contemporary Russia was all too reminiscent of the Russia of 1917, at least in terms of the primitive aspects of accumulation of capital and the consequent concentration of power. The Politburo had been replaced by the *bankburo*. It was as if the century had come full circle. The last parliamentary elections had produced a majority for the relatively unreconstructed Communist Party in the Duma, and the Duma had voted to seek a restoration of the Soviet Union.[2]

## Waiting for a Miracle

In 1997, the IMF, which had extended more than $9 billion in loans, was reasonably content with the performance of the Russian economy. The debt was being serviced in a timely manner and annual inflation, which had hovered in the range of three to four digits over the past six years, promised to drop to a single digit by the end of the year. Meanwhile, however, meeting the IMF's anti-inflation requirements had called for a withholding of government salaries and pensions totaling almost $7 billion. Teachers, scientists, miners, and soldiers had reported delays of up to a year in disbursement. A loaf of bread that had sold for 25 kopeks in the late 1980s was selling in 1997 for 2,500 rubles — a ten thousand-fold increase, and average family income had dropped two-fold.[3] Thought may be freer in political terms, but not in economic ones; children's textbooks that used to be free must now be purchased.

In August 1998, the Russian economy, so recently touted as the most promising of the emerging markets, once again slipped into crisis. Strained to the limits by the demands of foreign creditors and investors and the predations of its own version of "cowboy" capitalism, the economy could not withstand the hot money jitters unleashed by East Asia's financial meltdown. Despite promises of a Western bailout, the ruble plunged and with it an estimated 40 percent of total banking assets. Hundreds of banks went bankrupt or teetered on the brink. Already in default on billions of dollars in domestic debt, the government was hard-pressed to maintain service on the foreign debt.

For most Russians, however, the crisis was hardly new; they had failed to be blessed by the fleeting miracle. Since restructuring began in 1991 overall production had been cut in half. The domestic harvest in the fall of 1998, down by 48 percent from the previous year, was in fact the most meager in forty years. And the imported non-perishable goods that now make up 60 to 65 percent of the food products sold in Russia (up to 85 percent in Moscow) are for many simply unaffordable.

As winter approached, the food supply deficit in some areas, particularly the far east, was being described as dangerous. But Russians were drawing on deep reserves of ingenuity and fortitude. That much of Russia had fallen back upon a pre-modern subsistence economy was in a sense the good news. It meant that much of the population, even in the cities, was growing its own food, turning balconies and empty lots into gardens, and resurrecting barter on a major scale.

Russian men are fond of saying that there is no such thing as too little food — only not enough vodka; no such thing as an unattractive woman — only not enough vodka; no such thing as a silly joke — only not enough vodka; no such thing as *enough* vodka — only *not* enough vodka.[4] There is a lot of wealth to be tapped in Russia, and one can be sure that in a few years economists will be speaking again of the Russian economic miracle, but I fear that for most Russians for a very long time there will be not enough of anything, including vodka.

## Carpetbaggers and Suits on the Caspian

Such a friendly occupation force — no tanks or machine guns or khaki, just Mercedes and briefcases and pin-striped suits. And so well-meaning. The oil company carpetbaggers hovering over the Caspian Sea may know very well what they're after, but the foreign bureaucrats seem convinced that their missions are philanthropic. With respect to complaints by central Asians about the precipitous drop in their standard of living under Western-inspired economic reforms, an Agency for International Development (AID) contractee commented, "It's a shame they don't realize that all of this is a delayed reaction to the previous system and that, in the long run, it will be for the best" (perhaps what they realize is that, as Lord Keynes used to say, "in the long run, we are all dead").

One wonders if the Russians who swept across these steppes in the nineteenth century, bringing modernization to the descendants of Attila the Hun and Genghis Khan, saw themselves as equally well-meaning. Certainly the Soviet revolutionaries who displaced czarist nobility did.

Each newly triumphant set of *conquistadores* and carpetbaggers, missionaries and modernizers is convinced of the universality of its vision and the magnanimity of its mission, and each generates new rackets and new rich along with new categories of the wretched. In the wake of World War II there was talk of taming enemy nations, but in fact punishment was meted out only to leaders, and even then only selectively. Defeated peoples were to be subsidized with funds for relief and development.

Cold War conciliation, however, has offered up a new twist. This time it is the old enemy leaders who have become the new ally, to be courted and cut in on Western deals, while the people have been the victims of pillage. Of course the contemporary swarms of carpetbaggers and suits have not stolen the money outright in the manner, say, of Genghis Khan; they have simply stripped the currency of its value, then bought for a song the treasure and output of the region and the labor of its now desperate people.

## Some Less Equal Than Others

Historians elsewhere will not envy those who must create the birth legend of the modern independent Central Asian states. From this vantage point, too close in time, it seems that they were simply cast adrift — abandoned by their empire, as nationalist leaders of Russia, Belarus, and the Ukraine sought better deals for themselves. Likewise, the breakaway of the Central Asian republics from the residual economic market was not a planned escape. It resulted in a double whammy of devaluation — of the ruble against Western currencies and of Central Asian currencies against the ruble.

The prospects for economic transition vary greatly among the five Central Asian Republics, from Kazakhstan, the richest in per capita incomes, to the poorest, Tadjikistan. Perceptions of those prospects vary also within the new states, depending upon role and status. Well-placed regional bureaucrats, in the process of personal transitions from membership in a communist elite to membership in the capitalist elite, and the foreign bureaucrats who are sending them to Western capitals for economic retraining, seem abundantly optimistic.

In unguarded moments, even the Western purveyors of neoliberal reform might concede that optimism for the region as a whole was based in part on legacies of the Soviet System, particularly what is euphemistically known as human resources — that is, healthy, educated people — and that those legacies are now imperiled by dwindling public budgets. But in Kazakhstan, optimism centered on material resources. Until the implosion of the Soviet Union, 70 to 80 percent of Kazakhstan's trade in both directions was with what is now Russia, so economic dislocation has taken a heavy toll, including a precipitous drop in industrial production and national income. But Kazakhstan is not without its own cards to play. Its vast expanses of sparsely populated desert and steppe made it an attractive location for a major Soviet spaceship launching pad, which has been rented out since independence to the Russians.

Kazakhstan, moreover, is a major repository of mineral wealth, including gold. But the main reason Almaty's not-ready-for-prime-time airport is aswarm with anxious Western businessmen and self-important bureaucrats is petroleum. Known reserves around the Caspian sea are on the order of those of Kuwait, and potential reserves could make the sea — actually the world's largest lake — another Persian Gulf.

The catch is that, with respect to markets, the Caspian Sea is nowhere. Despite the unresolved pipeline problem, US companies had invested tens of billions by the mid-1990s. In 1997, however, China weighed in with an opening bid that stunned other players in the game. Distance and topographic obstacle course notwithstanding, China outbid two US-based companies for two major oilfields with a pledge to invest $10 billion to build a pipeline to its own territory.[5]

Meanwhile, the Kyrgyz people, under the shadow of the Tien Shan mountain range, where in winter the temperature drops quickly into the minuses, saw themselves in danger of freezing to death during the winter of 1994 when Uzbekistan cut off the gas. Kyrgyzstan had previously enjoyed a guaranteed supply of cheap — that is, subsidized — natural gas, but suddenly the Uzbeks wanted hard currency up front. The purchase was finally covered by a World Bank loan, but Kyrgyzstan will be harnessed in seeming perpetuity to foreign debt service. Perhaps it is no coincidence that Kyrgyzstan, with no material resources of interest to Western investors and nothing other than water of interest to its neighbors, is the only Central Asian republic to have made a convincing show of democracy. Its poverty has meant that the biggest thieves and snake oil salesmen have been lured elsewhere.

## The Environmental Downside

Kazakhstan's vast open spaces have proved to be a mixed blessing; along with the spaceship launching pad, they also drew the Soviet Union's nuclear bomb testing program. Open-air testing began in eastern Kazakhstan near the city of Semipalatinsk in 1949; some two hundred bombs were detonated in those skies before the practice was halted by the nuclear test ban treaty of 1963. Thereafter testing continued in underground chambers. Some four hundred underground detonations rocked the area before the complex was closed in 1991.

The nature of the legacy of that testing program is only beginning to be understood. Several hundred thousand people lived within a fifty-mile radius of the test sites. Within that population birth defects and leukemia are abnormally high. The government's own scientists have become highly concerned about long-term environmental contamination from nuclear fallout and many foreign agencies and NGOs, including even US Peace Corps volunteers, are addressing the problem; but at least twenty-seven sites are said to be beyond help. Meanwhile, testing goes on at the Chinese range at Lop Nor, upwind from Kazakhstan. Any climate irregularity is ascribed by the man on the street in Almaty to the Chinese tests.

The shrinking Aral Sea, on Kazakhstan's border with Uzbekistan, has also caught international attention, including a visit by US Vice President Al Gore. Once the world's fourth largest inland body of water, it has lost 60 percent of its volume and has dropped fifty feet. Upstream irrigation has diverted most of the water from the rivers that fed it. Salt and chemicals from the now exposed seabed blow over adjacent lands, spreading the contamination.

## Importing a National Ethos

Like other newly independent states, those of Central Asia have been faced with the challenge of creating a new national ethos. But they are handicapped in that task in that the crucial nation-building roles of designing economic policies and molding political institutions have been usurped by their new allies and "benefactors" from the West. Moreover, a shrinking public sector is in no position to play a unifying role.

At the same time that new forms of nationalistic expression are being found —revival of language and religion, for example, and discrimination against non-nationals, that is, those whose ethnic group does not coincide with the name of the republic — the social infrastructure that underpinned a national ethos is crumbling, and foreign products, from Coca-Cola to blue jeans to rap video, are overwhelming local markets. It is still possible to get *koomis* (fermented mare's milk) in Almaty's farmer's market, along with fruits and nuts and vegetables, but increasingly products that are processed at all, including even beer and champagne, are now imported.

Perhaps the greatest irony for those who would undertake nation-building is that the carriers of national culture, teachers of every level and every discipline, are being driven to the service of foreign companies just to feed themselves. My friend Raushan, a senior university professor of modern languages, showed me the sandals she had just bought in the market for the equivalent of a week's salary: US$27. The Kazakhi currency, the tenge, had lost nine-tenths of its value in a mere seven months. A single mother, Raushan now found herself paying for services like day care that used to be free, and supporting her aging parents, whose pensions had been rendered worthless. Her brother, a doctor, who might have helped, had lost his job, like so many others in discontinued government services and closed down factories.

Raushan enjoyed teaching and took very seriously her professional role as a conveyor of Kazakhi culture and values, but she was simply unable to get along on what was left of her salary. She was among the fortunate, however; she had options. With great sadness, she was contemplating accepting a position as interpreter for a US financial consulting firm that would pay ten times her university salary.

## The Newest "New" Class

The example of open ethnic strife in Tadjikistan has served to justify authoritarianism in Uzbekistan and has left many Kazakhs willing to settle for little more than a wave of the democratic wand over a leadership cadre that, apart from getting fatter (e.g., five hundred new black Mercedes), has changed precious little since independence. Foreign investors, financial advisers, and diplomats speak with relief of Kazakhstan's political stability. At a press conference following the country's first elections, when teams of international observers began to point out that the process had been less than edifying, the US Ambassador cut them off and terminated the conference. The election served to legitimate the ongoing rule of Communist leader Nursultan Nazarbayev.

The United States signaled the seriousness of its "security" interests in Kazakhstan in September 1997 by sending five hundred US paratroopers from Ft. Bragg, N.C., on a nineteen-hour flight to engage in "peacekeeping exercises" in the Kazakhi desert. Meanwhile, much of the hard currency floating around had been drawn from US taxpayers and privatized by the US government. Some of the NGOs through which US assistance has been filtered fit the usual image of people working long hours under hardship conditions for little pay out of commitment to a social cause — improved health, education, environmental preservation standards, or poverty alleviation. But the most flush of the "NGOs" were of a different sort entirely — the American Bar Association, the International Banking Institute, jet-setting consultants in legal and financial fine points of privatization, entrepreneurship, commercial banking, and other aspects of economic restructuring. The nature of the economic transitions in Kazakhstan and the magnitude of the profit-making potential at stake is a powerful disincentive to the kind of elections that might prematurely put decision-making authority at risk.

Can countries conceived without their consent and brought forth unarmed into the arena, like Christians waiting for the lions — a global arena crowded with predators poised to pounce — avoid disintegration or anarchy? Losses to date of industrial output and social infrastructure do not bode well for the region's short-term future. But this region, so rich in history and culture and in "human resources," has seen plunder and pillage and social dissolution before and has bounced back again and again. The question, as always, is how much and how many will be sacrificed to energize the next bounce.

## Notes

1. M. Elaine Mar, "The Dying in Moscow," *Harvard Magazine*, Sept.–Oct. 1996, p. 23
2. Grachev, lecture at St. Antony's College, Oxford University, Oct. 20, 1997.

3. Grachev, *loc. cit.,* and Katrina Vanden Heuvel, "Russia Waits," *The Nation*, Oct. 21, 1996.
4. This expression of sardonic Russian humor is on loan from my colleague and friend, Professor Sergei Baburkin of the University of Yaroslav.
5. James Meek, "China Joins Scramble for Black Gold," *The Manchester Guardian Weekly*, Oct. 5, 1997, p. 19.

## Chapter 11

# Cuba: Clinging to the Dream

*The laboratory for appropriate technology and sustainable development is usually the country that has no choice.*

*OLGA HAD A* winsome smile and the playful spirit that is so common to Cubans, but there was sadness in her pale blue eyes. It was not so much a matter of scarcity; she could deal with that. The worst was the uncertainty. At twenty-eight, she needed to be able to envision a future. Child of a Cuban soldier who went to Moscow for training and a Russian woman who returned with him to the magical island, Olga was a by-product of a world order that had collapsed.

Many of her friends had already left Cuba in search of more promising careers, or freedom of expression, or maybe just enough to eat. A journalist with Cuban television, she studied international relations in Moscow, but she was not tempted to return there to a situation she saw as even worse. Cuba was her homeland and the source of her identity. Yet like many others in the dark days of 1993, she lived with a nagging ambivalence about her country and her place in it. Cubans had shelter and day care, free education and cradle-to-grave health care, but there was no soap and no toilet paper and only one piece of bread per person per day. The rationing system meant that no one was starving but that a lot of people were hungry. Severe shortage of petroleum meant scarce transportation and daily electricity blackouts.

Doctors who briefed us at a clinic in Cienfuegos left on bicycles to make their house calls. In Havana, a nurse settled in for a long stay on the porch of our hotel, saying she was not anxious to go home to her eighth-floor apartment until the elevators started working again. Half of the country's tractors had been decommissioned, replaced in the fields by more reliable oxen.

## An Economic Freefall

For most of Latin America, the wretchedness of the early 1990s came about in a gradual descent over the course of the 1980s from the relative prosperity of the 1960s and 1970s. Not so for Cuba. What Cuba experienced was a free fall — a shrinkage in economic output of some 40% in two years.

What has become known in Cuba as the "special period," since the collapse of its Soviet-sphere market, is not so different from what the deprivations and conditionalities of globalization have done to most of the rest of the Third World. But the results are more stark in Cuba because the revolution has in a sense drawn the whole country into the middle class. Incomes may be low, consumer goods scarce, and perks hard to come by, but almost universal literacy, comprehensive education at all levels, and particularly the cost-free availability of higher education, have generated a very large proportion of professionals, and, in general, attitudes and expectations normally associated with a middle class. Moreover, the only available solution may be worse than the problem. While the threat of US military invasion served to unite, the recent invasion of dollars divides and alienates.

For the generation who made their own history, there is pride still in holding out against an increasingly virulent strain of capitalism. But that generation is being eaten by its children. Not knowing what they have to lose, because they've never been without it, young Cubans are mesmerized by the shiny gadgets sported by their affluent cousins from Miami. And the pride of Cubans, young and old alike, is shattered by the privileges extended to hard-currency-toting tourists and denied to them.[1]

The last set of the ex-Soviet troops left Cuba in 1993. With the Cold War over, one would like to think that more humane and more enlightened motives might come to the fore in US policy. Humaneness aside, simple greed might have suggested that US companies should move into the vacuum left by the collapse of the Soviet market. Instead, with the 1992 Torricelli Act, condemned by the United Nations, the US tightened even further its thirty-year-old trade embargo. The Helms-Burton Act of 1996 generated such indignation and legislative countermeasures among US trading partners that it had to be suspended immediately after passage.[2]

## Colonial Backwash: Occupied Miami

The initial shock to the US body politic delivered by the Cuban Revolution might be explained in part by the fact that, given the proximity of the island to the US mainland and the extent of US involvement in Cuban affairs, Cuba had been considered virtually an extension of Florida. The problem now for US policymakers is that that relationship has been reversed. It's the same ninety miles, but Florida, or at least Dade County, has become an extension of Cuba.

If US ownership of much of Cuba made extrication from Cuban affairs difficult, Cuban ownership of much of Florida makes it even more so. US politicians, including presidential candidates, who wish to do well in Florida do not have the luxury of fashioning a policy toward Cuba based on the US national interest; rather, they are held hostage to factional, or particularistic, Cuban interests. Meanwhile, the never-ending struggle between Cuba's revolutionaries and counterrevolutionaries that put such a chill on political expression in Cuba had done the same, according to human rights monitors of America's Watch, to the political climate of Miami. If the US government is to regain independence of action, policymakers must concern themselves less with how to isolate Castro in Havana than with how to isolate followers of Jorge Mas Canosa in Miami.[3]

Those Cubans who stayed at home and who blame the hardships they suffer on US policy are not just being peevish. At least until the mid-nineties, it was almost impossible for Cubans to get visas to visit with relatives in the US, but if the same Cubans came by boat and called themselves refugees, they were welcomed with open arms — and perhaps even paraded on television. Normal diplomatic relations would put an end to such absurdities and normal trade relations could easily relieve Cuba's most acute shortages while generating jobs for Americans, including Miami's Cuban-Americans.

## A Hostile World System

But the embargo is not a new problem, certainly not a systemic feature of the new world order; it is, rather, a vestige of the old — one that is now counterproductive in every particular to the Clinton Administration.[4] The worst news for Cuba is that even if a suddenly liberated US government chose to lift the embargo, Cuba's options would not look much better than they do right now.

Whether Cuba is an extension of Florida or Florida an extension of Cuba is less important in the long run than the fact that Miami has become the metropolis, or economic capital, of the Caribbean Basin. That does not mean that Cuba will automatically be swept back into the US sphere; it may mean that Miami is escaping that sphere to establish its own. But Cuba will still have to come to terms with a world economic system hostile not only to socialism but even to European-style mixed economies and social welfare systems.

By 1999, Cuba's antique cars were moving again and tractors were back in the fields. Foreign investment in tourism was restoring the colonial center of Old Havana and threatening the "Cancunization" of Varadero Beach. And a new elite, comprising those having access to dollars, was making its appearance. A story making the rounds featured Fulano de Tal, who was talking loudly about being a doorman at a new tourist hotel. "He has delusions of grandeur," friends explained. "He's really only a brain surgeon."

Since Cuban economic planners decided in 1994 to allow dollars to circulate freely, remittances from expatriates in Florida have proved a powerful stimulus to economic growth, if nonetheless an irritant to social harmony. By 1995, production had recovered to the 1988 level, and for 1996 economic growth registered 7.8 percent, according to the United Nations Economic Commission for Latin America and the Caribbean (ECLAC) the second highest in the entire region. It was the usual kind of miracle — a growth rate that could not and perhaps should not be sustained. Such reform has meant relief from crisis, though at some cost to revolutionary standards of fairness.

Political reform will encounter more resistance, particularly so long as resistance can be justified by US hostility. The stalemate leaves open the question that has haunted friends of the revolution since its inception. Is the worst of the system the price that must be paid for the best of it? Must universal literacy always be punished by an absence of anything worth reading? Is there an unavoidable trade-off between material equity and cultural and political creativity? Architects of the Cold War, on both sides, were bent on proving that such a trade-off was unavoidable, and the Castro government has yet to meet the challenge of disproving that thesis.

## Vestige or Vanguard?

Can Cuba succeed where all other Third World states have failed — in integrating the world capitalist system without loss of national sovereignty and, in particular, without loss of the social gains of the revolution? Maybe. Cubans are a remarkable people with much to offer, and not only in their highly developed pharmaceutical and biotechnology industries. Surely a world newly conscious of the need for conservation and recycling would seek guidance from a country that has no vehicular graveyards. In fact, necessity has made Cuba the mother of many inventions in the realm of organic agriculture and other aspects of sustainable development that should have great appeal elsewhere.

Could the US, then, learn to live with a more or less sovereign Cuba? Maybe, but even the best of American governments are more afraid of peace than of war. The beginnings of rapprochement would probably have to come from within the Cuban-American community. Just as those who fought the revolution have had to contend with a generation gap, the steadfast opponents of the revolution have a generation gap in their own community; young Cuban-Americans in search of their roots, as well as of business opportunities, may well break down barriers where others have failed.

# Notes

1. Despite US government restrictions, some eighty-three thousand US citizens visited Cuba in 1997.
2. The Torricelli Act calls for sanctions against third countries doing business with Cuba. The Helms-Burton Act allows that foreigners may be sued in US courts for dealing in properties claimed by Americans. The legislation was drawn up in such a way as to apply to virtually all properties nationalized by the revolutionary government, including that of Cubans who have since become naturalized US citizens.
3. Mas Canosa, President of the counterrevolutionary Cuban-American National Foundation, died of natural causes on November 23, 1997.
4. In October 1998, a record 157 countries in the UN General Assembly voted for a resolution calling for an end to the embargo. Only Israel joined the US in voting against the resolution, while twelve countries abstained.

# Part III: Second-Coming Capitalism and Comparative Disadvantage Suggested Readings


Andor, Laszlo, and Martin Summers. *Market Failure: A Guide to Eastern Europe's "Economic Miracle."* London: Pluto Press, 1998.

Barnet, Richard and John Cavanagh, *Global Dreams: Imperial Corporations and the New World Order*. New York: Simon and Schuster, 1994.

Brecher, Jeremy and Tim Costello. *Global Village or Global Pillage: Economic Reconstruction from the Bottom Up*. Boston: South End Press, 1995.

Burbach, Roger, Orlando Nuñez and Boris Kagarlitsky. *Globalization and Its Discontents: The Rise of Postmodern Socialisms*. London: Pluto Press, 1996.

Danaher, Kevin, *Fifty Years is Enough: The Case Against the World Bank and the International Monetary Fund*. Boston: South End Press, 1994.

Danaher, Kevin, ed. *Corporations Are Gonna Get Your Mama*. Monroe, Maine: Common Courage Press, A Global Exchange Book, 1996.

Cline, William R. *International Economic Policy in the 1990s* Cambridge, MA: MIT Press, 1995.

Ekins, Paul and Manfred Max-Neef. *Real-Life Economics: Understanding Wealth Creation*. London: Routledge, 1992.

George, Susan. *The Debt Boomerang: How Third World Debt Harms Us All.* London: Pluto Press, 1991.

George, Susan and Fabrizio Sabelli. *Faith and Credit: The World Bank's Secular Empire*. Boulder, CO: Westview Press, 1994.

Gray, John. *False Dawn: The Delusion of Global Capitalism*. New York: The New Press, 1999.

Griesgraber, Jo Marie and Bernhard G. Gunter. *World Trade: Toward Fair and Free Trade in the Twenty-first Century.* London: Pluto Press, 1997.

Harrison, Bennett. *Lean and Mean: The Changing Landscape of Corporate Power in the Age of Flexibility*. New York: Basic Books, 1994.

Herman, Edward S. "The Economics of the Rich." *Z Magazine*, Vol. 10, No. 7/8, July–Aug. 1997, pp. 19–25.

Hines, Colin and Tim Lang. *The New Protectionism: Protecting the Future Against Free Trade*. Washington, DC: Island Press, 1993.

Korten, David. *When Corporations Rule the World.* West Hartford, CT: Kumarian Press, 1995.

Isbister, John. *Promises Not Kept: The Betrayal of Social Change in the Third World.* West Hartford, CT: Kumarian Press, 1993.

Jatar-Hausmann, Ana-Julia. *The Cuban Way.* West Hartford, CT: Kumarian Press, 1999.

Mahon, James E. Jr. *Mobile Capital and Latin American Development.* University Park, PA: Penn State Press, 1996.

Mander, Jerry. *The Case Against the Global Economy and for a Turn Toward the Local.* San Francisco: Sierra Club Books, 1996.

Mittelman, James H. ed. *Globalization: Critical Reflections.* Boulder, CO: Lynne Rienner Publishers, 1997.

Nader, Ralph, ed. *The Case Against Free Trade.* San Francisco: Earth Island Press, 1993.

Phillips, Kevin. *The Politics of Rich and Poor.* New York: Harper Perennial, 1990.

Rich, Bruce. *Mortgaging the Earth: The World Bank, Environmental Impoverishment, and the Crisis of Development.* Boston: Beacon Press, 1994.

Reich, Robert B. *The Work of Nations: Preparing Ourselves for Twenty-first Century Capitalism.* London: Simon and Schuster, 1991.

Scholte, Jan Aart. "The International Monetary Fund and Civil Society: An Underdeveloped Dialogue." Presented at the International Conference on Non-State Actors and Authority in the Global System, University of Warwick, Oct. 31–Nov. 1, 1997.

Underhill, Geoffrey R.D., ed. *The New World Order in International Finance.* London: Macmillan, 1997.

United Nations. *World Economic Social Survey, 1996.* New York: United Nations, 1996.

Wallerstein, Immanuel. *The Modern World System II.* New York: Academic Books, 1980.

Wolff, Edward N. *Top Heavy: A Study of the Increasing Inequality of Wealth in America.* New York: Twentieth Century Fund, 1995.

The World Bank. *World Development Report 1997.* Oxford: Oxford University Press, 1997.

Ndebele Village in Zimbabwe

Part IV

# The Plundered Planet and Its Endangered Peoples

*The rich North has exported to the poor South its production models, its consumption habits, its polluting technology, and its garbage. Now it seeks to export as well the blame for environmental degradation and the responsibility for reversing it.*

*ENVIRONMENTALISTS AND* NGOs promoting grassroots development now find themselves swimming upstream against an ever stronger current, one which pushes accelerated production and consumption, limited only by profit-making potential. Governments harnessed to debt servicing schedules are in no position to resist the pollution of their water, the erosion of their soil, or the exploitation of their natural resources. Like the colonialists of centuries past, today's second-coming capitalists deplete, despoil, and depart.

## Missed Targets and Unperforming Treaties

The mood, as delegates gathered in New York City in June of 1997 for Rio Plus Five, was a grim one. Participants in this second world environment summit, a follow-up to the 1992 UN Conference on Environment and Development (UNCED or ECO '92) found that the firm goals and fond hopes expressed five years earlier in Rio de Janeiro had been illusory. On most scores — pollution of air and water, contamination of land and oceans, disappearance of rainforest and species — the degradation of the environment had accelerated.[1]

The World Wide Fund for Nature reported in 1997 that two-thirds of the world's forests had already been lost. Remaining forests are being felled and burned at an ever increasing rate. An area the size of England and Wales disappears each year.

More than eight hundred lobbyists were on hand to plot derailment when delegates from 150 countries met in Kyoto at the beginning of December 1997 to draw up a treaty addressing global warming. For all the dedication and enthusiasm invested by serious environmentalists, the conference promised little more than a much-needed tourism windfall for Kyoto and another inning in the North-South blame game. US calls for developing countries to discuss carbon emission targets were generally met with derision. Third World leaders considered such targeting as out of the question until rich countries started cutting their own emissions and pledged to help finance improved technologies in poorer countries.

Meanwhile, the richer countries were scarcely approaching agreement among themselves. The European Union, seeking more stringent controls, found the US proposal to stabilize emissions at 1990 levels to be feeble. The United States ultimately signed on to an agreement to reduce emissions of greenhouse gases to about 7 percent below 1990 levels by 2012, but to achieve that only through market incentives (e.g., higher energy prices, utility deregulation) rather than governmental regulation. Given the mood of the Republican congress, it was not likely to be ratified in any case.

In fact, should the US continue on its current course, emissions would be 34 percent above 1990 levels by 2010. Far from stabilizing, the US has seen emissions increase each year since 1990 for a total increase of more than 8%. Increases might be attributed to some extent to heightened economic activity, but pollution levels rose faster in 1996 than did economic output or energy consumption. The US alone contributes about one-fifth of the carbon being added annually to the atmosphere, a consequence largely of its inefficient transportation system; the average car adds its own weight in carbon to the atmosphere each year.

## The Overlooked Human Dimension

More important, perhaps, than the ongoing abuse of the material world, was the failure to follow through on the commitment to give equal weight to human needs and to highlight the intrinsic relationship between human and environmental poverty. The UNDP, in its 1997 Human Development Report, notes that Agenda 21, encapsulating UNCED commitments, recognizes an anti-poverty strategy as a basic condition for ensuring sustainable development.[2] But the global mechanisms established to promote and monitor implementation of Agenda 21 have failed to focus on poverty.

The connection? To begin with, the poor know more about environmental degradation in an immediate existential sense. They know because they occupy the front lines. That is not only the less assimilated indigenous peoples whose rivers are polluted and diverted and whose rainforests are receding; it is also the poor countries and poor neighborhoods that become garbage dumps and industrial wastelands.

Wealth does not mean invulnerability. Sooner or later the toxins dumped in or released over poor neighborhoods make their way into aquifers and rivers and drift uptown as acid rain. And the pesticides that first poison itinerant farm workers show up in suburbia in neatly packaged fruits and vegetables. But the poor in societies rural or urban, traditional or modern, occupy the front lines because they have fewer options, at least in the short term, than those who pollute with impunity.

Wherever there are hardships to be shared, the poor get more than their share of them. And to add insult to injury, the First World, having exported to the Third its consumption mania, its production-driven economic model, its polluting and energy-inefficient technologies, and its garbage, seeks to export finally the blame for the now visible threat to the planet's carrying capacity.

The combination of ever greater concentrations of capital, crazed to reproduce in a now global harem, and the desperation of debt-driven governments has set off a feeding frenzy for resources previously inaccessible by virtue of obstacle courses erected by nature or by governments. This frenzy is largely responsible for the extinction just since 1992 of some 130,000 species.

Mauritania's main source of wealth is the stocks of fish, particularly the sardines, off its coast. But that wealth is not now enriching Mauritanians. Local subsistence fishermen, banned by government edict from bringing in the overfished sardines, can only watch from the water's edge as European fishermen hawl them in to their giant factory trawlers.

The European Union had made the deeply indebted Mauritanian government an offer it couldn't refuse. The Europeans will pay more than $600 million over a six-year period for unlimited fishing rights in Mauritanian waters. European appetites, however, do not accommodate the hundreds of tons of sardines caught each day in those waters (Dutch trawlers alone take in three hundred tons a day); the main market for the catch, which is frozen, then canned in the Canary Islands, is West Africa.

The fish might then be available, in processed form, to the Mauritanian fishermen if they could afford them. But along with losing their main source of protein, the local population has lost its main source of income. They need not wait for the European payment to trickle down to the villages. It was destined to foreign financiers as debt service payments.

Some relief for local fishermen might be found in the moratorium on sardine fishing in those waters declared in October 1998. Green parties and organizations had shamed the European Commission into a temporary moratorium to consider the issue of overexploitation. But it may be too late. So great have been the combined catches in the region over recent years of EU, Japanese, Ukraine, and Russian vessels that the fisheries of the West African coast, previously among the world's most productive, now threaten to go the way of the Canadian cod banks into complete collapse.[3]

The threat to biodiversity has generated widespread alarm. It is curious that no such alarm has sounded with respect to cultural diversity. Among the species most endangered as we approach the new millennium are indigenous peoples.

## Cultural Diversity under Assault

The assault on indigenous people has been underway at least since the last millennium. It is as old as conquest, as old as greed; but the plight of unintegrated vestiges of so-called primitive cultures is set in relief as their numbers dwindle. The most common ways of measuring development — national aggregate data — tell us nothing about the fate of such peoples. High rates of GNP or per capita growth may well represent the success of conquering peoples or cultures in obliterating indigenous ones.

It is estimated that there remain some six thousand indigenous nations and 300 million indigenous people, about 5 percent of the world's population. They are categorized roughly as people having a unique language and culture and profound ties to ancestral homelands.[4] Such multi-generational attachment to, and familiarity with, places has made them at the same time valuable and vulnerable. They have suffered disproportionately from modern-day interstate and intrastate conflict, aggression against people as well as against nature.

In some cases, indigenous peoples have been intentionally targeted by *conquistadores* and carpetbaggers who coveted their land. In other cases, they have been exploited by war-makers, used as proxies and cannon fodder in strategic encounters they knew little about, or simply wiped out in passing when their ancestral homes got in the way of bombs or bullets and herbicides.

More recently, the resources rush has pushed such peoples onto ever more marginal land. The pollution of the indigenous lands by oil companies — Texaco in the Ecuadorian Amazon, Shell Oil in Ogoniland in the Niger River Delta in Nigeria — and the stripping of rainforests in Malaysia and Brazil have come to global consciousness only because of persistent and media-savvy resistance by the indigenous people themselves.

It had been hoped that recognition of the value of food, medicinal, and other products of the rainforest might not only serve as incentive to preserve flora and fauna, but might serve as well to bring new income and livelihoods to the indigenous peoples. That hope, however, is being dampened by new uses and interpretations of international intellectual property rights. Corporate "gene hunters" search for new materials for seed, pharmaceutical, and biotechnology companies, which would then "enclose" those materials and their uses in lucrative patents, removing them from, and possibly even prosecuting, hunter-gatherer and peasant societies, which have freely shared information about such products for centuries.

Many indigenous people have already been displaced from their mountains and deserts and rainforests. And in general, wherever they are found — with the possible exception of some US casinos — they are among the most disadvantaged. In Mexican *municipios* where 70 percent of the population is indigenous, 80 percent of the population lives below the poverty line, as opposed to 18 percent living in poverty in *municipios* where only 10 percent are indigenous. In Peru, the indigenous population is more prone to illness, twice as likely to be hospitalized. In Canada, infant mortality among the indigenous is twice as high as for the population as a whole. In Guatemala, most indigenous people, who constitute almost half the population, have no formal education.[5]

In Australia indigenous people, aboriginals, receive about half the average income of non-aboriginals. They were seventeen times more likely than other Australians to be arrested (the incarceration rate increased by 61 percent between 1988 and 1995) and seventeen times more likely than other prisoners to die in prison. They account for 2 percent of the population of eighteen million but 25 percent of deaths in police custody.[6]

In the US, more than one-third of the nearly two million native Americans live below the poverty line. Even as educational levels improved over the decade of the 1980s, average income dropped by about 13 percent. Native Americans have a higher percentage of children living in single-parent households than is the case in the non-native population, and death rates are higher.[7] Indigenous peoples almost everywhere, at the end of the twentieth century, excluded from meaningful political participation in captor societies, their livelihoods, communities, customs, and values under assault, have been particularly prone to self-destructive behavior — susceptible to diabetes and alcoholism, homicide and suicide.

## Colonialism Revisited

Nowhere has the clash between the logic of Second-Coming Capitalism and the needs of future generations been seen more clearly than in Brazil's Amazon Basin. Brazilian development has always been characterized by cycles of boom and bust — the booms fleetingly enriching mostly non-nationals, or at least non-locals, while the busts impact enduringly on plundered regions and communities. Starting half a millennium ago, with the first onslaught of European exploitation of the Amazon, and coming full circle since the 1980s back to the country's mineral-rich heartland and its last frontier, Brazil's boom fever sets in relief the limits of development as exhaustive production.

A central element of the neoliberal creed, along with "free trade" and privatization, that reinforces the thrust to exhaustive production is comparative advantage. Caribbean islands, used for centuries to the comparative advantage of European pirates and potentates, have seen their original inhabitants annihilated and several generations of Africans and East Indians enslaved or indentured to produce sugar and coffee, spices and tropical fruits for European markets.

Now as in the heyday of European colonialism, comparative advantage dictates that fertile land in the Caribbean, as elsewhere, be used in the production of export crops. But export earnings are rarely redistributed effectively to the population at large, while higher prices for imported food are.

The shifting winds and currents of El Niño that deprived Southeast Asia of its seasonal monsoons were attributed a measure of the blame for the forest fires that raged across Borneo in the fall of 1997, blanketing several countries with almost impenetrable smog. But even Indonesia's minister of agriculture conceded that plantations were the source of most of the fires. Fires are deliberately set to clear land for palm oil and pulp for export. A recent study by the Asian Development Bank found that over the past thirty years Asia had lost half of its forest cover. The continent had witnessed, also, the degradation of one-third of its agricultural land and the loss of half of its fish stocks.

Even in the most rugged and remote regions, like the highlands of Papua New Guinea, long ignored or avoided by the carriers of Western civilization, jungles and farmland and rivers that provided subsistence over the millennia to indigenous populations are being exploited and despoiled for logging, mining, and plantation agribusiness that have produced growth rates of up to 14 percent. While economists speak of economic miracles, the indigenous people are losing much more than land and livelihood; they are losing languages, cultures, and personal and community pride.

When the concept of sustainability took its place some two decades ago in the lexicon of development theory, it was as the beachhead of environmentalism. Modes of development were deemed unsustainable to the extent that they posed a long-term threat to the natural and human ecology. But words are prostitutes and power corrupts. While consciousness of the environment has taken proud place in the new world order, the catbird seat in that order is occupied by the purveyors of neoliberalism. Therefore, "sustainability" is being turned inside out to refer to the sustainability of economic growth and factors sustaining the growth model and to limit environmental regulations that might constrain it. At grassroots level, would-be beneficiaries of development all too often see the sustainability of their own community initiatives sacrificed to the sustainability of donor programs.

# Notes

1. The findings of Rio Plus Five are elaborated in the book's concluding chapter.
2. UNDP *Human Development Report 1997*. Oxford University Press, 1997, p. 114.
3. Paul Brown, "The Rich Have Inherited the Oceans," *The Manchester Guardian Weekly*, Oct. 25, 1998, p 23.
4. Douglas Watson, "Indigenous Peoples and the Global Economy." *Current History,* Vol. 96, No. 613, Nov. 1997, pp. 389–391.
5. UNDP, *op. cit.*, p. 43.
6. "More Aborigines are Dying in Prison," *San Francisco Examiner,* Nov. 10, p. A:10.
7. *San Francisco Examiner,* Sept. 22, 1996, p. A8; "Changing Numbers, Changing Needs: American Indian Demography and Health," a report on the National Research Council cited in Karen Macpherson, "Troubling Portrait of American Indians."

# Chapter 12

# Boom and Bust in the Brazilian Amazon

*The only reliable guardians of any*
*ecosystem are those who do not have the option of leaving.*

*In the land of the blind, the one-eyed man is a subversive.*

*IN THE AMAZON* Basin's Xingu River Valley, the Kararao project, a massive dam complex, was to be built by the Brazilian government in the early 1990s with World Bank funding. It would have flooded a portion of the valley, displacing members of eleven indigenous tribes. But the project encountered an unanticipated obstacle, in the form of the well-connected and public relations-savvy Kayapó tribe.

Kayapó chiefs, with help from social and natural scientists, took their case against the project to the World Bank, which was persuaded to suspend a US$500 million loan for dam construction. The Brazilian government responded by charging the chiefs, along with a US anthropologist, with conspiring against the national interest. With fine irony, the government brought the charges under the so-called Law of Foreigners, prohibiting foreign meddling in national affairs.

Summoned to give testimony at the Federal Courthouse in Belém, the Kayapó demonstrated their superior command of public relations techniques. They turned out some four hundred warriors and three dozen chiefs in full ceremonial dress (or undress), armed with clubs and spears, to confront riot-control police bearing automatic weapons, before a generous sampling of the world press. International pressure soon forced the government to drop the case.

## Regeneration versus Depletion

Since the beginning of European civilization, Brazil has been subject to an exaggerated version of boom and bust development. Unlike the indigenous peoples who had lived in a state of equilibrium with their environment, European colonists tended to exploit the resources of a newly claimed area until they were depleted and then to move on. A non-regenerative approach to finite resources, along with dependence on fickle export and capital markets, has dictated periodic shifts in the country's geographic and sectoral centers of gravity and has shaped the nature of political competition as well.

Among the resources to be nearly depleted early on, along with the turtles and manatee of the Amazon, were the indigenous peoples, enslaved to stoke the sugar boom in the Northeast. Subsequent boom and bust cycles drew population, resources, and political intrigue to the mines and the dairy farms of Minas Gerais and then farther south, to São Paulo, where coffee was competing with sugar for first place among export earners.

Since the 1980s, however, Brazil's boom fever had zeroed in once again on the Amazon — the country's mineral-rich heartland and its last frontier. Brazilian leaders, particularly "strategic thinkers" — military or civilian — have always looked lustfully and anxiously at the Amazon Basin, fearing that if Brazil did not explore, develop, and settle it, she would lose it to her neighbors. From the end of the rubber boom until the middle of the century, however, such concerns had little material consequence. The beginning of the contemporary assault on this new frontier might be traced to the building of the new capital, Brasilia, by the government of Juscelino Kubitschek (1956–1961) in the underdeveloped interior state of Goias. A new road linking Brasilia with Belém bisected the Amazon Basin and opened up the area to settlers and fortune-seekers.

The pace of opening quickened in the 1960s, as the military government established the Superintendency for the Development of the Amazon (SUDAM) and began the construction of the Trans-Amazonic Highway. The population of Manaus has doubled, to more than a million, since 1967 when it was declared a free-trade zone. Ranching, logging, and public and private mining ventures have also been undertaken increasingly since the beginning of the 1980s. Such ventures call, in turn, for more massive infrastructure projects — roads and bridges and dams — projects which predictably have unpredicted consequences. The joint public-private enterprise venture Companhia Vale do Rio Doce (CVRD), largest iron mine in the world, carved out an estate in Goias that continues to grow like a jungle plant, voraciously consuming trees and water to maintain its energy level.

In the mid-1970s, the government began to offer incentives for clearance of the rainforest, a ploy which at the same time offered tax shelter to major corporations and appeared to constitute an alternative to desperately needed and fiercely resisted land reform. The offers drew large numbers of peasants displaced by drought in the Northeast and mechanization in the Southeast. Most have found, after inordinate investment of time and labor, that the leached soils respond very poorly to farming and not much better to grazing. Worse still, land titles in areas cleared or to be cleared have been poorly drawn, with overlapping and under-lapping and outright fraud making it easier for major landholders or speculators to push peasants off the land they had cleared.

By the 1980s this frontier free-for-all had produced hundreds of deaths and a land concentration pattern comparable to parts of the country settled centuries earlier. The ejected peasants, lacking options, have become an itinerant labor force, concentrated in instant slum towns on the margins of the land they had cleared. Reconcentration of the land has also meant food shortages, since 80 percent of the food crops have been produced by holders of small plots. Major landholders were more likely to be engaged in export agribusiness. Even so, since the land is so infertile, they have often earned more from tax write-offs than from anything cultivated. Forest clearance incentives were finally revoked in 1987, in response to international pressures, but speculation in land continued until the mid-1990s to be fueled by hyper-inflation.

Adding to the Wild West ambiance of the Amazon Basin has been a new gold rush that began in 1980 and before the end of the decade made Brazil the world's third largest producer. Mercury, used to process the ores, has contaminated the water and lowered the fish catch over a large portion of the Basin.

## Endangered Peoples

Among the many species of plant and animal life endangered by the latest and most multifaceted boom in the Amazon is its people. It is estimated that only some 200,000 of Brazil's indigenous tribal people have survived, with perhaps fifty thousand of them still living deep in the rain forest. The largest tribe, the Yanomamö, their numbers reduced to about nine thousand, have recently seen their territory overrun by some forty-five thousand gold prospectors. *Caboclos* (mestizos or non-tribal Indians) who live in symbiosis with the rainforest — by hunting, fishing, and subsistence farming — see their livelihoods, and sometimes their very lives, threatened as well by the activities of prospectors and other fortune seekers.

At its peak in the 1980s, the Gold Rush drew some 150,000 miners to the Brazilian Amazon Basin and produced ninety thousand tons of ore annually. By the late 1990s output had dropped to twenty thousand tons annually and only some fifty thousand miners remained in the area. But mercury contamination remained. In several Amazonian villages where US and European aid agencies in the mid to late 1990s tested hair samples of mothers and children for levels of contamination, it was found that most registered levels well above those considered tolerable by the World Health Organization.[1]

A shallow reservoir backed up by a dam built in the 1980s near Manaus has become yet another breeding ground for mosquitoes. Another dam, generating power for the CVRD's Carajó mine, displaced thirty-five thousand people. The growing number of reservoirs has contributed to a malaria epidemic, building since the 1970s, with more than a million cases reported by 1990. Incidence of infection has continued to rise. In 1996, 1,775 cases were reported in the shrinking population of the Yanomamö. In the late 1990s, as new strains, resistant to antidotes, appeared, malaria was considered the most serious threat to health in the Amazon.

Though links with First World scientists and environmentalists are essential, it stands to reason that the first line of defense for the rainforest, and its most effective defenders, would be the people who depend on it — as a rainforest — for their survival. The fact that the now endangered cultures of the Amazon Basin are also the area's foremost ecologists was recognized by the convening of the First International Congress of Ethnobiology in Belém in 1988 in order that some six hundred scientists from thirty-five countries might learn from the Kayapó and other native peoples. The need for international solidarity has been recognized as well; leaders of indigenous groups from all over the Western Hemisphere met in the village of Altamira in the Xingú Valley in 1989.

There have also been efforts to organize across broader ethnic divides to defend common interest. Accelerated ranching and logging in Acre and Rôdonia, on Brazil's borders with Peru and Bolivia, threaten the livelihood of unacculturated tribes as well as *caboclo* rubber-tappers. Efforts to organize against the assault have brought the threatened groups together and have been successful enough to generate an exceedingly violent backlash. Union leader Chico Mendes, murdered in December 1988, was the best known of many popular leaders in the Amazon targeted for assassination. Amnesty International and other human rights organizations believe that such assaults represent a systematic attempt on the part of property owners to suppress union activities and inability or unwillingness on the part of civil authorities to prosecute.

## Still the Land of the Future

The government of President Fernando Collor de Mello, elected in 1989 — in the first direct presidential election in three decades — showed some seriousness about environmental issues in general and the protection of the Amazon in particular. Collor de Mello established a cabinet-level secretariat for the ecological preservation of the Amazon (SEA) and appointed a widely recognized environmentalist, José Lutzenberger, to head it. Collor de Mello did not reject out-of-hand — as had his predecessor — the concept of debt-for-nature swaps; but he one-upped those calling for international controls on rainforest clearance by proposing an international tax on the emission of carbon. His most dramatic gesture was that of authorizing the bombing of airstrips used by gold prospectors in Yanomamö territory.

On this and other important issues, Collor de Mello proved to be no mere cipher at the service of private and bureaucratic interests. Nevertheless, his Center-to-Right constituency was essentially that of the land-holding, commercial, and financial elites who have the most to gain and the least to lose from a continuation of boom and bust development, including the recent frenzied consumption of the Amazon. Most of the country's environmentally conscious organizations supported his rival, Labor Party leader Luis Inácio da Silva (Lula), who ran him a close race for the presidency in 1989.

Under siege over an influence-peddling scandal, Collor was forced to resign at the end of 1992 and was subsequently impeached. Vice President Itamar Franco, a conscientious but weak political centrist, then assumed the presidency. Fernando Henrique Cardoso, internationally noted social scientist and Finance Minister in the cabinet of Itamar Franco, was elected to the presidency in 1994 with the support of the Center-right and the blessing, of international creditors and financial institutions. Since he had been in times past a leading theorist in the cause of economic nationalism, many of his old friends hoped that after the elections he would break free of his new, strange bedfellows and reassert his concern for local control of resources. That was not to be.

Environmentalists and defenders of the rights of indigenous peoples were stunned by the issuance of a presidential decree on January 9, 1996, allowing loggers, miners, farmers, and businessmen to contest in court the boundaries of territory (about 11 percent of the Brazilian Amazon) previously set aside as nature and indigenous reserves. The OAS in late 1997 reported a 95 percent increase over the past year in the invasion of indigenous land.

By late 1997, a response in part to the generalized growth spurt of the Cardoso presidency, dozens of new large-scale infrastructure projects were being launched in the Brazilian Amazon, underwritten by multinational agencies and US, European, and Asian investment banks. Industrial waterways, railways, roads, and oil and gas pipelines were to serve as export corridors, providing Brazil with outlets on the Pacific, Caribbean, and North Atlantic coasts. Ten new hydroelectric dams were to provide energy for the expansion of mining operations and for new townships, and millions of acres of new farmland were to be devoted to export crops, particularly soya beans.

Investments planned for the next five years amounted to ten times what the G-7 was investing in its Pilot Programme to Conserve the Rainforest.[2] Most of this new development is taking place without environmental impact studies, without consultation with indigenous or other local populations, and without serious political debate as to the merits and drawbacks of such a course.

There is no parallel or compensatory project planned to benefit indigenous communities. But indigenous organizations in Brazil, Guyana, and Venezuela met in late 1997 to explore strategies to counter the onslaught, and more than 400 NGOs focusing on the environment were reinvigorating participatory democracy in Brazil.[3]

## Notes

1. David Cleary, "Mercury Contamination in the Amazon Basin: Problems and Solutions," Seminar presentation at St. Antony's College, Oxford, Oct. 14, 1997.
2. Anthony Hall, International Advisory Group of the G7 Pilot Programme to Conserve the Rainforest, "Brazil: Toward the Twenty-first Century," Inaugural Conference of Oxford University's Center for Brazilian Studies, Dec. 8–9, 1997.
3. Darrell Posey, Dir., Programme for Traditional Resource Rights, Oxford Center for Environment, Ethics and Society. Receipt of Sierra Club International Chico Mendes Award and the UN Global 500 Award, "Brazil: Toward the Twenty-first Century."

Chapter 13

# Papua New Guinea: Modern Materialism and the New Cargo Cult

*Most consequences are unintended.*

*Species and cultures come to be valued only when they are almost extinct.*

*LINGUISTS HAVE NOTED* that until very recently the indigenous people of Papua New Guinea were so proud of their collective individuality, or clan distinctiveness, that clan members made a point of holding on to languages only a few hundred people spoke; and some clans intentionally adopted new words to distinguish themselves from others. What seems to be different now is that the children are sliding toward the English-based pidgin that is fast becoming the common language of working classes in the modern sector. Apparently, in ways so subtle that only children can see them clearly, all things indigenous are being discredited vis-à-vis the ways of the foreigners.

## When Worlds Collide

The Global Village has swallowed up the last of its hinterland. In the early 1990s it reached out, almost overnight, and took in Papua New Guinea. The island of New Guinea, which Papua New Guinea (PNG) shares with the Indonesian province of Irian Jaya, is among the world's largest and accounts for 85 percent of PNG's present total land area. The modern state of PNG comprises the eastern half of the island and hundreds of smaller islands to the North and East, including Manus, New Britain, and New Ireland in the Bismarck Archipelago, Bougainville and Buka in the Western Solomons, and the Trobriand, Woodlark, D'Entrecasteaux, and Louisiade Island groups.

Most of this extensive territory was unexplored and virtually unnoticed by outsiders until relatively recent times.

The eastern shores of the big island were first visited by Spanish and Portuguese fleets in the sixteenth century, but there was no European settlement there until 1884, when Germany laid claim to the North coast and Britain followed suit in the South. In 1901, Britain turned its protectorate over to a newly autonomous Australia. Australian troops seized German outposts on the northern coast during World War I. Australia then retained control (or the illusion of control) under a League of Nations mandate and subsequently, after a period of Japanese occupation during World War II, a United Nations trusteeship. Australia granted limited home rule in 1951, followed by more extensive autonomy in internal affairs in 1960, and full independence in 1975. That, at least, was the virtual reality of Western colonialists.

For the region's indigenous peoples, whose ancestral roots date back some fifty thousand years, reality was something else entirely; and few Westerners dare pretend to understand it very well. Rugged mountainous terrain and dense tropical rainforest, together with the tradition of fierce defense of clan autonomy, account in part for the survival into modern times of more than seven hundred languages (by some accounts, about one-third of the world's known languages — English is the official national language, but the trade languages, Motu and Melanesian Pidgin English, are in more common use). There are still few roads into the interior, and until the advent of the airplane most language groups remained isolated not only from the outside world, but also from each other.

The astonished faces of indigenous highlanders were captured on film when Australian pilots first penetrated their territory in the 1930s. When my husband and I visited in the mid-1980s, there were still tribal elders to be found in the vicinity of Mt. Hagen who remembered when the first of the great silver birds descended and disgorged the strange, pale figures they took to be the ghosts of their ancestors. The visitors were clearly otherworldly because they carried talking boxes and other magical devices that could not possibly have been made by man.

## On Underdevelopment, Poverty, and Powerlessness

The experience of Papua New Guinea during its first two decades of independence suggests that underdevelopment, poverty, and powerlessness are not always synonymous. The first European visitors found a culture that was literally of the Stone Age in that tools were made of stone, bone, and wood; metal-working was unknown. Even so, agriculture was highly developed. In fact, archeological finds indicate that farming was practiced in the region during the same period when agricultural settlements were being established in Egypt and Mesopotamia.

Indigenous traditions include a strong attachment to the land and to village life along with assumption of kinship obligations extending far beyond nuclear families. Though most land ownership is communal, there is a tendency to acquisitiveness and a strong sense of what constitutes private as opposed to communal ownership. Relationships are generally egalitarian, based on acquired rather than inherited status, and equity is maintained through traditions in which conspicuous consumption is collective. Community members who earn more than their neighbors are expected to expend it in the form of gift-giving or of sponsorship of village or clan-wide fiestas marking weddings, funerals, and other family affairs. Such egalitarianism has generally made for lively, if not necessarily orderly or efficient, politics.

By the usual standard-of-living indices, PNG even now would have to be considered among the world's least developed countries. The population has more than doubled in the last three decades. Some 44 percent of the mid-1990s population of 4.2 million is under sixteen years of age. Only about half of those over sixteen are literate. It is estimated that 38 percent of the children under five years of age are malnourished. Infant mortality, though dropping, remains very high at 114 per one thousand live births, while maternal mortality, at nine hundred per 100,000 births, is the fourth highest in the world. Along with childbirth, diarrhea, malaria, and acute respiratory infections are the main causes of death. And death comes early. Life expectancy is fifty-six years.

More than 80 percent of the population is rural, dependent on subsistence agriculture employing low-level technology. Most produce some surplus, however, for exchange in local markets, and, at least until recently, they were not necessarily poor. There was surplus enough, it seemed, to provide a most eventful social calendar.

Driving through the highlands in 1985, my husband and I, in the course of two days, came across a lavishly provisioned funeral, a wedding, a *wontok* (in pidgin, "one talk," or language group) *payback* (explained below), a fiesta, or *sing-sing,* a parade, a groundbreaking ceremony, and several markets, complete with games, story-telling, mock fights and other forms of entertainment. At the site of the funeral, where a thousand guests were expected, scores of pigs were being slaughtered.

Pigs also had a literally central role at the wedding we attended. Two dozen of them were tied to stakes in the center of a field, while the bride's family sat on one side of the field and the groom's on the other. The pigs, whose squealing and grunting punctuated the ceremony as if they were a hired chorus, constituted about half of the bride price. The other half was paid mostly in cash, but included also one cassowarie, an ostrich-like bird valued for its plumage and its bone marrow, which is used in the preparation of a poison for the tips of spears and arrows. The total bride-price amounted to the equivalent of about US$23,000. (After staring at me for a while, a wedding guest, dressed in the *lap-lap,* a wrap-around waistband holding large leaves or grasses in strategic position, commonly worn by indigenous men in the highlands, approached my husband and, in pidgin, asked how much he had paid for me. Marty responded that he didn't know yet. "Our customs are different," he told the highlander. "We don't pay all at once, but continuously over the years. You see, I'm still paying.")

I have rarely seen so much cash in one place as graced another field in the highlands. The kina bills (the kina exchanged then for slightly more than one dollar) were attached to forked sticks planted in the ground or carried by dancers, clad in grass skirts, face paint, feathers, and cuzcuz fur. The drumming and dancing that was to go on from sun-up to sundown was devoted to consecrating the ground for a new Lutheran Church and community center. The forest of cash represented contributions by villagers to the project. We were aware that the fur and feathers worn by the dancers also represented major financial outlays. One man had told us that he spent two or three thousand dollars a year on feathers for his family.

## The Reckoning: Corruption and Violence

In Papua New Guinea, as in so much of the world, but more recently there than elsewhere, rumors of immense troves of exploitable riches have drawn immensely ambitious exploiters, some of whom are not averse to the use of fraud, bribery, coercion and intimidation. Violence and materialism were by no means alien to indigenous tradition, but the newcomers and the "Wild East" frontier boom they have generated have timewarped those tendencies into a new and more menacing manifestation.

PNG has 145,000 square miles of tropical forests (an area almost as large as the state of California) thick with particularly valuable hardwoods, like walnut, mahogany and pine. Moreover, unlike some of its Southeast Asian neighbors, PNG, which has no large sawmills, permits the export of raw logs. The amount of wood exported annually has quadrupled since 1980, amounting by 1993 to about three million trees a year. Local environmentalists estimate that at current rates of depletion forests of commercial value will be gone within ten to twenty years.

PNG legislation allocates ownership of the forests to the people who live in them rather than to the government, an arrangement more enlightened in principle than that available to indigenous peoples in many other regions. However, Tim Neville, Forests Minister in the early 1990s, observed that "this is a battle that pits people wearing loincloths and bird feathers against fast-talking, fast-moving foreign loggers." Bird-feather headgear may be deceptive; some villagers have held their own remarkably well in negotiations with ambitious outsiders. Nevertheless, the government estimates that a village receives about $24 for each tree, a tree which the logging company will sell for about $600. Forest Ministry figures show that for the $500 million worth of logs shipped out last year, the tribes claiming ownership were paid less than $15 million.

A government commission found in 1989 that the logging industry, largely Malaysian-owned, had been "bribing politicians and leaders, creating social disharmony and ignoring laws." When results of the investigation were made public, the chief investigator, Judge Tos Barnett, was attacked and almost killed by thugs wielding sharpened screwdrivers. Forests Minister Neville, whose plan would have banned the export of raw logs and required practices ensuring the sustainability of the forests, was also assaulted on at least two occasions by armed thugs.

A more serious clash over resources has been underway since 1988 on the island of Bougainville in PNG's North Solomons Province. Islanders became disgruntled over the conviction that they were being denied their rightful benefits from the enormous Panguna copper mine owned by an Australian company. Such sentiment gave rise to a separatist movement led by the Bougainville Revolutionary Army.

Insurgency and counterinsurgency, continuous over more than six years, have claimed some ten thousand lives and have allegedly resulted in summary execution, "disappearances," and torture on the part of PNG defense forces, police, and correctional personnel. Conflict has also closed down the Panguna mine, once responsible for almost half of PNG's foreign exchange earnings. Talks have been underway since 1994, and government and opposition leaders alike continued in early 1997 to speak of the "peace process," but in fact conflict appeared to have escalated. Amnesty International drew attention to forty-four Bougainvilleans who had been "disappeared" during 1996; and at the beginning of 1997 it became known that the PNG government had sent in some forty mercenaries from Europe, Africa, and Australia, supplied by South African subcontractors of a British-registered security consultancy firm. The revelation drew expressions of consternation from several governments, including that of Australia, PNG's main source of foreign aid. Such protest, along with rising army insubordination, brought down the government of Sir Julius Chan in April 1997.[1]

## The Modernization of Tradition

Meanwhile, however, new forms of violence were spreading on the main island, and particularly in Port Moresby. Gangs of unemployed young men, known locally as rascals, roam the streets engaging in muggings and gang rape. The Port Moresby police estimated that there might have been as many as three hundred rascal gangs in the capital in 1996. They appeared to be undeterred by the 10:00 PM-to-dawn curfew in effect in 1997.[2] (Newspapers in the South Pacific, when we first visited, had been full of accounts of gang rapes in Port Moresby of white women. Arriving there, I asked our travel agent, an indigenous highlander named Norbert who spoke English with a German accent, if there were any truth to these accounts. Norbert was indignant. "Of course not," he said. "Such charges are just a reflection of racial prejudice. The 'rascals' don't make a point of going after white women; they rape all women.")

House-breaking appears now to be a major source of employment and income, and a family's wealth may be measured by the amount of barbed wire ringing their home. Some social scientists at the national university in Port Moresby believe that an urban variant on the cargo cult has come into use to explain and justify theft, particularly against foreigners. The belief, in general, is that the miraculous gadgets arriving with Westerners must be provided to them by their ancestors in the spirit world. It follows that the ancestors of the indigenous people must also be trying to send such gifts. Earlier versions assumed that the goods could arrive only in large silver birds that needed specially prepared landing strips. Port Moresby's modernized version holds that the gifts already sent by the ancestors of the local people to their own descendants had been waylaid and appropriated by the foreigners in their midst.[3]

The dramatic increase in street crime in Port Moresby over the past decade, and the pervasive fears so generated, along with the presumed requirements of counterinsurgency in Bougainville, have emboldened security forces and led governments to encroach upon civil rights. The Internal Security Act, passed in 1993, has been roundly criticized by legal experts and human rights monitors. In some cases, for example, arrests could be carried out without judicially issued warrants, and persons could be listed as members of proscribed organizations solely on the basis of the police commissioner's affidavit. Efforts had also been launched to establish a national identification system and to tighten official regulation of the media.

PNG security forces were notoriously undisciplined, a situation that appeared to be deteriorating in the 1990s. Instances of torture and abuse were reported from regions throughout the country. Police were accused of firing live ammunition into crowds, of staging revenge raids on villages and of burning homes — even, in a 1993 instance, of beating a government minister during a detention for traffic violations.

One explanation for such behavior on the part of security forces is that they tend to operate much like just another *wontok* in traditional *payback* skirmishes. The *wontok payback* system is one of collective retribution, a practice that generally has all the outward appearance of preparation for war: men in warpaint and a special array of feathers face off in a field or clearing, wielding their clubs and spears and bows and arrows. (On one occasion, I tested the authenticity of such belligerence by raising my camera to take a picture of a fearsomely feathered and painted warrior who was waving his spear at me. It turned out, fortunately, that he was posing.) It may, in fact, lead to all-out clan warfare, but its function is more nearly that of a primitive judicial system. The collectivized "eye for an eye" tradition, like that of Appalachia's legendary Hatfields and McCoys, held that a transgression — anything from minor theft to murder — by a member of one clan against a member of another was to be paid back in kind, but against any member of the offending clan rather than necessarily against the one guilty of the offense.

Since offenses to be avenged included traffic accidents, and since Westerners, to many indigenous clans, constituted a single *wontok,* vulnerability was very general. (An Australian woman told us about driving her jeep through a mountain pass and coming suddenly upon a tree trunk blocking the road. From the hillside, a man in war paint and feathers came racing toward her, spear in hand. Reaching the jeep, he laid down his spear and started to move the tree trunk. "I'm sorry," he said, "I was just waiting here to kill somebody.") As accidents increased in frequency, however, in the 1980s, the negotiation of compensation, rather than payback in kind, became more common, and clansmen were becoming quite accomplished in the fine art of tort litigation.

In the 1990s, however, the situation took a turn for the worse, as automatic weapons began to show up in the highlands. They are sent by relatives in the city or sold to the tribesmen by soldiers or by foreigners, arriving in helicopters, who come in search of "Niugini gold," the marijuana that grows wild there. With the influx of guns, what had been largely ritualistic battles providing a context for negotiation became very real and deadly battles, in which competitive body-counting replaces measured retribution or compensation. In 1994 the central government classified large areas of the highlands as "fighting zones," to be entered at one's own risk.

## Resources and Human Resourcefulness

Longer than most of the so-called Third World, and longer especially than most areas with exploitable riches, PNG managed to hold its own against the relentless onslaught of modernization. Underdeveloped did not necessarily mean poor, and it certainly did not mean devoid of resourcefulness. In fact, in the case of many PNG highlanders it meant guardianship of resources and preservation of traditional ways that foreign investors and other would-be exploiters, accustomed to dealing with elections and courts, strikes and riots, did not know how to handle.

Well into the 1980s some indigenous communities had their own means of persuading developers to take their interests into account. We were told of a tribe that had been paid $2 million for the land on which a dam and electricity-generating station were built. Some while later the tribe concluded that they had sold short, that they should have asked for $3 million.

The company responded that the transaction had been completed and would not be reopened, whereupon the tribal negotiators pointed out that if there were general resentment in the community, the staff manning the dam and power station might become uncomfortable around villagers with their bows and arrows and poison-tipped spears. The company saw the wisdom of that argument and came through right away with another million.

Thus, an array of unfortunate trends, apparent especially since the early 1990s, by no means constitutes the whole story of PNG's present and future. It still has far more of its original resources, cultures, and self-sufficiency than most countries colonized, settled and exploited earlier. For the indigenous peoples, however, holding the line against further deterioration of their rights and assets will call for a sharp reversal of current trends and a policy agenda that promotes regeneration over depletion.

## Notes

1. *The Manchester Guardian Weekly,* Mar. 30, 1997, p. 4, and April 6, 1997, p. 4.
2. It was estimated that up to 90 percent of Port Moresby's young men were unemployed. See Seth Mydans, "In Lush Tropics, a Flowering of Murderous Gangs," *The New York Times,* May 1, 1997, p. A4.
3. Professor Yaw Saffu, Political Science, University of Papua New Guinea, Port Moresby, Conversations, July 1985.

# Chapter 14

# Greenpeace: An Ecowarrior's Belated Victory

*It is dangerous to make waves*
*when you are in a small boat.*

*With enough enlightenment, self-interest*
*can be the functional equivalent of ethics.*

*JUST BEFORE MIDNIGHT* on July 10, 1985, Lloyd Anderson, forty-one, of San Francisco, asleep on his bunk in the radio operator's cabin, was jolted awake by the first explosion. By the time he had pulled on his pants and scrambled to the main deck, there had been another blast. *Rainbow Warrior,* a vessel owned and operated by Greenpeace, was listing sharply to starboard and the stern was already partly under water. Within four minutes of the detonation of the first bomb, the ship had been sunk at her moorings in the Auckland harbor. The ship's photographer, Fernando Pereira, thirty-six, of Portuguese birth and Dutch citizenship, had been trapped below deck near the site of the second blast and was drowned.

On the following day, the sympathetic and the curious, braced against wind and rain, lined up along the dock like mourners filing past a casket to view the partially submerged remains. The tall mast leaned wearily toward the horizon, starboard stern resting on the harbor floor, while the protruding portside bow displayed the vessel's emblems — a rainbow and a dove bearing an olive branch.

In the best of times, the Auckland offices of Greenpeace are probably adequate, but in the aftermath of the bombing of the *Rainbow Warrior* they seemed cramped and chaotic. Volunteers from among New Zealand's two thousand members and sixteen thousand financial supporters of Greenpeace took calls from media around the world. Walk-ins brought flowers and food, money, and even offers of boats. Telegrams arrived by the hundreds, and volunteers manning donation boxes around the harbor area streamed in with plastic sacks full of New Zealand dollars. Some $6,000 was deposited in Auckland's donation boxes during the first day after the bombing. Meanwhile, trust funds for Pereira's two children and funds for Greenpeace were being established around the world.

*Rainbow Warrior*'s thirteen crew members, representing nine countries, were tired and dazed, grief-stricken, and unable to contemplate the next move. Skipper Peter Willcox, a US citizen, said that Greenpeace had prided itself on its stance of nonviolence and had imagined that stance afforded it a modicum of protection. The ship's doctor, Andy Beiderman of Switzerland, said that ocean-going vessels are inherently vulnerable. Greenpeace might change some of its tactics, but it would be impossible to make boats and harbors and oceans safe for the would-be peacemakers.[1]

New Zealand's Prime Minister, David Lange, said he had been deluged with telegrams urging the government to supply a substitute ship to escort the flotilla of yachts already assembled in the Auckland harbor for a planned protest voyage to the Mururoa Atoll, a French nuclear test site, later that month. Lange said the government had seriously considered the requests, but that providing a naval vessel or offering the protection of New Zealand's Navy would have represented a militarization of what was intended to be a process of peaceful protest. Meanwhile, New Zealand's parliament, unable to afford much protection to Greenpeace, beefed up its own security.

In the aftermath of the bombing, Auckland itself seemed to be in a state of shock. The sports stories that usually dominated the daily newspapers' front pages were crowded out by coverage of the crime and the investigations. A local newsman commented that New Zealanders don't like "foul play" and that many saw the attack on *Rainbow Warrior* as an attack on the nation that had welcomed the ship. Indeed, in closing its harbors some months earlier to a US naval fleet that might have carried nuclear weapons, New Zealand had identified itself with the primary goal of the Greenpeace campaign — that of a nuclear-free Pacific.

## Youthful Davids Take on the Nuclear Goliath

The Pacific campaign, which began in February, 1985, was launched to protest and to focus world attention on US nuclear tests in the Marshall Islands, particularly current testing relating to Star Wars strategies; the mining of uranium in Australia and Japanese plans to dump low-level nuclear waste in the Pacific; and ongoing French underground nuclear weapons testing in the vicinity of the Mururoa Atoll. On the positive side, visits by *Rainbow Warrior* and its companion vessels were intended to celebrate the efforts of New Zealand and of several island micro-states to make the Pacific a nuclear-free zone. Palau and Vanuatu, for example, had adopted anti-nuclear policies, and Nauru and Kiribati had presented a resolution at the 1983 London Dumping Convention urging that all nuclear waste dumping be permanently banned.

Opposition to nuclear testing and waste dumping represents only a part of the raison d'être of Greenpeace. The organization came into being in 1971 as an expression of outrage at the abuse of nature around the world by governments and industries. Greenpeace has sought to protect endangered animal and plant life, but as Kelly Rigg, Wildlife Coordinator of the Washington, DC, office noted, environmental preservation and peace are inseparable. Of all the many contemporary threats to wildlife and not-so-wildlife, none is so menacing as that of nuclear contamination and ultimately of nuclear war.

Even before the bombing, Greenpeace had national offices in fifteen countries. It was particularly strong in Western Europe, and it had about 400,000 contributors in the US, with several offices on both coasts. Almost all of its protest actions had taken place at sea or in harbors, but it had engaged in a few inland operations. In 1980, it staged a food lift to isolated Navajo and Hopi communities in Arizona and New Mexico.

The flood of contributions in the wake of the bombing and the Babel of condolences by political leaders around the world made it clear that Greenpeace had a global following of impressive proportions. However, the organization's enemies were also numerous, far-flung, and powerful. Investigators, including divers and explosives experts called in by New Zealand military and police authorities and by Interpol, concluded early on that the bombing, employing about twenty kilograms of explosives, was not likely the work of crazed amateurs, but, rather, a highly professional job.

Curiously, given the organization's many adversaries, Greenpeace officials gathered in Auckland at the time of the bombing were convinced from the beginning that French military intelligence operatives were responsible. Time and the investigative efforts of New Zealand police and French journalists proved them right.

Two French intelligence agents, held in connection with the bombing and charged with murder, went on trial in Auckland in November 1985, and pleaded guilty to a reduced charge of manslaughter. Only July 7, 1986, France agreed to pay New Zealand $7,000,000 in compensation and to apologize officially for the sabotage. In return, New Zealand allowed the convicted agents to be transferred to the military garrison on Hao, the atoll that serves as a supply base for France's nuclear testing station in the Pacific, where they were to remain for a period of three years.

## An Impressive Enemies List

The investigation was made all the more difficult by the fact that several governments around the world might have had motives for sabotaging Greenpeace. The first direct action taken by Greenpeace was intended to obstruct a US nuclear bomb test in the area of Amchitka in the Aleutian Islands. In 1970, a group of Canadian and American Quakers in Vancouver began to call attention to the upcoming test. They soon captured the attention of Canadians living on the Pacific Coast, who feared that the explosion might disturb the region's geological fault and generate a tidal wave. The Quakers and their like-minded associates then decided on a strategy of nonviolent action on the high seas. The broken-down boat, christened *Greenpeace*, that was to be the first vessel of the "econavy" never reached Amchitka, but it attracted plenty of media attention along the way. As a consequence, world attention was focused on the area, the atomic test was canceled, and public outcry soon led to the designation of Amchitka as a bird sanctuary.

Greenpeace has since engaged in direct action, on-site "witnessing," in protest against nuclear explosions elsewhere, against ocean dumping of radioactive and other toxic waste, and against the slaughter of whales, dolphins, and seal pups. It was only after several years and many Greenpeace encounters with the dumping ships of several nations that the London Dumping Convention voted for a ban on the dumping of nuclear waste at sea.

## In Defense of the Endangered

Defense of the endangered whale has brought Greenpeace into nonviolent confrontation with several governments, including those of the former Soviet Union, Japan, Spain, Peru, and Iceland. Attempts to stop the slaughter of seal pups have brought clashes with sealers from Scotland, Norway, and Canada, and befriending the dolphin has meant encounters of the unfriendly kind with US and Japanese fishermen.

In 1975 and 1976, with a membership of some ten thousand and an enlarged econavy, Greenpeace took on Soviet whaling fleets. On the first occasion, the whalers continued to fire their explosive harpoons, despite the fact that Greenpeace crew members, on inflatable Zodiacs, had placed themselves between the whalers and the whales. With the second confrontation, however, the whalers, in their six hundred-foot factory ship, *Dalniy Vostok*, abandoned the hunt.

Direct actions on behalf of dolphins began in 1978. Greenpeace members traveled to Japan's Iki Island that year to protest the slaughter of dolphins. On Japan's Izu Peninsula, Greenpeace halted the intended killing of six thousand dolphins and a Greenpeace member was jailed in Japan in 1981 after freeing 150 captive dolphins. Dolphins were also being killed in large numbers as a consequence of being caught in the nets of tuna fisherman. As a result, in 1982 and 1983, *Rainbow Warrior* confronted US tuna fleets in the South Pacific to urge concern for the victimized dolphins.

Greenpeace adopted the cause of the seals in 1976. That year, its members went to Newfoundland to protest the slaughter by Norwegian and Canadian hunters of harp seals. Greenpeace protesters stood in the path of a Norwegian icebreaker with their own bodies, seeking to protect baby seals from the hunters' clubs. Through the efforts of Greenpeace, the slaughter of whales and seal pups has been dramatically curtailed. Casualties in Canada's massive harp seal hunt, for example, dropped from 204,000 in 1981 to 5,401 in 1985. In the Orkney Islands, the seal hunt has been permanently banned. Several European countries have prohibited the importation of seal skins.

Almost too late — all nine species of great whales were considered to be endangered — Greenpeace efforts on behalf of the whales have proved remarkably successful. The gray whale, in fact, was removed in 1994 from the endangered list. Several countries had already abandoned or prohibited whaling when the International Whaling Commission (IWC) agreed to a phase-out of commercial whaling in 1982. However, some countries, particularly Japan, the former USSR, and Norway, continued the practice; thus Greenpeace remains vigilant and prepared for further confrontations at sea.

Greenpeace concerns also embrace the welfare of other sea creatures. The organization is working, for example, with the Wider Caribbean Sea Turtle Conservation Network to formulate and promote national and international laws for conservation, implementing nesting beach management, eliminating trade in sea turtle products, and curbing the impact of petroleum spills.

## Protecting Human Beings

Efforts to protect human beings have aroused more controversy and encountered more resistance. Marshall Islanders have suffered intensely from the fallout of sixty-six US atmospheric nuclear tests conducted some 30 years ago. A test in 1954 exposed the people of the tiny island of Rongelap to about half of a lethal dose of radiation. Although the extent of the exposure and the nature of the risks were well-known to US authorities, the islanders were not moved until three days after the rain of radioactive particles began to fall on them. According to Greenpeace spokesmen, 70 percent of the survivors have thyroid cancer, burn scars, or symptoms of premature aging. Among the offspring of those so exposed, there has been a high incidence of deformation and mental retardation. While insisting that islanders who subsequently returned to Rongelap were in no danger, US authorities advised them against eating locally grown food or locally caught fish. American government scientists continued to monitor living conditions there, but the US and Marshall Islands governments ignored the islander's pleas to be moved to another island. (Greenpeace activists believed that the islanders were being used as guinea pigs.) The desperate islanders finally appealed to Greenpeace. Thus, the first task of *Rainbow Warrior* in connection with Greenpeace's Pacific Campaign of 1985 was the evacuation of Rongelap's 306 inhabitants to the relatively unpolluted island of Mejato, a part of the Kwajelein Atoll.

After the fateful docking in Auckland, *Rainbow Warrior* and the accompanying vessels of its flotilla were to sail to Rarotonga, lending their presence to the South Pacific Forum, then on to Mururoa. The atoll, in French Polynesia, had been the site of some one hundred nuclear weapons tests since 1966. Greenpeace vessels had sailed in protest to Mururoa four times previously. In 1974, the French government bowed to widespread protests at home and in the Pacific and ceased its atmospheric nuclear testing, but underground testing in the Mururoa area continued, including, according to Greenpeace, tests of the neutron bomb.

Greenpeace protesters had been arrested subsequently and jailed for brief periods in the former Soviet Union, Spain, Japan, and several other countries. The bombing in Auckland harbor, however, was a response of a different dimension, setting in relief the extraordinary vulnerability of the nonviolent, but demonstrating as well the extraordinary potential of nonviolent protest. As Gandhi and Martin Luther King, Jr., knew so well, in a contest for hearts and minds, the party that overreacts and responds with violence to nonviolent protests plays into the hands of its adversaries. With its sloppy sabotage, the French government both paid tribute to Greenpeace's effectiveness in the past and contributed enormously to its subsequent stature.

With a contributing membership in 1986 exceeding 1,500,000, Greenpeace continued to promote a comprehensive ban on the testing of nuclear weapons. It was not able to prevent the French from following through on their Fall 1985 tests, but its influence was felt at the South Pacific Forum, where the thirteen participating nations, on August 6, 1985, signed a treaty banning the testing or placement of nuclear weapons, and the dumping of radioactive waste, in the South Pacific.

## The French Surrender the South Pacific

A decade later, a Greenpeace flotilla, led by a second-generation *Rainbow Warrior*, was on hand at the Mururoa atoll to protest and obstruct a series of six nuclear tests. But this time Greenpeace was not alone. International indignation at the French government was such that the test conducted on January 27, 1996, was declared to be its last. The government of Jacques Chirac cut short its planned sequence of tests, signed the South Pacific Nuclear

Free Zone Treaty, and began the process of permanently closing down its nuclear test sites at Mururoa and Fangatanfa atolls.

Nuclear war remains for Greenpeace the ultimate environmental issue, so its priority for 1996, its twenty-fifth anniversary year, was to promote the signing of a strong Comprehensive Test Ban Treaty. Now five million members strong, with affiliates in thirty-two countries and a budget in 1997 of $145 million,[2] thanks in part to the exposure, sympathy, and interest focused on the organization by the French sabotage of the original *Rainbow Warrior*, Greenpeace is able to employ a broad array of effective techniques in its public information and policy campaigns, from a slick quarterly magazine to celebrity press conferences and meetings with policymakers. But its trademark continues to be high visibility guerrilla theater and nonviolent but risky encounters on the high seas. As China continued to engage in nuclear arms testing in the summer of 1996, Greenpeace was attempting to dock its fleet in Chinese ports.

Greenpeace continues to champion the cause of marine life — whales, dolphins, seals, sea turtles and other creatures — and some species appear to be stabilizing or even making a comeback, due in no small measure to the organization's efforts. But its campaigns to create a green and peaceful world address a broad range of abuses and engage a powerful set of adversaries.

In 1997, Greenpeace U.K. was campaigning against the dumping of oil and gas rigs at sea and against the expansion of the North Atlantic oil fields. Shell Oil had been forced by the Greenpeace campaign to abandon plans to sink the Brent Spar oil storage buoy at sea. Greenpeace was involved in a court action against the British Department of Trade and Industry and twenty-two oil companies, including British Petroleum (BP), with respect to the exploration of the frontier oil fields of the North Atlantic.

The engagement with British Petroleum was a particularly frictious and risky one. Following a week-long occupation of a BP-chartered rig off the Shetland Islands, four Greenpeace activists were arrested and BP obtained a court order freezing the organization's assets and demanding $2.2 million in compensation. A month later, however, the British government announced that for the first time in twenty years it was bringing its policy into line with the rest of Europe on disposal of oil rigs, nuclear submarines, and a range of toxic chemicals. The decision was announced as fifteen European nations met in Brussels to discuss eliminating pollution from the North Sea.[3]

Greenpeace targets in the late 1990s include over-fishing, particularly by commercial operations using mammoth trawl nets and high-tech floating seafood factories; deforestation, conducted in part by a $100 billion logging industry largely controlled by fewer than two dozen industry giants, threatening peoples and cultures, and local economic options; and nuclear and other unsafe energy sources (Greenpeace has proposed an "environmental Marshall Plan" for the newly independent states of Eurasia to help them replace dangerously degenerated nuclear plants with sound and sustainable energy generation systems).

Other campaigns address toxic substances — production, use, and disposal, and the environmental injustice that ensues as those who have less voice, greater needs, and fewer choices must see their neighborhoods degraded first, selected as sites for toxic substance production and toxic waste dumps. Greenpeace is also researching and calling attention to the threat of global warming and the connections between environmental pollution and public health, and it is promoting organization at the community level to protect local environments and monitor abuses.

It might be said that the real target of Greenpeace's many and far-reaching campaigns is a value system. "All of us are threatened," according to Greenpeace literature, "by those who live for profit only."

## Notes

1. Personal interviews with *Rainbow Warrior* crew members and officers and volunteers of Greenpeace, Auckland, New Zealand, July 1985.
2. *The Washington Post,* National Weekly Edition, Aug. 24, 1997, p. 18, reported that Greenpeace had been losing ground in the US, its membership having fallen from 1.2 million in 1991 to 400,000 in 1997.
3. *The Manchester Guardian Weekly,* Aug. 24, 1997, p. 1, and Sept. 14, 1997, p. 7.

# Part IV: The Plundered Planet and Its Endangered Peoples Suggested Readings

Broad, Robin and John Cavanagh. *Plundering Paradise: The Struggle for the Environment in the Philippines*. Berkeley: University of California Press, 1993.

Brown, Lester. *The Worldwide Reader on Environmental Issues*. New York: W.W. Norton & Co., 1991.

Brundtland, Gro Harlem, Chairperson. *Our Common Future*. New York: Oxford University Press, 1987.

Carson, Rachel, *Silent Spring*. New York: Houghton Mifflin, 1962.

Clark, Roger and Madeleine Sann. *The Case Against the Bomb*. Marshall Islands, Samoa and Solomon Islands before the International Court of Justice Advisory Proceedings on the Legality of the Threat or Use of Nuclear Weapons. London: Joint Publication of the Foundation for International Environmental Law and Development (FIELD), Rutgers University of Law at Camden, and the UN Mission of the Marshall Islands, Samoa, and the Solomon Islands.

Durning, Alan. *How Much is Enough? The Consumer Society and the Future of the Earth*. New York: W.W. Norton, 1992.

Dwivedi, O.P., and D.K. Vajpeyi, eds. *Environmental Policy and Developing Nations*. Boulder, CO: Lynne Rienner Publishers, 1995.

Flavin, Christopher and Hal Kane. *Vital Signs: The Trends That Are Shaping Our Future*. New York: W.W. Norton/ Worldwatch Institute, 1996.

Foster, John Bellamy. *The Vulnerable Planet*. New York: Monthly Review Press, 1994.

Gore, Al Jr. *Earth in the Balance: Ecology and the Human Spirit*. New York: Houghton Mifflin, 1992.

Grainger, A. *Desertification: How People Make Deserts, How People Can Stop, and Why They Don't*. Washington, DC: International Institute for Environmental Development, 1982.

Kelly, Petra. *Thinking Green*. Berkeley: Parallax Press, 1994.

Schnailberg, Allan. *The Environment: From Surplus to Scarcity*. New York: Oxford University Press, 1980.

Sell, Susan K. *Power and Ideas: North-South Politics of Intellectual Property and Antitrust*. New York: SUNY Series in Global Politics, 1997.

Van Cott, Donna Lee. *Indigenous Peoples and Democracy in Latin America*. Boston: St. Martin's Press, 1995.

Wolbarst, Anthony B. *Environment in Peril*. Washington, DC: Smithsonian Institution Press, 1992.

Tlaxcala, Mexico

# Part V

# Input Democracy and the Unemployed State

*The only effective balance of power is a balance between political and economic power — that is, between the power of money and the power of organized people. The role of government is not to mediate between private and public interest; it is to represent and advance the public interest.*

*The difference between the major parties in the United States is simple; the Democrats do with chagrin what the Republicans do with glee.*

*ONE OF THE* very positive developments of the last several years in Latin America, Eastern Europe, parts of Central Asia and East Asia, and even Africa, has been the spread of democracy — or at least of elections — and the generalized requirement of elections as the sole acceptable means of rule legitimation. It would be very dangerous, however, to view this trend as unidirectional — "the end of history"[1] — or as the best we can do toward achieving the popular ideal of democracy. It represents, rather, a change in the nature, rules, and venues of the game of power competition that offers both new opportunities and new vulnerabilities. Over the longer term, the spread of elections has by no means been an unbroken trend; it has come in fits and starts, waves and cycles, incomplete and always subject to reversal.

The development or redevelopment of democracy (understood as popular, as opposed to elite, rule) should not be simply equated with or tracked through national elections. Elections are a means, not an end, and means are always subject to subversion or corruption. There may well have been more democracy in "primitive" or pre-modern societies than is common in contemporary democracies. In the absence of more reliable means of recording choice in complex societies, however, it has become difficult to speak convincingly of democracy without reference to elections.

The nation-state system is itself a fairly recent social construct, and national elections did not become commonplace, even in Europe and its liberated offspring, until the mid-nineteenth century. At the beginning of the twentieth century, by some assessments, there were only nine countries that could legitimately be considered democratic, and by 1960 only twenty-nine. A similar survey in 1990 found sixty-five countries engaging in creditable elections.[2]

Thereafter, with the implosion of the Soviet Union and the spread of separatist fervor, there was an explosion in the number of recognized states and thus in the number of national elections. Qualitative considerations aside, there were some 118 states in the late 1990s having elected governments. This era of electoral democracy is by no means the century's most effective in terms of output, or accountability, but in terms of input, the staging of and participation in elections, it is certainly the most far-reaching geographically and the most firmly entrenched in international law, from the political covenant of the 1948 Universal Declaration of Human Rights, now signed by more than one hundred countries, to the spreading practice of international and non-governmental monitoring of elections.

## Making Waves: Gravitational Forces and New Frontiers

This new era of democracy is not simply a by-product of the end of the Cold War. Like any development so unlikely, it has been over-determined, produced by many factors. This new wave of democratization might be traced to Western Europe in the mid-1970s. Having developed strong domestic economies and a strong democratic vocation, having discarded the costly last throes of straight-forward colonialism (as opposed to neocolonialism) and found economic strength in unity, the European Community exerted a strong pull on the continent's unconverted fringes. The lure of membership in the Community clearly gave an edge to democratic forces confronting authoritarian regimes in Portugal, Spain, and Greece.

The influence of Europe was felt in the Western Hemisphere as well, but a climatic change in the post-Vietnam War United States made a greater difference in Latin America. The first clear-cut reversal for Latin America's devastating era of militocracy came with President Jimmy Carter's insistence on respect for the electoral outcome in the Dominican Republic in 1978.[3]

With the ending of the Cold War, the proliferation of new states — shards of the Soviet Empire — constituted a new frontier, an irresistible challenge to seekers of power and profit as well as to those of more benign motives. But whatever the motive, whether revision of property and investment codes or the facilitation of new forms of expression and participation, the staging of elections launched the reorganization and offered the essential legitimation.

For the Third World in general, the end of the Cold War meant both liberation and resignation. For the Right it meant the loss of their cover story, for the Left the loss of their dream. First World potentates and profiteers lost their rationale for openly propping up monsters like Mobutu Sese Seko on security grounds.[4] But then, they no longer needed such monsters. In an unregulated globalized capitalist economy, there was little danger that hungry natives could compete successfully under any form of government for a share of Africa's riches. In such a context, both revolutionary and militarist-modernizer legitimation have shrinking constituencies; and the forces that had constituted at times the political extremes, at times the political options, are left with no marketable alternative to elections.

## Politics and Market Power

Perhaps the weightiest factors in explaining the trend to democratization, or electoral legitimation, are best illustrated by reference to the exceptions to the rule: the countries that scarcely bother to put up a democratic façade. The most obvious and numerous in that category are China and its expanding sphere of influence, and the oil-producing Muslim states. That is not to support the Huntington thesis of cultural causation and the coming "clash of civilizations."[5] Far from it. Muslim religion and culture have no more to do with the major powers' acceptance of dictatorship in the Persian Gulf and Brunei than has Communism, Confucianism, or any other "ism" with acceptance of it in China.

In a sense, virtually all states in the now globalized economic system are vanquished states — that is, the public sector has been eaten by the private sector. China is, of course, another matter — the five hundred-pound panda who sits anywhere he pleases. The disinclination of the West to challenge the legitimacy of China's government or even seriously to protest its systematic human rights abuses might be attributed to prudent caution in dealing with powerful states. But prudence in international politics is not customary; single-mindedness in profit-seeking is. The power that takes precedence now is market power. It happens that the most powerful constituents of Western governments — the money-movers — are not anxious to risk disruption in China or with China as they are busily moving their money there.

In sum, apart from players holding trumps, like China or Saudi Arabia, states, as such, hold weak hands. Elections are becoming the modus operandi for selection of governments in large part because economic interests are less threatened now than they were two or three decades ago by the formal processes of democracy. That is, global concentration of economic power is such that elected leaders have very little latitude in economic policy-making anyway; and elite interests are well served by allowing elected governments to absorb the blame for policies punishing to the poor. Faced with the expense of an increasingly high-tech, media-led, professionalized game of electoral politics and finding the vestments of office akin to a straitjacket, leaders unable to deal with the needs of the un-affluent are regularly discredited and defeated by leaders uninterested in doing so. At any rate, the frequent turnover of heads of government from one party to another, long viewed as evidence of electoral transparency and systemic stability, gives evidence also of the inability of elected leaders to deal with the most urgent needs of their constituencies.

## The Vanquished Public Domain

At this moment in the eternal struggle to determine means and ends of power distribution, the norm of elections occupies the winner's circle. But how are we to see democracy as having won while in so much of the "democratized" world winners in both political and economic terms are the very classes, sectors, agencies, even individuals, who engaged in every imaginable maneuver to obstruct democracy?

There is a great danger in welcoming so many "ringers" into the celebration of this ritual. It is that they will succeed in redefining electoral democracy, re-drawing its parameters in such a way as to trivialize it — to further marginalize governments from economic policy-making, to equate free thinking with free markets, the right to compete with the right to destroy competition, to such an extent that no matter how large a majority preferred that a function (e.g., campaign finance) be removed from the private realm or that a service (e.g., running water or health care) be offered in the public realm, such a policy would be seen as anti-democratic. The initiative for setting boundaries between public and private domains has been seized by the private; re-drawn borders are rapidly being codified into national and international law, and border regions vacated by the public are being homesteaded by the private.

To say that this wave of democratization is not so meaningful as the cheerleaders would have us believe is not to say that it offers no hope. But it offers hope only if those who are serious about democracy understand the players and the game well enough to treat elections as an opening pitch rather than the final clearing of bases — i.e., "the end of history." A party or sector or movement that is able to mount a campaign and win an election, like one that mounts an effective insurrectionary campaign, proves only that it cannot be ignored — that it is a contender, not the major wielder of power. In fact, real power almost always lies elsewhere.

Democracy understood only or mainly as elections misses the essence of politics as the action at the top of the food chain. To find the arena where the crucial decisions are made, one would do well to take the advice that Deep Throat offered to the journalists investigating the Watergate break-in: follow the money.

Democracy is more likely to be found where the money isn't: in small and/or resource-poor states, or at local levels of government. When democracy breaks out in a particular constituency, the power game just shifts to a larger, more encompassing arena. In the nation-state system, there has been a tendency for control over resources, including tax revenues and taxing authority to move up the system; from local levels to state or regional and national, while responsibility for social well-being, especially over the last two decades, moved down.

As elected governments here and there, in First World and Third in the 1960s and 1970s, became accountable to broader constituencies, creditors and corporations with the greatest interests at stake on the one hand threw their weight behind anti-democratic forces within state systems and on the other sought protection for their assets and freedom from regulation beyond the reach of any nation-state. Globalization, made possible finally by the collapse of the alternative market, is the completion of that great escape. It is the ultimate centrally planned economy, in which taxes are paid in the Bahamas and campaign contributions are paid in Washington, Tokyo, Berlin, and Bombay. That pattern, along with the ever-present threat of capital flight and currency speculation, leaves governments around the world working for and competing for the favors of the same banks and corporations. Meanwhile, as governments divest, disintegrate, and proliferate, the corporations they serve fold and merge, becoming fewer and larger, richer and ever more powerful. More than a quarter of the world's economic activity is conducted by its two hundred largest corporations, and up to one-third of world trade takes place among different units of individual global conglomerates.[6]

But states that are no longer representative to any meaningful degree of popular sovereignty, no longer able to respond to popular need or majority interest, are not likely thus to wither away. They simply come to be dependent upon and at the service of a different set of masters. Even if the decisions that most fundamentally affect the allocation of resources and opportunities are not made at the national level, there are still many rewards to be gleaned by state-holders, as well as by domestic and foreign private stake-holders who will be making the former offers they cannot refuse. Thus, to the extent that national leadership is really to be determined through elections, it must be expected that great resources will be expended in manners legal and illegal, democratic and anti-democratic, to control the process. Little wonder then that corporate taxes shrink as campaign contributions grow.[7] Worse yet, obsession with controlling electoral outcomes leads to population displacement, resettlement, even ethnic cleansing.

## Redemocratization in Latin America

The struggle for re-democratization, or democratic transition, in Latin America in the late 1970s and early 1980s, particularly in Brazil and the Southern Cone, was undertaken at great personal risk and sacrifice by popular leaders and movements. But it left no celebrated heroes, no monuments, no holidays or commemorative stamps. In fact, for those most engaged the conflict never really ended; it simply moved inside and lodged in their souls.

In Central America, where abortive democratic movements had given way to popular insurrection, the Reagan Administration finally recognized what more seasoned conservatives had long understood — that in a client state a civilian government that is uninterested in acting upon or unable to act upon a popular mandate and unwilling or unable to control military and paramilitary forces is a better hedge against social change than a repressive military government. That learning process was expedited by a US Congress that under popular pressure to end support for human rights violations insisted on taking a firm position on both sides of the fence; particularly with respect to Central America, it made the maintenance of a democratic civilian façade a condition for the ongoing provision of military aid — aid, that is, to anti-democratic forces.

The new round of elections in South America has served in some cases to edge countries away from authoritarian systems. In other cases, however, it has served to legitimate older authoritarian systems, thus giving them a new lease on life. The Paraguayan elections of May 1993 aroused particular interest in that they offered the prospect that after almost a half-century of military dictatorship Paraguay might at last undergo a transition to democracy. Such was not to be — at least in the short term. Swarms of international election monitors and journalists notwithstanding, those elections served to legitimate a presidential election "show" in which the outcome was never really put at risk.

Throughout the world, as elections become freer, the elected become less so. Where electoral outcomes have unmistakably represented the triumph of a long-suppressed popular will, as in Haiti and South Africa, investors and creditors and the First World governments and international financial institutions that serve them have laid out in no uncertain terms the dangers that accompany precipitous promotion of equity. The surrender of economic sovereignty has left elected governments without the wherewithal or the inclination to deal with new forms of violence or with the growing income gap that spawns them. For many, memories of the horrors of military rule have begun to fade and, as developments in Peru, Venezuela, and elsewhere suggest, "democracy" itself, coinciding with economic devastation, is once again falling into disrepute.

For the most part, contemporary manifestations of authoritarianism take the form of police power, its relevance to politics shrouded as unrest degenerates into anomic street crime and economic problems giving rise to it become increasingly untreatable at the national level. Still, to say that democracy in the 1990s is failing to live up to its promise is not to say that parties and elections and parliaments are likely to be abandoned. In many countries, though progress in demilitarization has been halting and exasperatingly slow, military power has continued to ebb. Few other than would-be autocrats see promise, at this point, in autocracy. And only those having very short memories could fail to find hope in an increased measure of respect for human and civil rights.

## Notes

1. In reference to the much cited article by Francis Fukuyama, "The End of History?" *National Interest,* Summer 1989. Fukuyama sees the end of the Cold War as the end of ideological struggle.
2. Greg H. Fox, "The Right to Political Participation in International Law," *Yale Journal of International Law,* Vol. 17: 539, 1992, pp. 539–607.
3. In 1961 all but about three of the Latin American countries were generally considered democratic. By 1976 all but about three were considered authoritarian. By 1991 all but one or two were considered democratic.
4. Mobutu, whose ghoulish kleptocracy ruled Zaire for thirty-two years, had come to power as a CIA asset. He died in September 1997 after his regime was toppled by the rebel forces of Laurent Kabila, who renamed the country "Congo."
5. Samuel Huntington's thesis is elaborated in *The Clash of Civilizations and the Remaking of World Order* (New York: Simon and Schuster, 1996).
6. Richard Barnet, "Stateless Corporations: Lords of the Global Economy," Chap. 1 in Kevin Danaher, ed. *Corporations Are Gonna Get Your Mama* (Monroe, Maine: Common Courage Press, A Global Exchange Book, 1996).
7. According to a 1993 US General Accounting Office study, more than 40 percent of the corporations with assets of $250 million or more doing business in the United States paid no income taxes or taxes of less than $100,000. The corporate share of federal income tax, 23 percent in the 1950s, was down to 9.2 percent in 1991.

Chapter 15

# Redemocratization in the Southern Cone: A Legacy of Abuse

*The buck stops short.*

*Truth is a lonely traveler,*
*the bastard at every family picnic.*

*AT CÓRDOBA'S* University City one can still see the concrete and steel foundations of the military bunkers that some fifteen years ago surrounded Argentina's oldest college of philosophy and letters. But the casual visitor would not notice such things. Unlike international wars, civil wars, and revolutionary wars, counterrevolutionary wars — of governments against their own citizens — leave few visible scars; but the wounds take longer to heal.

In late 1994, Brazil and South America's Southern Cone seemed caught in a time warp. One who was there thirty years earlier, as I had been, might have expected to have a sensation of déjà vu. When I was a Peace Corps Volunteer in Chile in the early 1960s, President Alessandri, a Conservative, was about to be replaced by a Christian Democrat named Eduardo Frei. In Argentina at that time, a civilian of the Radical Party had just replaced a military regime, with the help of the Peronist vote. In Brazil there was a president backed by organized labor and a nationalist movement promoted by dependency theorists like Fernando Henrique Cardoso.

In Chile thirty years later, a second-generation Christian Democratic president named Eduardo Frei had defeated a Conservative named Alessandri. (On the campaign trail, Frei quipped that he had just two things going for him: one was his last name, Frei; the other was his first name, Eduardo.) In Argentina, a Peronist had replaced a Radical who had taken over from the military. In Brazil, a popular labor leader running for the presidency on a nationalist, dependency-type platform had been overtaken and defeated by a candidate representing the Center-right — the same Fernando Henrique Cardoso, runaway father of dependency theory.

Does that mean that the political and economic game had come full circle in thirty years? No. The ghosts of democracies past are still ghosts. Now, as in the early 1960s, most Latin American governments are considered democratic because elections have taken place. Now, as then, there is less to such democracy than meets the eye. But the obstacles and deceits are of a different order.

In the early 1960s, "democracy" was being discredited — in Central America and the Caribbean by fraud,[1] in the Southern Cone by vulnerability to military intervention. Now, in the 1990s, democracy is being discredited by irrelevance — by the absence of options and expectations.

The democracy of the 1960s was unstable precisely because there was hope, hope that political democracy might lead in the direction of economic democracy. The democracy of the 1990s is more nearly stable because there is little such hope (and consequently, little fear). More than ever, electoral politics is the moral equivalent of sport.

In the 1960s, the United States was promoting growth, but also social change — within limits. Not surprisingly, Latin American leaders chafed at the limits. Those who rejected the limits were labeled by the US and its Latin American allies as subversives. Those who accepted the limits were labeled by their own people *entreguistas*, or sell-outs. The *entreguistas* then began to lose their political bases to the "subversives," a trend highly perturbing to those who had the most to lose.

Whereas some parties on the Left rejected liberal electoral democracy in principle but accepted it in practice, parties of the Right did just the opposite. They embraced electoral democracy in principle but rejected it in practice. So the region suffered a decade or more of counterrevolutionary terror and another of economic disaster — of unemployment and hyperinflation, disintegration of social infrastructure and dissolution of social fabric. With the beginning of the 1990s, the region was celebrating the completion of a trend towards redemocratization and was even experiencing spurts of economic growth — major accomplishments, achieved at great social and personal costs; but what do these things mean now, in the context of the global village?

One of the problems for the analyst, as for the voter, is that of confusion between what is old and what is new in this regional and global new order. It seems to me that three old problems, closely linked then and now, have taken on new dimensions and perhaps a new order of significance:

1. *Violence*. Violence of political inspiration, instigated at regime level, has almost vanished, but its legacy has not. Police continue to be among the major perpetrators of violence, though most often off-duty, on a free-lance basis. For most the greatest vulnerability now

is the burgeoning random, or seemingly random, street crime, which in itself tears at the social fabric and has a chilling effect on civil and human rights.

2. *The growing gap.* The economic booms of the nineties like the awful busts of the eighties have fallen unevenly on classes, sectors, regions, races, genders, and generations and have exacerbated what were already shamefully bifurcated distribution systems. Moreover, the touted solutions tend to pit categories of the insecure and disadvantaged against each other, fracturing the coalitions that built and might sustain elements of a welfare state.
3. *The surrender of sovereignty.* Even as elections become freer, the elected become less so. In the 1990s, the mantle of office looks ever more like a straitjacket.

## Pervasive Violence and the Battered Population Syndrome

Brazil's observation in 1994 of the thirtieth anniversary of the military counterrevolution that so profoundly affected its political and economic course was a very low-key affair. Commenting on a newly released book in which military commanders of the 1960s and 1970s conceded for the first time that torture had been a systematically employed policy tool, an active duty general shruggingly asked why such matters should be brought up now.

Ariel Dorfman's play, *Death and the Maiden,* dealing with the toxic residue of the Pinochet dictatorship, played well in London, and a movie version played well in the United States, but in Chile it quietly bombed. Argentine and Uruguayan friends tell me that the topic of the "dirty wars" — of military repression and popular resistance — is generally avoided because the hate and fear that lie just beneath the surface of public, and even private, relationships are best left untapped.

The celebrated redemocratization of the Southern Cone — the reconciliation of the privileged and the wretched, of the armed and the unarmed, of abusers and victims — leaves whole populations with something akin to the battered wife syndrome. In the absence of punishment of the perpetrators, of open and definitive social condemnation of their deeds, victims tend to blame themselves, either for somehow causing or inviting the assault or for allowing themselves to be victimized, or both. Rather than a cause for moral outrage, the episode or epoch becomes a source of social embarrassment. As open resistance had been limited and abuse to some degree selective, victimization is unevenly experienced. Thus the national soul-searching that should be expressed in social analysis is expressed instead in individual angst and psychoanalysis.

In fact, the withdrawal of the military has not been to a safe enough distance to allow democracy free rein. Coup attempts and threats and other acts of military insubordination surfaced from time to time throughout the 1980s in Uruguay and Argentina, and in Chile there was no pretense of subordination of the armed forces to the elected civilian leadership. Instead, there was talk of co-government — a recipe, the British might say, for horse and rabbit stew; equal parts, one horse, one rabbit. In July 1994, President Frei publicly declared that the commander of the Carabineros, or National Police, accused of responsibility for a massacre in years past, did not enjoy the confidence of the government. But under the rules of the game — the stacked deck that civilian leaders saw no choice but to accept — Frei could not remove him. Despite Chile's real progress toward redemocratization, the leader of the Communist Party was arrested in 1996 for publicly criticizing Pinochet.

In general, the abusers of the era of militocracy, from the tyrants to the petty freelance torturers, continued to enjoy impunity. Attempts by civilian governments in Argentina and Uruguay in the 1980s to prosecute had met with such ominous military countermeasures that henceforth the amnesties that military conspirators had granted themselves were treated by civilians as if they had the sanctity of law. Several former members of governing juntas in Argentina who had been convicted of human rights abuses and imprisoned under the government of Raúl Alfonsín were subsequently pardoned by the government of Carlos Saúl Menem. In Uruguay, in 1996, the admission of a former military officer that during the military regime detainees had been tortured and killed and buried secretly on military property caused a brief stir in the media, but it did not spill over into the political arena.

It was not until 1998 that the issue began seriously to be revisited. At that time Argentine jurists concluded that amnesty laws protecting the murderers of mothers did not relieve them from liability for trafficking in their orphaned children. Former junta leader General Jorge Videla was imprisoned on such a charge early in the year, and a similar change was pending at year's end against Admiral Emilio Massera.

The most dramatic breach to date in the wall of impunity was the arrest of Chile's retired dictator, General Augusto Pinochet (now, by his own rules, Senator for Life) in London on October 16, 1998. He was being held on a Spanish request for extradition to stand trial for the murder of Spanish citizens who had been serving the United Nations in Chile. A British high court ruling that Pinochet enjoyed diplomatic immunity as a former head of state was overriden by the House of Lords, but as the year drew to a close it remained to be seen whether he would, in fact, be extradited to Spain. In the meantime, Switzerland had lodged its own request for extradition and it appeared that other European governments would follow suit.

In Chile, the arrest had led to much rejoicing but also much concern and, in some quarters, anger. The government's defense of Pinochet, the degree of unease and polarization and the extent of hedging and evasiveness among those, even on the Left, who enjoyed a political forum, suggested that Pinochet, or Pinochetismo, still cast a long shadow across the land and that the need for exorcism remained acute. (The trial of Pinochet might also give elements of the US government the unsought but much needed opportunity to unburden themselves with respect to their complicity in Pinochet's reign of terror.)[2]

Even so, selective political violence, "democratized" during the years of militocracy in the sense that the affluent were also susceptible, has abated. Official violence is generally limited once again to the poor, who were always vulnerable. Assault by the police, on their own or in the hire of businessmen or landowners, against the poor was particularly notorious in Brazil.[3] But, along with the poor, the middle class has fallen prey to another kind of violence — a cultural import, some say, from the United States — a sort of street-level tax collection. Throughout Latin America locals now suggest "safe" taxis and a firm grip on wallets.

In Rio de Janeiro, the tunnels that move traffic through the mountains to connect the principal parts of the city in the early 1990s had become "toll tunnels," as heavily armed thugs blocked the entrances and systematically collected; and the nightly sounds of machine gun shoot-outs as drug lords competed for control of *favelas* (shantytowns) had generated a siege mentality in a city so recently famed as fun-loving. Such menacing anarchy is almost as subversive of democratic prospects, as certain to sever links among races and classes and generations, as is tyranny. With the metropolitan murder rate running at twenty a day, most Cariocas (the people of Rio de Janeiro) seemed relieved when the federal government, in late 1994, launched Operation Rio, a series of assaults involving several thousand troops, against the *favelas* assumed to be the most heavily infested with narcotraffickers.

## Economic Polarization and Social Dissolution

One need not see the latest figures from the UN Economic Commission on Latin America to know that the region's income gap is widening dramatically, at a pace accelerated by the growth spurts of the 1990s. On all sides in the private sector one sees monuments to new wealth.

Cutting a swathe across virgin forests in the mountains above Rio de Janeiro, the property of a Coca-Cola franchise heiress sports an incongruent modern mansion, with matching mini-mansion for the security guards and a city pound-size kennel for guard dogs. In Uruguay's Punta del Este and Rio's Barra de Tijuca, in Santiago's Barrio Alto and La Paz's Barrio Abajo there is a flourishing of gated and guarded communities, of ghost towns and palaces used only for holidays and parties. A single Christmas party in Punta del Este (at the estate of the Scarpa family, brewers of Brazil's Brahma beer) is said to have cost a million dollars.

But shantytowns — *favelas* and *poblaciones populares* and *villas miserias* — are growing, too. Such growth is a consequence, in part, of rural to urban migration, as shown in a recent study in Córdoba, but also, as indicated in a study of Brasilia's "satellite cities," by slippage from the middle class. Of course, the poor are the front-line victims of the new-style urban anarchy, and in the shantytowns, too, those who can afford them are buying guard dogs.

Meanwhile, for the public sector the new free-market order has been very expensive. Throughout the region that sector has been asset-stripped. Most who serve the public, from garbage collectors to university professors, have seen their standards of living dropping for two or three decades. Services that might pay for themselves or even, at higher cost to consumers, bring in a profit are privatized, while local, state, or national governments with no visible means of support are left to pick up the rest. For this they resort generally to regressive taxes, like Chile's 18 percent value-added tax.

In Argentina a frenzy of privatization — a government going-out-of-business sale — brought several years of rapid growth, but that growth in the private sector has come at the expense of deterioration of basic services in the public sector — education, health, housing. Argentine friends tell me that most services, now privatized, are as bad as ever; but now they cost more. Argentina's economy grew by some 8 percent between mid-1996 and mid-1997, but representatives of the country's largest teachers' union, marching along with thirty thousand others in a protest in July 1997 against double-digit unemployment, claimed that their current real wages were only 37 percent of what they were earning in 1980. Chile's "economic miracle" of the late 1980s (6–7 percent annual growth) was a catch-up in part after the disaster of the early 1980s (–13 percent). Attempts of the Christian Democratic governments in office since 1990 to deal with the social deficit are said to have lifted more than a million people out of poverty; but it was not until 1996 that real wages in the formal sector climbed back to the levels attained in the early 1970s, and some 40 percent of the population remained stuck in the unprotected hand-to-mouth informal sector.

In Brazil, as in Argentina, exhaustion with hyperinflation has led the public to accept currency stabilization plans that mean First World prices and Third World salaries. (Brazil's minimum wage was about $70 a month in 1994 when I spent $10 in Brasilia for a single serving of coffee and ice cream.) Like Argentina's Menem, Fernando Henrique, whose Plano Real is credited with his meteoric rise in the polls and his stunning first ballot victory on October 3, 1994, gambled that consumers would opt for currency stability above all. Unlike Argentina and Chile, Brazil could not court the favor of international capital through a policy of deindustrialization. Though in many ways it is one of the world's least developed countries, it is also now among the world's most highly industrialized. Brazil has belatedly launched the courtship, however, through large-scale privatization — and thus denationalization — of industry.

The price that has generally been demanded of heavily indebted countries in Latin America and elsewhere for reentry into the game of international commerce is a price that Brazil, at least until the mid-1990s, had been reluctant to pay. That price is relinquishment of economic sovereignty, the denationalization of economic decision-making. The state itself under that circumstance comes to be unemployed, except to the extent that it serves as a collection agency for creditors. The otherwise beached ship of state is then subcontracted as a receivership.

## Democracy on a Short Leash

What has come to be the operative definition of democracy in Latin America as elsewhere in the 1990s is a curiously lopsided one, one that disregards representation and accountability. This is not necessarily the fault of the elected. Taking office is not the same as taking power; the ritual of an election does not confer power if power does not reside in the electorate.

The main elements of power are material resources and force, or money and guns, and in Latin America election offers neither. Elections may offer free expression and association and the illusion of participation, but in the 1990s they rarely offer economic gains or even protection against losses for middle and working or marginalized classes. In fact, it seems that increasingly, in rich and poor countries alike, the role of the elected leaders and parties with broad, popular bases is to sell out their own constituencies. In fact, any suggestion of an upward shift in burden-bearing would likely dry up credit and set off a stampede of fleeing capital. The rules set by creditors and enforced by international financial institutions are such as to ensure that borrowers and beneficiaries of credit are able to pass "shared sacrifice" down the social scale to classes that did not benefit. Otherwise the game would soon be stalemated. The ultimate collateral, after all, of a loan to a government or other collectivity is the resources and/or labor of those least able to defend their interests.

Meanwhile, the kind of democracy that is compatible with the new version of free enterprise turns out to be very expensive. With campaign contributions routinely in the millions of dollars, corruption becomes institutionalized and virtually all politicians are in some degree vulnerable — the most vulnerable often being those who steal least and spread it around the most. In other words, to the extent that money fuels the process and all politicians are dependent, the charge of corruption becomes just another weapon in a conflict in which the side with the best-stocked armory has the advantage. British economist John Maynard Keynes's sardonic take on the "long run" was modified in Brazilian political circles, where indictments were being handed down wholesale in the early 1990s; the proverb came to be "In the long run we are all in jail." In the end, with options so narrowed, pressures so fierce, and vulnerability so great, elected leaders, especially those with the largest and most hopeful followings, are in danger of being utterly discredited, along with their parties or movements and perhaps the ideal of democracy itself.

In this context, the entire political spectrum in Latin America has shifted sharply to the Right. Programs elaborated in Chile by Christian Democrats in coalition with Socialists and in Argentina by Peronists — supposedly a labor party — in the 1990s, might have seemed embarrassingly anti-nationalist and anti-popular even to Conservatives two decades ago. The Left has not disappeared, but now, chastened and pragmatic, it has slipped over to occupy what used to be the Center. In Uruguay, the traditional Blanco and Colorado parties have become almost indistinguishable; where the Colorado party used to be, more or less, is the previously "subversive" Frente Amplio. The programmatic limb Frente Amplio is out on includes sparing from privatization those government services that are being frugally and efficiently run.

For Brazil's general elections of 1994, Lula (Luis Inácio da Silva), the fearless champion of the working class, tutored by media advisers and lectured by First World economists, clipped his beard, donned coat and tie, and tempered his rhetoric. Engaging in time travel, one might say that Lula had run as Fernando Henrique (the Fernando Henrique, that is, of the 1960s and 1970s) while Fernando Henrique had run as José Sarney (the conservative president of the mid-to-late 1980s). Brazilians on the Left found grounds for optimism in the fact that as a candidate Fernando Henrique had already sold out his friends in order to appeal to his enemies. They figured that as president he could only sell out his enemies. There were no such illusions in 1998 as Fernando Henrique, who had held on, at great cost, to a stable currency, won another decisive victory over Lula, despite capital flight — an echo of the Asian crisis — and a crippling austerity package designed to lure that capital back.

Actually, Brazil's presidential contests of the 1990s point up the difficulty in sorting out illusion and reality, good news and bad news. The good news was that both of the major candidates — Fernando Henrique, the extraordinarily sophisticated and insightful social scientist, and Lula, the skillful community organizer and eloquent spokesman of popular interests — were a cut above the best in the political stables of most countries North and South. The bad news was that that is no longer enough to convert participation in elections into participation for the majority in the fruits of their labor. (Privatizations of the late 1990s have attracted foreign investment on a massive scale, but such riches do not trickle down and the income gap remains the widest among the world's democracies.) Even if these two remarkable men and their constituencies had seen fit, directly or indirectly, to cooperate or coordinate, it is not clear that they would have been able to hold off the creditors and carpetbaggers and the muggers operating in the streets and suites long enough to make a measure of that great country's resources available to its marginalized masses.

# Notes

1. In Haiti, the referendum that legitimated the assumption by "Baby Doc" — Jean Claude Duvalier — of the late Papa Doc's lifetime presidency registered two million votes for and one against. I always imagined that lonely one vote had been cast by Baby Doc himself.
2. Dr. Brady Tyson, who in 1979 had apologized on behalf of the US delegation to the UN High Commission on Human Rights for the US role in the military seizure of power in 1973, was quietly edged out of government service. US government documents released following the arrest of Pinochet indicate that in the aftermath of the execution of two US citizens the US Ambassador had assured the Pinochet government that "this small matter" would not be allowed to stand in the way of cordial relations.
3. Only two of the fifty-two police charged in a 1993 massacre of twenty-one people in the Rio de Janeiro shantytown of Vigario Geral had been convicted by the end of 1998. Most involved in the infamous murder of eight street children that same year on the steps of Candelaria Church had also gone unpunished. Nor had there been convictions in the 1996 massacre by military police of nineteen landless peasants in Pará.

## Chapter 16

# Election Monitoring in Paraguay: The Show and the Critics

*Most hen houses are guarded by foxes.*

*Most social and political systems are underpinned by denial.*

*NEWSPAPER HEADLINES* in Asunción the morning following Paraguay's general elections on May 9, 1993, might have led one to believe that government and opposition papers were covering different elections in different countries. About all they had in common was generous coverage of the activities of the entourage of former President Jimmy Carter and other international election observation teams. The foreign presence — some three hundred official observers and a swarm of media people — was not so overwhelming in this case as in that of the 1990 elections in Nicaragua, when it seemed there were more observers than voters. Even so, the experience left many of us with the uneasy feeling that our mere presence served to lend legitimacy to a process that in fact left much to be desired.

The intensity of international interest in this case derived from the prospect that after almost a half century of military dictatorship Paraguayans might at last be able to participate in open and honest elections. In the case of such a benchmark election, one that may serve as a step forward in the process of transition to democracy, there are several good arguments for having observers on hand. The most important, perhaps, is a potentially preventive role; that is, one might hope that the presence of foreign observers would inhibit would-be perpetrators of the most egregious abuses, such as the government thugs who assaulted voters and candidates at the polls and on the streets in Haiti in 1987 and in Panama in 1989.

Election observers may also delegitimize, and thus weaken, governments "elected" by clearly fraudulent means or may pressure reluctant incumbents to relinquish power to duly elected opposition groups. There are, however, other less edifying roles for observers. With something less than the best of intentions, major powers may use observers to delegitimize obstreperous governments within their spheres of influence that were in fact freely elected. And even independent observers with the best of intentions are vulnerable to being used to legitimate governments that manage to get themselves reelected through unfair but more or less invisible misuse of incumbency.

The Paraguayan general elections of 1993, complete as of June 2 when the Congress promulgated final results, set in relief many of the problems and pitfalls of observing and passing judgment upon elections. Latin Americans are better equipped conceptually than Anglo-Americans to deal with electoral processes and results like those witnessed in Paraguay. They might speak of *dictablanda* (soft dictatorship) or *democradura* (hard democracy), acknowledging that most elections and most governments fall somewhere on a continuum between fully democratic and utterly undemocratic, but US constituencies want their answers and their labels in absolutes.

The misuse of observers comes about in part because only those most intimately involved in the electoral process or most likely to be affected by the outcome will read observer reports in their entirety. For most, the judgment of observers will be passed on in headlines and sound-bites, and all complexities and subtleties will be lost. Moreover, such reports will be used in the manner of any people's bible — that is, selectively. Any such reports will carry a certain amount of diplomatic fluff, if only as praise for the democratic vocation demonstrated by voters, and headlines are often drawn from the fluff rather than from the more important observations found in the report.

Finally, in most cases, the focus of observers, or of the media's use of observers, falls too narrowly on what transpires on election day at the voting precincts and on the outcome or projection of the vote count. In the Paraguayan case, most observers, including the Latin American Studies Association (LASA) team on which I served, accepted the government's finding that the official candidate had received a plurality of the popular vote, but that was far from the whole story and far from a finding that the election represented a breakthrough to democracy.

## An Environment of Fraud

A more serious assessment of the process and the validity of its outcome should take into account what the LASA team called the undemocratic character of the macro-political process, or what observers from the World Council of Churches referred to as "fraude ambiental," or an environment of fraud. In other words, how much legitimacy should we attribute to a game that takes place on a playing field with a 60-degree tilt? And finally, how much congratulation is due a regime that demonstrates its willingness to accept victory — but not defeat — in an election?

The ruling triad of military, bureaucracy, and official party, popularly known as the Colorados, had control of most of the money, all of the guns, and all of the electoral machinery. Over the past century, the Colorados have built a patronage system stretching into every hamlet, wherein the appeal of carrots has been reinforced by the omnipresence of sticks. Yet Paraguay has come a long way since the ghoulish thirty-five-year rule of General Alfredo Stroessner was ended by a coup d'état in 1989. The coup, led by General Andrés Rodríguez, was motivated by palace intrigue and intra-military rivalries, but a new generation of democratic activists in the universities, professions, unions, churches, and non-governmental organizations took advantage of the incident to force a democratic opening. Gradually, the newly demanded freedoms of expression and assembly came to be generally respected.

The election immediately following the coup, which confirmed Rodríguez in the presidency, was scarcely a model one, though few doubted that the coup had earned Rodríguez great popularity. Municipal elections in 1991 — the first in the country's history — gauged the potential of a newly mobilized democratic opposition. A coalition known as Asunción Para Todos (Asunción for All) swept the capital while the Liberals, the traditional opposition to the Colorado Party, carried the second largest city and more than thirty other municipalities.

The new constitution, promulgated in 1992, was drawn up by a Colorado-dominated assembly, but was far more democratic than the previous document. As the elections of 1993 approached, the Liberals, subject in the past to co-optation and schism, were more nearly united under the leadership of Domingo Laino. Laino's dogged opposition to Stroessner through the years had subjected him to imprisonment, torture, and exile, but it had earned for him widespread respect.

While the Liberals marshaled their traditional following in the rural areas, newer and smaller parties, including the Febreristas and the Christian Democrats, joined forces with newly mobilized groups, such as those who had formed the winning coalition in Asunción, to form a new party, Encuentro Nacional, or National Convergence. As the election approached, Encuentro's charismatic presidential candidate, Guillermo Caballero Vargas, enjoyed the lead in most public opinion polls, including some commissioned by the Colorado Party itself.

Meanwhile, within the Colorado Party a schism had developed between the loyalists of Stroessner and those of Rodríguez. Pre-election chicanery had included a blatantly rigged primary that threw the nomination to the Rodriguista candidate, Juan Carlos Wasmosy. A multimillionaire, Wasmosy had made his money the old-fashioned way — on government contracts, in this case for the construction of Itaipú, the world's largest dam.

The environment of fraud leading up to election day also included public statements by military and party leaders to the effect that they would continue their "co-government" regardless of the outcome of the elections; pressure on government officials to mobilize their employees in support of Colorado candidates, pressure that intensified as opinion polls showed opposition candidates leading; and withholding or belated delivery to opposition parties of the voter registration lists and information on the location of precincts or polling places.

Opposition party poll-watchers were not surprised to find on election day a pattern of *urnas con patas* (ballot boxes with feet), or voting precincts that were not where they were supposed to be, and to find that registration lists had been tampered with; having already traveled a considerable distance to the village or town where he or she last voted, the prospective voter would be told that he was registered in some other town.

The most dramatic "irregularities" on election day itself were a grenade and machine gun attack on the only opposition television station and the closing of national borders by the military, so that Paraguayan citizens working in Argentina and Brazil were prevented from returning to vote. Even at the airport in Asunción, foreigners were admitted on election day while citizens found their entry blocked until time for the polls to close. By comparison, most other election-day infractions seemed relatively minor, though the litany was long, constituting a comprehensive course on election chicanery. Commonly heard complaints against the ruling party included the purchase of identification cards; the overrepresentation of Colorado party precinct officials and poll-watchers and the underrepresentation of those of the opposition; instruction of voters in booths; misuse or absence of indelible ink (to mark thumbs and prevent repeat voting); detention of trucks or buses carrying opposition voters; and particularly in outlying areas, outright intimidation of opposition poll-watchers and voters.

Even so, since many of the alleged infractions were invisible to most of the observers, and since what most observers saw most of the time was a relatively orderly and uncontentious process, and since the Colorado candidate's lead turned out to be a commanding one, there was an inclination among observers to assume that in themselves election-day irregularities would not have been sufficient to alter the outcome. (In the case of US-based observers, a fairly casual attitude with respect to corruption of electoral procedures derived also from familiarity. Americans tend to assume that if it happens in Cook County it can't be all that bad. Maybe we should be thinking instead about inviting international teams to observe our own elections.)

## Taking No Chances

If observers' reviews of voting precinct procedures were "mixed," there was no such ambivalence about the sequence of events that followed the closing of the polls and that pertained to the vote count. The radio and television *cadena,* or hook-up, that had been established for keeping the country informed on the progress of election-day activities had begun, long before polls closed, to issue reports, based on rather casual exit polling procedures, of percentages of votes cast. Revelation of the standing of individual parties in exit polls was prohibited by law, but broad hints had the effect of skirting that prohibition. The moment polls closed, at five o'clock, those totals were given with party labels. That is, it was announced before the formal vote count had even begun that the Colorado Party had won. On the strength of that announcement (by a media personality beholden to the government), Colorado candidate Wasmosy declared victory and party militants began a raucous celebration, with fireworks (in some cases, gunfire) and honking, parading vehicles throughout the city. Whether or not intimidation of the opposition was intended, it was certainly experienced.

More ominous, however, was the interruption of communications in early afternoon on election day between central offices of Saka and the organization's field operators. Saka (Guaraní for "transparency") is an umbrella organization embracing a number of NGOs. With financial support from public and private sources from a number of foreign countries and in-kind contributions from domestic organizations, it had engaged in voter education and was conducting a vote tallying operation parallel to that of the government. The seven dedicated telephone lines that were to allow Saka volunteers to call in their own calculations, precinct by precinct, were cut from about 2:00 PM on election day until about 2:00 AM on the day following. The government's explanation, echoing that of the telephone company, was technical difficulties; but when former US President Carter complained directly to General Rodríguez, the company managed to restore the service for some ten minutes — until Carter left the Presidential Palace — after which it was cut again. The Carter group's conclusion was that the interruption could only have been intentional.

In the meantime polling stations in many locations were surrounded by police, and Saka messengers, who were to have delivered the parallel count, by prior agreement with election officials, were prevented from entering or leaving those stations. In other places, Saka volunteers were physically abused, and there was an episode of a vehicle carrying Saka messengers being forced off the road and overturned.

## The Catch-22

On the evening of the day following the elections, Saka nevertheless presented its findings to that point, figures that differed only slightly from the unofficial count of the Central Electoral Commission (JEC) — a count reflecting totals called in by the principal officers of each voting precinct. The official count, however, had scarcely even begun, and by the second day after the election, complaints were being heard about *actas oficiales*, or voting records, that had arrived at JEC headquarters unsealed or unsigned or that had been lost or damaged.

This was particularly disturbing in that while marginal differences that might result from tampering with the vote count would not affect the outcome of the presidential election, they might well determine whether or not the opposition parties would maintain the congressional majority registered in unofficial early computations taken by both Saka and the JEC. Indeed, as the official count continued during the week after the election, the initial lead of the opposition in Congress was gradually eroding.

The general impression conveyed by such irregularities at this stage of the process was that the vote from various locations would have to be challenged and perhaps nullified, all of which would throw the structuring of the conflict to the Colorado-controlled JEC and the resolution of the matter to the Colorado-controlled Congress. This might occasion no particular concern if the Congress in question had been freely elected in accordance with a democratic tradition, but that was not the case. Moreover, the incumbent military-Colorado Party regime had already signaled that it was not predisposed to accept election results not to its liking.

Provisional results released by the JEC a week after election day gave a plurality of 40 percent to Colorado candidate Wasmosy versus 32 percent for Laíno, the Liberal candidate, and 24 percent for Encuentro's Caballero Vargas. The fact that the combined vote of the opposition, even by official count, exceeded that of the official candidate was of little consequence since there was no provision for a run-off election. The opposition total for the Congress, however, was another matter. In the case of the Senate, the five-seat margin for the opposition projected the day after the election was holding a week later; but the 4-seat majority for the opposition in the lower house projected early on by the JEC and confirmed by Saka had given way by May 17 to a two-seat majority for the Colorados. Opposition outrage had little resonance at that point as most election monitors had left and Paraguay had slipped elsewhere from news coverage and public consciousness. Meanwhile, echoing pre-election threats, Colorado Vice President-elect Angel Seifart warned that the Colorados would use force if necessary to defend the "results of the elections."

By June 2, however, when the Congress declared electoral results final, the opposition majority in the Congress (five seats in the Senate, four in the House) had been restored. Perhaps the turnabout in the vote count had been influenced in some way by foreign or international pressure. The primary reason, however, was the resolve of the major opposition parties to boycott the Congress unless they were able to occupy the seats they were confident they had won, and their agreement to concede the presidential election if the Congressional result was respected. The Colorados were not prepared to face the public embarrassment of a boycott by the Congressional opposition.

Despite the contextual and procedural problems surrounding Paraguay's 1993 election, the importance of those elections should not be understated. The prospect of such elections gave purpose to the mobilization of a new generation and to their determination that freedom of expression and assembly should be respected. And the electoral process, flawed as it was, gave the opposition a leverage point from which to extract concessions. By 1996, the judiciary and the electoral tribunal had undergone major reform in the direction of transparency and expanded participation.

## A Learning Process

There are a number of hard lessons to be learned from Paraguay's 1993 elections. Among them:

1. For opposition forces pushing against the odds for a democratic opening, the rule demonstrated elsewhere in potentially transitional cases is reinforced by the outcome here. That is, absent provision for a run-off election, only a united opposition stands a reasonable chance of prevailing over an entrenched authoritarian government.
2. While public opinion polling may serve as a hedge against governmental fraud and abuse, it may also become a tool for would-be power abusers. This case shows how readily exit polling and premature projection of results, especially in conjunction with convenient communications failures, might be used to pre-empt an actual vote count and create a fait accompli.
3. In cases of potential transition, election observers and other would-be legitimators should insist that there be no such Catch-22 as control of electoral procedures, including computation of ballots and resolution of disputes, by incumbent governments that are also contenders in the elections.
4. Finally, election monitors should be very cautious about how we permit our roles and our presence to be used. It is not enough to cover ourselves with a balanced report, when we know full well that it will be used in an unbalanced way.

Relative orderliness on election days pales to insignificance when it has been demonstrated that what we are observing is an election show rather than a genuine contest whose outcome is uncertain. Election shows are not new to Latin America or even to Paraguay. Stroessner had himself duly reelected every five years. What made the election so different this time was that the opposition parties and the voters chose to take it seriously. Can election observers take it any less seriously without becoming accomplices in giving "democracy" once again a bad name?

## Chapter 17

# Magic Realism and Mexican Elections

*In truly democratic elections,*
*all money is foreign.*

*With the help of a great many adjectives*
*(limited, tutelary, illiberal, etc.) democracy*
*has become almost universal.*

*CONTRARY TO EXPECTATIONS,* the only Mexican warlord on the rampage during the week of that country's benchmark municipal and congressional elections in 1997 was Popocatépetl. Its eruption, adding tons of ash to Mexico City's already highly visible air, was its most dramatic since the Institutional Revolutionary Party (PRI) started its unbroken and until recently unchallenged tenure in power sixty-eight years before — a preview, perhaps, of the message voters were to deliver on July 6.

Carlos Fuentes, interpreter laureate of the Mexican soul, declared that Cuauhtémoc, having lost the city to Spanish conquistadors in 1521, had come back to reclaim it. Cuauhtémoc Cárdenas, namesake of the defeated Aztec leader and son of Lázaro Cárdenas, most popular of the revolutionary party's former presidents, swept the first mayoralty election of the world's largest city with almost half of the votes cast — in a well populated field of candidates, a landslide. His party, the Revolutionary Democratic Party (PRD), formed by a PRI schism and a merger of small leftist parties, prevailed in the Federal District's legislative body by a wide margin.

Together the PRD and the National Action Party (PAN), the latter traditionally representing business and Roman Catholic Church interests but with a broadening base particularly in the North, deprived the PRI of the majority it had always enjoyed in the lower house of Congress. In the Senate, there were too few seats at stake for PRI control to be put at risk, but under new electoral laws all seats are to be contested in the year 2000, and PRI confidence is severely shaken.

Cárdenas, a mild-mannered, gracious, even seemingly modest civil engineer, had challenged PRI candidate Carlos Salinas in 1988 and was widely believed to have been denied the presidency by fraud. Since that time, as both the PAN and the PRD mounted stronger regional challenges and encountered a smorgasbord of obstructionist practices, Mexican elections have come under greater scrutiny.

## Elections in a Fishbowl

The PRI, weakened by a Job-like barrage of disasters — internal schisms, assassinations of leaders, currency collapse, corruption scandals involving narcotraffic, and mounting social unrest, expressed in the capital through strikes and demonstrations (some four thousand in 1996) and in the South through real or virtual guerrilla activity — has been unable to resist domestic and foreign pressures for electoral reform, including formation of a newly non-partisan Federal Elections Institute (IFE). The IFE, during the summer of 1997, oversaw the credentialing and training of more than 1,400 election observers, most of them Mexican but about 320 of them "foreign visitors."

I was one of the 135 foreigners, from the US, Canada, South America, the European Community, even Africa and Asia, invited by the national nonpartisan organization Alianza Cívica, or Civic Alliance. As election day approached, teams of observers fanned out across the country, particularly covering areas where races were expected to be close and where violence, intimidation, or ballot tampering had been reported in the past. My election-day team of two American academics, two Canadians (an artist and an Episcopal archbishop), an Argentine businessman, and a local school teacher — visited forty-four voting stations in nineteen precincts in the state of Tlaxcala.

Overall impressions within our micro-brigade as well as among observers around the country varied somewhat by age and experience, younger observers being more conscious of the problems while the more seasoned were more impressed by the progress achieved. We observed a few cases of ill-prepared precinct officials, incomplete party representation, inadequate sealing of ballot boxes, campaign propaganda in the vicinity of voting precincts, violations (perhaps innocent ones) of ballot secrecy, apparent attempts to vote more than once (attempts that were in fact resisted by precinct officials), ink for staining fingers after voting that often failed to work properly, and finally and more seriously what appeared to be attempts at voter intimidation: unauthorized, thug-like characters (dark glasses worn indoors conveyed the mood) hanging around voting stations. On balance, however, what we saw was an orderly, well-run and monitored process in which officers, from IFE central controls to the precinct level, were conscientious and competent, and voters, turning out in record numbers for a mid-term election (58 percent of those eligible), participated with new hope and enthusiasm.

Elsewhere the outcome was much the same, though a few major races were challenged, including the governorship of Campeche. For the Alianza Cívica and its invited foreign election observers, the most chilling event took place on the second day after elections. Observers who had been posted to different parts of the country had been brought together on the premises of an NGO for a major press conference. Suddenly, two men flashing police badges (of the *judiciales*, or federal judicial police) burst into the courtyard, seized one of the observers, an American, dragged him out and threw him into an unmarked vehicle where more police were waiting. They drove him around for a while, interrogating him, roughing him up, taking all his money (about $300) and finally dropping him several blocks from the site of the press conference.

Alianza Cívica viewed the event as remarkably straightforward government intimidation, albeit with a little freelance profit-taking on the side. In such a case, though, one could not be sure where the buck stopped. The kind of indiscipline, even anarchy, among security forces (and still protected and contracted ex-security forces) that was once a media caricature seems now to have a greater measure of reality.

## Scoring the Game of Spin

Observers had been braced for disturbances in the poorer, more largely indigenous and conflict-ridden South, which indeed occurred, though on a lesser scale than many had feared. The relatively new guerrilla organization Popular Revolutionary Army (EPR), active particularly in the states of Oaxaca and Guerrero, had declared a truce for the electoral season and stuck to it. In Chiapas, where counterinsurgency operations had taken a toll of more than one hundred casualties over the last year, the Maya-based Zapatista Liberation Army had pledged to boycott elections. The government confirmed its inclination to confrontation and intimidation in the region by sending in some three thousand troops shortly before the elections. The Zapatistas responded in kind by seizing and burning ballot boxes and otherwise engaging in electoral sabotage. For the Mayan population in general it appeared a sad waste of opportunity for more creative activism, and for Subcomandante Marcos, commander of the Zapatista rebels, in particular a sullying of his reputation for public relations genius.

While it might be said that the Zapatistas had a fair hand (at least in the sense of sympathetic international attention) and played it badly, the PRI government managed in the now globalized arena for the election to make the most of a bad hand, claiming a victory for its electoral reform and democratization process. That positive media spin served as a perceptual buffer to the actual losses suffered by the PRI, and the tight focus on election-day procedures distracted attention from more serious campaign infractions and from obstacles to democratization that may or may not be legal.

## Tilting the Playing Field

Pressure on members of PRI-controlled unions may not have been visible at voting booths, but it was so clumsily handled that, at least in the federal district, it generated a powerful backlash. Taxi drivers organized by the Central Labor Federation (CTM) were angry enough to tell anyone who would listen that they were voting PRD out of resentment of having several days' pay, or even their jobs, held in the balance if they failed to donate time to deliver PRI loyalists to rallies and to the polls. Sidewalk vendors and others in need of licenses or subsidies were also angry about threatened fines or withholdings if they failed to attend PRI rallies.

Other tactics that have tilted the playing field over the years were not necessarily illegal — after all, the PRI was making the laws — but testify both to the wealth of means of subverting democracy and to the political acuity that, along with the tangible popular gains of revolution and the more lasting intangible ones, has made the PRI the world's most durable political party. One such tactic has been generating or co-opting minor parties to fill any inviting vacuum on the political spectrum and to split the otherwise threatening opposition. A crude specimen, the Cardenista Party, designed to draw votes away from the PRD, failed miserably, but the Workers' Party (PT) proved rather more useful, retaining the 2 percent vote that entitles it to congressional representation.

The new Green Party (PVEM), which garnered almost 4 percent of the vote, aroused suspicion among some accustomed to divide-and-conquer or "brilliant pebbles" (confuse-the-voter) tactics, as its leadership derived largely from the PRI while its vote was presumed to have cut more deeply into the PRD constituency. But European Community Greens who had investigated and nurtured it believed it would play a genuinely independent and wholesome role in the Congress, which has proved in fact to be the case.

Long accused of diverting public funds to partisan purpose, the PRI succumbed this time to opposition demands for a formula for generalizing public subsidy. The subsidy may, in fact, have proven advantageous to opposition parties, though the PRI, with by far the greatest congressional representation, received the largest allocation, and amounts in general were so high as to be seen as abusive to the taxpayer.

As in the US, however, public subsidy has not displaced private subsidy. In Mexico, as in the US, it has become more difficult for parties and candidates to get away with buying votes; but high rollers, domestic and foreign, who seek to influence Mexican policy, have found it easier, cheaper and more efficient to buy candidates and elected officials. PRI financial records, unearthed in response to a PRD challenge to the declared PRI gubernatorial victory of candidate Roberto Madrazo Pintado in Tabasco in 1994, indicated that the Madrazo campaign had spent about $70 million (sixty times the legal limit) on the race. Though the documents were authenticated by the Attorney General, the investigation ordered by the Supreme Court has yet to bear fruit.

## The Triumph of the Caricature

The Mexican status quo might have survived exposure of unedifying campaign practices and of mounting financial corruption. It might even have ridden out a few more loops on the roller coaster of economic globalization. The revolution and the party that grew out of it had in fact produced a highly resilient system, utterly unrelated to the caricature that pervaded the US media. The disaster that has befallen Mexico since the mid-1980s is that of the loss of its uniqueness, the absorption of influences and responses to pressures from elsewhere in the hemisphere to such an extent that it has finally come to resemble the caricature.

Mexico, the first country of Mesoamerica to experience revolution, sought in the late 1970s and the early 1980s to offer at least moral support to Central American states whose time seemed to have come. Since then, though, Mexico has lost the last of the moorings laid by its own revolution and so has been dashed about by the backwash of failed revolutions farther south. The fate of more than 470 PRD leaders murdered since the founding of the party in 1989 would have been a predictable fate of democratic reformers until recently in Guatemala or El Salvador, but not in Mexico.

Mexico has long been famous for the *mordida,* or petty bribe, but such bribery seems almost democratic, or at least redistributive, compared to the scale of corruption that has come into play of late. The kind of corruption that has placed a wretchedly poor country about seventh in the world in number of billionaires (at least twenty-four) began with the oil crisis of the 1970s but found its greatest impetus in the privatizations that got under way in the 1980s and the drug trafficking of the 1990s.

Each of these major influences is exogenous in origin. The transplantation of big-time narcotrafficking has been dubbed the Colombianization of Mexico. But to blame Colombia would miss the point. It was US policymakers who chose not to understand the fallacy of a supply-side strategy for a war against a cash crop in inflexible demand. So long as demand persists and the "war" keeps profits in the stratosphere, the shutdown of production or transit operations in one area can only mean the opening of new theaters of operation.

Perhaps the most demoralizing of recent developments — assassinations at political altitudes where evidence evanesces — should be regarded as North Americanization. Mexico has always had more than its share of violence — bar fights and bandits and brawls in broad daylight — but not since the revolutionary era had it reached into the process of presidential succession. The candidacy of Luis Donaldo Colosio — young, charismatic, idealistic — for the presidency in 1994 had aroused new hopes that the PRI might actually be reborn as a democratic party attuned to the needs of the common people. His assassination, followed in short order by that of José Luis Ruiz Massieu, PRI congressional leader, had an effect on the Mexican polity not unlike that of the assassinations in the US in the 1960s. Many lost all faith at that point not only in the PRI but more broadly in the government and the system that sustained it.

The elections of 1997 did not restore faith to all who had lost it. But the amount of optimism available to be tapped in a country that has suffered so much in so short a time is truly remarkable. Perhaps it has to do with the fact that while most of us settle for virtual reality, Latin America insists on the higher realm of magic realism.

## Magic Realism and the Mexican Miracle

Only in the realm of magic realism would the chronicle of the death of an era be foretold by the eruption of a dormant volcano and the passing of the last living symbol of that era: Fidel Velásquez, ninety-seven-year-old leader of the PRI's central labor federation. To compound the other-worldliness of the setting, news of the election results had to compete with the news of the death of the country's most wanted drug warlord, Amado Carrillo Fuentes. He reportedly died at the hands of a plastic surgeon while having his face remodeled. At any rate a corpse with blurred features bounced around and came to rest with the US Drug Enforcement Agency. We are not likely to get the full story from the media because the surgeon and others who attended him were murdered before they could be questioned; but I imagine novelist Gabriel García Márquez could handle it.

Some aspects of the electoral outcome also suggest magic realism. First World governments and the financial interests they represent had been pressing the PRI toward allowing greater competitiveness, the general assumption having been that the advantages would fall to the business-friendly PAN. (The PAN candidate had a strong early lead in the Mexico City mayoral race.) The PRD was thus able to slip in, as Mexicologist Martin Needler put it, under the PAN's radar shadow. Potentates and profit-takers were geared to react to competitiveness or the lack of it rather than straightforwardly to leftward or rightward movements in the political spectrum; so instead of the guarded official language and money market mayhem that might have been expected to accompany a left-of-center victory, there were laudatory words and upward adjustments in Mexican stock market activity and peso value.

Cárdenas would need more than magic to govern Mexico City. He had little time (two and a half years until the presidential campaign was to get underway), high expectations to fulfill, and few resources at his command. The federal government, whose leaders' interests hardly lie in promoting Cárdenas, controlled the city's police force and a major portion of its budget. The choices left to the mayor were not easy ones.

Sad to say, the most realistic learning experience of the elections of 1997 may have been that of the children who participated in the UNICEF training poll. UNICEF's noble intent was to teach children the virtues of political participation while linking that participation to the protection of rights. But the exercise turned out to be more realistic, surely, than had been intended. The ballot offered them no candidates, but a choice among rights such as to health, education, housing, potable water, breathable air, freedom of expression, freedom from abuse and discrimination, and freedom from premature participation in the workforce. In other words, what children might have learned from the exercise is that unless we all learn how to use political participation to change social and economic direction we will continue for the indeterminate future to find ourselves choosing among rights rather than enjoying all the rights to which we should consider ourselves intrinsically entitled.

Mexico's elections of 1997 represent real gains. The country acquired a three-party system with the immediate promise of new representation in legislative decision making. The all-important capital city received a popularly elected mayor. There was reason to hope for real competition at all levels in the year 2000. Still, Mexico needs a miracle.

Economists, feeling omnipotent these days, like to speak of miracles every time an economy that has been trashed begins to rebound. (Where else could it go from the bottom?) And Mexico has had more than its share of economic trashings to rebound from. But there is a Mexican miracle; it is that despite trials worthy of Job visited upon them at ever shorter intervals by economists and bureaucrats, politicians and profiteers, and all manner of large- and small-scale thugs, most people manage somehow to survive and to create and procreate and even to keep hope and humor alive.

# Part V: Input Democracy and the Unemployed State
## Suggested Readings

Black, Jan Knippers. *Development in Theory and Practice: Paradigms and Paradoxes*. Boulder, CO: Westview Press, 1999.

Boyer, Robert and Daniel Drache, eds. *State Against Markets: The Limits of Globalization*. London and New York: Routledge, 1996.

Cavanagh, John and Richard Barnet. *Global Dreams: Imperial Corporations and the New World Order*. New York: Touchstone Books/ Simon and Schuster, 1995.

Chomsky, Noam. *Deterring Democracy*. London: Verso, 1991.

Chomsky, Noam and Edward S. Herman. *The Political Economy of Human Rights, Vol. 1, The Washington Connection and Third World Fascism*. Boston: South End Press, 1979.

Crook, Clive. "The Future of the State," *The Economist*, September 20, 1997, pp. 55–57.

Domínguez, Jorge and Abraham Lowenthal. *Constructing Democratic Governance*. Baltimore: Johns Hopkins University Press, 1997.

Gills, Barry, ed. "Globalization and the Politics of Resistance," *New Political Economy*, Special Issue, Vol. 2, No. 1, March 1997.

Gills, Barry, Joel Ricamora, and Richard Wilson, eds. *Low Intensity Democracy: Political Power in the New World Order*. London: Pluto Press, 1993.

Haggard, Stephan. *Developing Nations and the Politics of Global Integration*. Washington DC: Brookings Institution, 1995.

Hahn, Jeffrey W., ed. *Democratization in Russia: The Development of Legislative Institutions*. Armonk, NY: M.E. Sharpe, 1996.

Kelly, Phil, ed. *Democracy in Latin America*. Boulder, CO: Westview Press, 1998.

Lambert, Rob. "Bargaining on Stability: Indonesia's New Labor Movement: Class Interests, State Authority and Global Trade" presented at the International Conference on Non-State Actors and Authority in the Global System, Oct. 31–Nov. 1, 1997. University of Warwick, UK.

Needler, Martin C. *Identity, Interest and Ideology: An Introduction to Politics*. New York: Praeger, 1996.

*Our Global Neighborhood. The Report of the Commission on Global Governance*. Oxford: Oxford University Press, 1995.

Payne, Anthony and Paul Sutton. *Modern Caribbean Politics*. Baltimore: Johns Hopkins University Press, 1993.

Reich, Robert B. *Locked in the Cabinet*. New York: Knopf, 1997.

Robinson, William. *A Faustian Bargain*. Boulder, CO: Westview Press, 1992.

Sassen, Saskia. *Losing Control? Sovereignty in an Age of Globalization.* New York: Columbia University Press, 1996.

Schuman, Michael. *Towards a Global Village: International Community Development Initiatives.* London: Pluto Press, 1994.

Stepan, Alfred and Juan Linz, eds. *The Breakdown of Democratic Regimes: Europe.* Baltimore: Johns Hopkins University Press, 1978.

Stepan, Alfred and Juan Linz, eds. *Problems of Democratic Transition and Consolidation.* Baltimore: Johns Hopkins University Press, 1996.

Strange, Susan. *The Retreat of the State: The Diffusion of Power in the World Economy.* Cambridge: Cambridge University Press, 1996.

Walker, Thomas W., ed. *Nicaragua Without Illusions: Regime Transition and Structural Adjustment in the 1990s.* Wilmington, DE: Scholarly Resources, 1997.

Whitehead, Laurence. *The International Dimensions of Democratization: Europe and the Americas.* Oxford: Oxford University Press, 1996.

Wronka, Joseph. *Human Rights and Social Policy in the 21st Century.* Washington DC: University Press of America, 1992.

Asunción, Paraguay

# Part VI

# Security States and States of Insecurity

*The most insecure states, classes, and individuals are those that have the most to lose.*

*Don't let people mistreat you; they'll never forgive you for it.*
*Forgiveness is easier for the abused than for the abuser.*
*For the abuser, forgiving anyone, including himself,*
*must begin with acknowledging guilt and assuming responsibility.*

*THE STORY IS* told of a little Polish grandmother trying to enter the United States in the heyday of McCarthyism. A bored bureaucrat recites the standard security question, "Do you intend to overthrow the US government by force or violence?" With dawning wonder, she asks, "Could I?"

Operative definitions of security and insecurity and the official concerns and policy prescriptions flowing from those definitions have always been set by those who were in absolute terms the most secure. Thus the prevailing concept of security has been a highly elastic one in which the most insecure states, classes, and individuals are those who have the most to lose. The idea of what is to be secured stretches to encompass not only what the "haves" have, but what they think they have and what they think they should have. Perhaps the Reagan Administration's alarm in the 1980s that Harlingen, Texas, might be invaded by Nicaragua was taken with a grain of salt; but, in general, the position has been accepted straight-facedly and expressed in public expenditure that the richest and the most powerful states and persons are sorely threatened by the poorest and the weakest.

Emerging from World War II with some 50 percent of the world's wealth and only 3.6 percent of its population, the United States was obsessed with security. And at one time or another it made repressive authoritarian security states of most of its clients. Likewise the Soviet Union, trying to hold together an expansive, continental empire, devoted so much of its resource base to security that it finally imploded. For the largest shard of that union, Russia, such paranoia is no longer affordable. In fact, the Russians have been selling their arms on a massive scale to the Chinese. The US, now suffering from an enemy shortage, is forced into a Keynesian rationalization (job creation) for creating and maintaining burdensome military budgets and subsidizing arms sales.

Good news on the arms control front — the signing by 125 nations on December 3, 1997, in Ottawa of a treaty banning land mines — was dampened by the fact that the US, Russia, and China were not among the signatories.[1] The US continues to lead the world in arms sales, its share in the global market having increased from 25 percent in the late 1980s to 52 percent in 1996. The size of the market has shrunk by more than half during that period, however, as Russia, apart from major sales ($9.1 billion) in 1995, mainly to China, has almost dropped out of the business.

In August 1997, the United States lifted its twenty-year ban on the sale of sophisticated weapons to Latin America. The expansion of NATO is also expected to give a boost to US and Western European arms sales. NATO requires that each of its members invest at least 3 percent of GDP in national defense. The NGO in the forefront of lobbying efforts in the US, the US Committee to Expand NATO, was headed by Bruce Jackson, director of Strategic Planning for Lockheed-Martin; a major arms manufacturer, Lockheed-Martin, incidentally, had contributed $2.3 million to political campaigns in 1996.[2]

China, for its part, is clearly in an expansive mood. Its leadership now shows little patience with those within its borders or on its periphery who would question their authority or their priorities. And their highest priority appears to be that of opening markets without opening minds — at least to new political ideas and ambitions. Thus, China poses both a formidable obstacle to the spread of democracy, even of "virtual" or input democracy, and a propaganda challenge for those to whom "democratization" was essentially a cover for prying markets open.

The democratization thrust of First World governments and financial institutions represents a strange-bedfellow seduction, or a double con. Those genuinely concerned about freedom for people understand that they have no clout without the backing of big money. Those primarily concerned about freedom for money find it easier to get government assistance for leveraging market reforms and designing congenial commercial codes in transitional states if the project is sold as promoting democracy.

But the arrangement breaks down when target governments refuse to go along. When goals clash and bedfellows become estranged, the monied interests almost always win. In those cases, security states reappear and traditional human rights concerns, about freedom from persecution for political beliefs and associations, come to the fore.

Outrage over the prime-time massacre of unarmed pro-democracy students in Beijing's Tiananmen Square in 1989 and the increasing suffocation of Tibetan tradition has given way in the 1990s to hushed embarrassment, as high-rollers and the governments on their payrolls become fixated on a market of a billion consumers and low-wage workers. Likewise for countries on the Chinese periphery, support from the West for political freedom and human rights will likely become ever harder to muster.

The Taiwanese and their allies have been given notice of China's intentions through missile "tests" and other military maneuvers since mid-1995; and the huge digital clock in Tiananmen Square that for years counted down to Hong Kong's 1997 return to Chinese suzerainty denoted an unambiguous attitude. Western governments and international agencies had little to say about authoritarianism in Indonesia until the financial crisis of 1997–98 made President Suharto's position untenable; and questionable practices in other emerging markets of the East and Southeast have drawn little attention. But the courage and tenacity of Burma's democratic movement, and especially of its leader Aung San Suu Kyi, have made hypocrisy more costly for Western leaders and have energized those in the West who are serious about human rights.

In South America's Southern Cone, official violence has diminished but has not disappeared. Few of the torturers and executioners of the period of militocracy have been called to task for past crimes, and few civilians want seriously to test the durability of the social truce. Meanwhile, freelance violence has exploded, deepening the tendency to anomie and social isolation. Latin America is both richer and poorer than it was during the last brief flowering of democracy some three decades ago — a consequence of trends both regional and global and of policy decisions, not of policy failures. The Latin American states are not in danger of disintegrating in the manner of East European and Central Asian ones, but — as in the United States — their societies are fragmenting nonetheless, between those made insecure by opulence and those for whom security means nothing left to lose.

Likewise in South Africa and the neighboring so-called front-line states, official violence has for the most part been supplanted by private, syndicated or anomic, street crime. While the end of apartheid and the advent of Black majority rule has been accepted with relatively good grace by most whites and coloreds in South Africa, street crime has raised tensions once again and threatened the implementation of the all-important reconstruction and development program. Elsewhere in the region, the combination of years of drought and of social conflict with the requirements of structural adjustment programs have made food security — that is, the avoidance of starvation — a matter of overriding concern.

"The war to end all wars," as US President Woodrow Wilson referred to World War I did not end them, nor did World War II or the Cold War. More than fifty million people have been killed by war since 1945. War itself remains a major threat to human security, as do official and freelance violence, disease, and starvation. In most parts of the world, however, in the late 1990s, concerns about insecurity were expressed most frequently in connection with jobs. It had finally become unavoidably clear that the flip side of flexibility for owners and managers is inflexibility — the loss of rights and options — for employees.

For several years, in the late 1980s and early 1990s, the job and wages shrinkage accompanying globalization was ignored or denied by the money-movers, the politicians who had bought in or been bought, and the major media, or treated as an aberration. Now that the trend is beyond deniability, it is being treated as it if were inevitable and, in fact — in the long term — in the general interest.

The job insecurity that begins at the bottom of the pecking order necessarily moves up the corporate ladder. But the anxieties of the late 1990s were not simply about job security; they were also about the fact that the shrinking paycheck was virtually the only security.

Flexibility for globe-trotting business has also come to mean inflexibility for down-sized governments; even the most popularly based ones were engaged in the trimming of benefits and the dismantling of social services and safety nets. For so many, then, without extended family systems to fall back on, maintaining a livelihood had become a daily high-wire act.

Security does not lie in a wall or a missile or a gun. It lies in the reasonable expectation of being able to maintain dignity and human connectedness from day to day.

## The Face of Security

Norway, though relatively poor, was almost 100 percent literate at the beginning of the twentieth century. By 1913, the country had an electoral system characterized by universal suffrage. In 1997, women held 39 percent of the parliamentary seats, as opposed to 11 percent in the United States.

Public expenditure on education in the mid-1990s was more than 9 percent of GDP, about twice that of the United States. There were eight times as many books published per capita, but less than half the printing and writing paper consumed. Fifty-six percent of the work force was represented by unions as opposed to 16 percent in the United States.

Norway, in 1997, had the lowest murder rate of any country of the world. Under the national health service, coverage was universal and virtually free. Norway's total expenditure on health, as a percentage of GDP, is less than two-thirds that of the US, but the US maternal mortality rate is twice as high. On the birth of a child in Norway, either parent may take leave from work for forty-two weeks at 100 percent of salary or for one year at 80 percent.

In general, Norway's expenditures on social security benefits, as a percentage of GDP, are about twice those of the US. Of course, Norway's taxes are also high and highly progressive. The country's Labour Party government stepped down in 1997 leaving government in the hands of a coalition of three more conservative parties. The new government, promising more equitable taxes and more benefits, pledged to "work actively to create a warmer society in which people feel that they have a responsibility for each other."[3]

## Notes

1. Land mines laid for wars long lost continue to kill or maim some twenty-six thousand people, largely children, each year. It is estimated that there are some 100 million mines lying in wait in sixty-nine countries.
2. Bill Mesler, "NATO's New Arms Bazaar," *The Nation,* July 21, 1997, pp. 24–28.
3. Prime Minister Kjell Magne Bondevik, Inaugural Address by the Government to the Storting, Oct. 21, 1997.

## Chapter 18

# When Democracy Fails: The Legacy of Burma's Abortive Uprising

*Success and greatness lie on different tracks.*
*One does not achieve success with powerful enemies;*
*one does not achieve greatness without them.*

*The appeal of going for greatness is that you don't*
*have to compete with the opportunistic and the unscrupulous.*

*STRANGELY ENOUGH,* even on the eve of the massive popular uprising of 1988, the rhythm of life along the Irrawaddy River seemed not to have changed much since it was immortalized by Rudyard Kipling in his poem "The Road to Mandalay." On the fourteen-hour journey by train from Rangoon to Mandalay, the antique "upper class" coach was cooled in principle by ceiling fans. It was utterly devoid of shock absorbers, and inhabited by extended families of spiders, mice, and other assorted tropical fauna.

The coach also accommodated travelers of higher status. There were, for example, two senior monks, barefoot and draped in simple saffron robes; the younger monks or novices who attended to their needs prostrated themselves fully, touching their foreheads to the filthy floor of the coach, before withdrawing.

Across the aisle from the monks was a slender, middle-aged man in uniform. He too had an entourage of servants — mostly enlisted men. One of his orderlies lowered the heavy metal window beside him at the beginning of the trip, even though the heat was oppressive. The monks referred to him deferentially as "the General."

While the monks chewed on their betel nut in detached tranquillity and other passengers gazed through open windows at people and oxen at work in flooded rice paddies, the general appeared to be meditating or praying for hours on end, with clasped hands, closed eyes, and furrowed brow. Finally he stirred, and an orderly laid out for him a multi-course meal, kept piping hot in a portable, five-layered metal container. (There was no dining car; passengers bought from vendors at whistlestops along the way or brought their own meals, commonly a rice dish with fish paste wrapped in a leaf that served also as a plate.)

At that point the general began to take note of fellow passengers and even very graciously offered to share his tea. During the several remaining hours of the trip, before he alighted to a heel-clicking military welcome at Meiktila, some three hours short of Mandalay, he often stretched to peer out of the window ahead of and behind his own; but he never raised the metal sheet that shielded him from the world beyond our coach. The episode began to make sense when one of his attendants confided that he was the commander of the People's Police Force (PPF) in Rangoon. The next day a newspaper reported that Rangoon's police commander had been demoted and transferred. His superior, the director-general of the People's Police Force, had been fired and other PPF officers reprimanded in connection with an incident that had occurred during the student riots of the previous March.

Burma's official news agency was conceding for the first time that forty-one detainees had died in police custody. They had been squeezed into a single police van, along with thirty others who survived, and left for two hours after police, using tear gas, broke up a crown of demonstrators. An official inquiry found that they died of tear gas inhalation and suffocation. It was hard to imagine that our traveling companion — frail, contemplative, even genteel — was the villain of that piece, but in Burma many things are not as they appear.

The grim profile that emerged a couple of weeks later when the country caught the international media spotlight — the profile of a rigid military dictatorship, a tightly controlled socialist economy, and a population languishing in abject poverty — failed utterly to capture the ironies and eccentricities of the struggle and its setting. Burma certainly lacked most of the appurtenances of the modern world. Even the traces of eighteenth-century technology left by the British constituted an awkward overlay on a way of life that belonged to earlier centuries. But the country's heartland was exuberantly green and fertile, and compared, for example, to the grinding poverty in much of neighboring India or Bangladesh, Burma's slow-paced, unpolluted towns and villages seemed pleasant — almost idyllic — and the people remarkably healthy and animated.

If there were serious shortages, they must have been of the imported goods that middle classes everywhere find essential. The impact of inflation, however, deriving from a sinking currency and a thriving black market, was very real and disconcerting. The dollar's value on the black market was six times that of the official exchange rate, and those who dealt in money and other illegal goods and services showed little concern about being apprehended. Far from the kind of "tight ship" one might expect of a socialist military regime, business in Burma, legal or otherwise, bordered on anarchy. Government employees did not seem to take official regulations very seriously; in fact, they often volunteered advice on how to circumvent them. And illegal operations were profitably "protected" by the putative enforcers.

Foreigners were not allowed to travel overland by bus or taxi except by arrangement with the official agency, Tourist Burma; so drivers of the unauthorized taxis — actually modified pick-up trucks — that routinely hauled visitors over the strung-together potholes that passed for roads peeled off bribes at security checkpoints to uniformed officials who showed no hint of embarrassment about the transaction.

It almost seemed to work, but a government so cravenly corrupted could not hope to enjoy legitimacy. And what little authority it retained was being squandered by its heavy-handed and unimaginative response to opposition. Even so, on the part of such a graceful and gentle-spirited people, an uprising as massive and unrelenting as that of August 1988 was incongruous.

## Mounting Resistance to Militarism

A province of British India until World War II, Burma has had little experience with democracy. Members of the same coterie of rebels who supported the Japanese invasion in 1942, believing the Japanese to be liberators, then supported the British in 1945 in expelling the Japanese, established the first government of independent Burma, a multi-party, parliamentary one, in 1948. Civilian rule was weakened over the years, however, as the military, called upon to suppress separatist movements among ethnic minorities around the fringes of the national territory, grew bolder.

In 1952, armed forces commander General Ne Win, under criticism for brutality in the suppression of minority tribes, turned on his erstwhile colleague, U Nu, the prime minister, and deposed him. Ne Win established a new party, the Burma Socialist Programme Party (BSPP), outlawing all others; but his power rested for the most part on an increasingly privileged military establishment.

Ethnic minorities, in some cases led by warlords and funded by traffic in opium and heroin, continued to engage the forces of the central government. The struggle was also joined early on by the country's educational and religious institutions. Students and Buddhist monks, prominent in the burgeoning resistance movement in 1988, were among those who had resisted the coup d'état thirty-five years earlier and who had suffered scores of casualties. Grievances mounted as Ne Win's troops burned down the student union building and outlawed student organizations. The riots that erupted at the national university in Rangoon in March 1988 left some three hundred dead and added hundreds more to the list of political prisoners students sought to free. So anti-government rioting broke out again in June, and Rangoon remained under curfew until the end of the month.

The university remained closed in July, but faculty sources reported that the students had actually won the latest showdown; the government had yielded to many of their demands, including demands for the release of political prisoners. I asked a professor who also held a responsible government position at that time if her co-workers in the ministry held her under suspicion because of her university connection. On the contrary, she said, they were all in sympathy with the students.

Nor was contempt for the government limited to an urban middle class; rather, it drew upon a wellspring of frustration that had no apparent class or regional bounds. In the small town that is present-day Pagan, where five thousand Buddhist temples rise from the plain in silent tribute to an ancient civilization, a horse-carriage driver recited in some detail and with barely suppressed anger the recent history of government atrocities against the opposition.

Security forces generally kept a low profile during the month of July. On July 22, 1988, however, heavily armed troops lined the major thoroughfares of Rangoon in preparation for an extraordinary congress of the ruling party, called to consider economic and political reforms. At the congress, General Ne Win, seventy-seven years old, stunned his compatriots and the world by announcing his resignation from the chairmanship of the party. (He had earlier stepped down from the presidency, but without relinquishing authority.)

To the assembled leaders, that must have sounded like partycide, because they selected, as a successor to Ne Win, the one man most likely to hold the line against democratization. Retired General Sein Lwin, BSPP Joint Secretary and the person responsible for riot police and internal security since the coup d'état of 1962, was also the choice most certain to bring students, monks, and other groups back into the streets. In fact strikes and demonstration on the streets of Rangoon, alternating with government crackdowns, spread in August to Mandalay and other cities. The tens of thousands of demonstrators, had become hundreds of thousands, and more than a thousand had been killed.

Meanwhile the general had been replaced by a reputedly moderate civilian politician; but he was overthrown on September 18 by the military, under the leadership of General Sau Maung, who unleashed a new reign of terror. Some three thousand militants of the democratic movement, mainly students, were murdered and more than ten thousand others fled into exile, some to Europe and North America, but many to the rugged region along the Thai border controlled by ethnically distinct and rebellious hill tribes, united in the National Democratic Front in opposition to military rule.

Military leaders organized a new junta, known as the State Law and Order Restoration Council (SLORC). The SLORC set about to open up the economy, beginning with characteristic grace, by offering resource concessions to the Thai military in exchange for repatriation of Burmese exiles. The SLORC promised to schedule elections in the near future and even invited political parties to form and register; but all the while it maintained martial law, kept schools closed, and prohibited gatherings of more than five people.

Undaunted, Burmese democrats persevered into 1989 with their antigovernment demonstrations, led in particular by Aung San Suu Kyi, daughter of Burmese independence leader General Aung San, who was murdered in 1947 on the eve of statehood. Aung San Suu Kyi was placed under house arrest in July 1989, triggering further mass protests and mass arrests.

Much to the dismay of military leaders, the long-awaited elections in May 1990 produced a landslide victory (an 82 percent majority of parliamentary seats) for Aung San Suu Kyi's National League for Democracy. The elected assembly was never allowed to convene. The SLORC dug in its heels. It changed the name of the country to Myanmar (a change that many regime opponents have simply refused to recognize), but it did not change its form of government.

## A Protracted Struggle: Aung San Suu Kyi vs. the SLORC

In 1991, Aung San Suu Kyi's valiant efforts on behalf of democracy and human rights were recognized by the awarding of the Nobel Peace Prize; and that award brought her movement much needed foreign support. An international campaign for Aung San Suu Kyi's release, spearheaded by former Costa Rican President Oscar Arias and other Nobel Peace Laureates, finally bore fruit, and she was released in 1995.

Aung San Suu Kyi immediately and straightforwardly defied the conditions of her release, returning to the mobilization of her National League for Democracy and speaking out to all who would hear about the abuses and the illegitimacy of the Burmese junta. As the Association of Southeast Asian Nations (ASEAN) prepared to meet in mid-1995 with the adoption of observer status for Burma on the agenda, she mounted a campaign, with the help of support groups around the world[1] to block that adoption.

The campaign yielded a great deal of attention and outrage around the world about the oppression of the Burmese, but ultimately it failed. The ASEAN states (Brunei, Indonesia, Malaysia, the Philippines, Singapore, Thailand, and Vietnam), few of which could themselves pass any very stringent test of democratic standing, argued the utility of "constructive engagement" and the need to draw Burma away from dependence on China. China, of course, had a long head start and in fact had provided extensive military and economic assistance to the regime in recent years, but trade with and investments from Japan and the ASEAN countries were mounting sharply.

The European Union, the United States, Canada, and Australia mounted vigorous protests of the actions of ASEAN, but their own commitment to democratic conditionality fell short of effective economic sanctions. While the seriousness of some elements of the foreign affairs leadership of the Western states about resisting the Burmese dictatorship is beyond question, they appeared to have lost out once again to elements answering to more immediate material interests. The largest corporate investors in Burma in the late 1990s, Total and UNOCAL, were French- and US-based. Their gas pipeline construction, undertaken in partnership with SLORC, has displaced some thirty thousand people in more than fifty villages, and pressed villagers into unpaid labor.

The US Congress passed new legislation, signed into law by President Clinton in early October 1996, mandating the imposition of sanctions in the event of "large-scale repression." In fact, that same month Aung San Suu Kyi, attempting to hold a peaceful meeting of her National League for Democracy, was once again placed under house arrest and some eight hundred democracy activists were rounded up and arrested, but US investors and merchants were not deterred.

In May 1997, the United States moved closer to effective sanctions with an embargo against future US investment in Burma. Previous investment, like that of UNOCAL, was not affected, though a number of companies with lesser investments have in fact moved out. There are serious implications, however, for the interest of UNOCAL as of other foreign investors in Burma and elsewhere in a lawsuit pending in 1998 in the United States District Court for Central California. The opinion of Judge Richard A. Paez, issued on March 25, 1997, in the case of John Doe I vs. UNOCAL Corporation, denied the defendant's plea for dismissal. The ruling holds that despite arguments to the contrary with respect to jurisdiction, time lapse, sovereign status of the business partner, and other matters, those filing on behalf of Burmese farmers and their families are entitled to sue a US company in US courts for compensation for human rights violations allegedly committed by that company's governmental business partner.[2]

Changes in regime window-dressing — some shuffling of personnel and a new name, State Law and Development Council (SLDC), to replace SLORC — followed Burma's incorporation into ASEAN in July 1997. On the occasion of Burma's national holiday, November 24, Aung San Suu Kyi was allowed to entertain diplomats and supporters in her home; but she remained closely watched and other League leaders were continually harassed.

## Open Markets and Closed Minds

Meanwhile Burma's uniformed rulers are reconfirming the viability of the Chinese model — of free trade without free thought, of open markets and closed minds. Serene, timeless Burma has been switched onto fast-forward in material terms. High rises hover over graceful dilapidated British colonial buildings, and in streets once filled with people, animals, and carts, one can see irritated drivers growling into cellular phones while stuck in traffic jams.

Department stores that didn't exist in 1988 are filled with high-tech toys that most of the population a decade ago had yet to dream of. And there are buyers. Hard currency is more plentiful than ever before[3] — from foreign investment (some $6 billion since 1989) and the remittances of Burmese exiles (about $3 billion) and perhaps most of all from the heroin trade (global opium production has doubled since 1988 — Burma is the world's largest producer). But the bounty is not invested in human resources. The army, primary beneficiary of the new boom in trade and investment, has also, since 1988, absorbed more than 60 percent of the national budget. Only about a fourth of the children entering school go past the fourth grade. Nor does the bounty trickle down by other means; rather, it contributes to a growing gap between rich and poor. Most of the population of some forty-five million continues to live in poverty made all the more stark by the contrast.

## Notes

1. The Free Burma Coalition, launched by exiled graduate student Zar Ni, had chapters on at least ninety US campuses in 1996.
2. Lucien J. Dhooge, "A Close Shave in Burma: UNOCAL Corporation and Private Enterprise Liability for International Human Rights Violations," *University of North Carolina Journal of International Law and Commercial Regulations*, Vol. 24, Fall 1998, pp. 1–69.
3. That was the case at any rate until late 1997, when US and European embargoes and, more importantly, the generalized financial meltdown in East and Southeast Asia, began to take their toll. Currency values plummeted in Burma, as elsewhere in the region, at the end of the year.

## Chapter 19

# Anarchy at Street-Level: The New Security Threat in Southern Africa

*Before a people can chart its own future,*
*it must reconstruct its past — that is,*
*it must reinterpret a history fashioned by its oppressors.*

*APPROACHING THE* Johannesburg airport, the South African Airways pilot announced, "You are now completing the safest part of your journey. Drive carefully and lock your car doors." He might have been particularly mindful of the recent rash of vehicle hijackings (more than ten per day), but it appeared to be generally accepted by locals and visitors alike that Johannesburg is now the crime capital of the world.

The adoption of a new democratic and color-blind South African constitution in spring of 1996, just two years after the historic election that brought Nelson Mandela from prison to the presidency and broke the stranglehold of apartheid, passed almost unnoticed in the international media. The withdrawal of de Klerk's National Party from the cabinet in June might be seen as marking the final parenthesis around the transition period. At least in terms of global politics and perceptions, South Africa — and by extension its front-line neighbors who have undergone their own democratization or re-democratization processes — leaves to now re-writable history the heroic liberation struggle and becomes just another country with seemingly insuperable problems.[1] Perhaps the most intractable of those problems, and surely the one most threatening to the newly woven social fabric, will be that of freelance violence — street crime. A public opinion survey in 1997 found that 58 percent of the population considered crime a major problem, compared to only 6 percent in 1994.

# An Expanded Free-Fire Zone

Dormitories at Johannesburg's prestigious University of Witswatersrand have the ambiance of a high-security prison; getting out is almost as hard as getting in. Parking lot attendants at exits ask to see the car restarted with keys to ensure that it has not been hot-wired. Security guards are spread strategically around the campus. Even so, four participants in a conference I was attending — men, walking together in broad daylight — were assaulted and robbed.

Snuggled against the soaring cliffs of Table Mountain, Capetown, seat of the South African parliament, is one of the world's most enchanting port cities and an increasingly popular tourist destination. It does not yet share Johannesburg's reputation for crime infestation; but apart from the Victoria and Albert Waterfront, where security guards are omnipresent, the streets are deserted in the evenings. Residents claim that anyone on downtown streets after dark is probably either a tourist or a mugger.

The Cape has always had a reputation for being more tolerant and socially fluid than other regions of South Africa. But Blacks and Coloreds had been moved out of prime real estate to preserve it for Whites. Coloreds comprise more than half of the population of Capetown, but Blacks are moving in now from townships and homelands, looking for work. Squatter communities on the periphery of the city, and particularly around the airport, have a population already of some 750,000. Such a build-up is frightening to Whites and Coloreds, for whom crime is now a major concern. A university professor in the Cape told me that six of his friends had been murdered just in the last few years.

During the first nine months of 1997, an average of sixty-five murders were reported each day in South Africa, most of them in and around Johannesburg. Police had identified 481 criminal syndicates, many of them operated by former members of the state security forces.

Throughout Southern Africa cities are walled and gated one establishment at a time. Streets and sidewalks are regarded as a kind of free-fire zone. In the Namibian capital, Windhoek, hotel doors were operated from behind the reception desk. It was impossible to open them at any hour from the outside — good protection, one assumes, for the staff, though not necessarily for the guests.

In Mozambique's capital, Maputo, my husband and I were warned not to go out for a stroll, even in the daytime, and to be very careful of the kind of taxi we engaged.[2] Friends in the diplomatic community in Zambia were told not to go to downtown Lusaka at night, even in a car. The residence they had taken over from other European diplomats came with full-time maid and gardener and a twenty-four-hour security guard. Like most other European or expatriate homes, it was walled and gated, and windows and doors were double-barred. There was an electronic burglar-alarm system for the entire property, along with the pervasive "panic button" that is supposed to summon the police instantaneously. Inside the house, the hall leading to the bedrooms had an additional padlocked and alarm-wired "rape gate." Whether such systems are seen as practical precautions or as paranoia, the fear they reflect is very real and has real political and socioeconomic repercussions.

Even in Maun, Botswana, a rural town of rounded, thatched huts and mostly unpaved roads, from which safaris set off for the Okavango Delta, European expatriates complain about burglary. Of course, diplomats, expats, and tourists are by no means the most likely victims of freelance crime. Those most devastated in Southern Africa as elsewhere are the local under-classes, those who had been victimized already by prevailing economic and political systems and generally lack the wherewithal to protect themselves. A poll conducted by the Institute for Security Studies found that compared to 58 percent of Whites, 67 percent of Blacks and 84 percent of Coloreds in the Johannesburg metropolitan area felt unsafe at night in their neighborhoods.

Edward, a taxi driver in Victoria Falls, was a Shona from the southern part of Zimbabwe. His wife and three children still lived there, seven hundred kilometers away. He said it was really tough to live like this, as he was able to see his family only a few times a year; but it was better than what they had tried before — living together in Harare. The cost of everything — housing, transportation, water, electricity — was very high; but the worse problem was crime, and taxi drivers were particularly vulnerable. There was always a danger, he said, when he picked up a fare that he might be robbed at gunpoint.

In Namibia, for a newly independent government lacking both the resources and the unscrupulousness of its colonial predecessor, maintaining public order has been an acute problem. In some outlying areas, villagers have taken matters into their own hands, resorting to vigilante operations.

In Namibia, as in South Africa itself, it has been very hard for some of the freedom fighters, especially those who did not go into exile, but chose to stay and to face great risks, and in many cases great loss, to accept the idea of reconciliation, not only without revenge, but without any pretense of justice against the worst rights abusers. In a gentle voice, with wisdom and compassion welling from deep blue eyes, Buddy Wentworth says, "I really came to Namibia to kill White people." A Cape Colored, he had been active in the Communist Party and the ANC (African National Congress, the largest anti-Apartheid political organization, now the governing party in South Africa). When he was forced out of South Africa in 1969, he went to Namibia to fight for SWAPO. His first act as Deputy Minister of Education in the new Namibia was to ban corporal punishment in the schools. Things got out of hand during the first year or two of the new regime, as the only discipline that children had known had been removed, but then they settled down again. The same cannot yet be said of the lack of discipline on the streets, but

Buddy and his colleagues say that violence is not the solution; violence is the problem.

## The Legacy of Official Violence

Violence is by no means new to South Africa or its neighbors. The toxic residue of a half century of official violence — of violence instigated by White rulers — continues to poison relations and, in some areas, to generate open conflict among poor Blacks. Throughout the 1980s, RENAMO guerrillas spread terror among Mozambique peasants in an effort, organized and financed by the South African government, to bring down FRELIMO, the movement that led Mozambique to independence in 1975. RENAMO fighters are now being integrated into the Mozambique security forces, but the UN calculates that there remain some two million landmines, lying in wait like old enemies, along dusty country roads.

In South Africa itself, well into the period of transition to majority rule, unreconstructed security forces continued to subsidize the sabotage operations of Inkatha movement leader Mangosuthu Buthelezi in order to portray South Africa's struggle as essentially Black-on-Black. The deadly struggle still under way in Kwazulu-Natal province, between ANC and Inkatha Zulus, has spilled over into metal-working areas of the East Rand, or the east ridge, above Johannesburg. There migrant workers, ANC and Inkatha, from Kwazulu-Natal are housed like sardines in separate hostels in Black townships like Tokoza, Vosloorus, and Katlehong; and their battles, fought with guns, knives, machetes, and explosives, have engulfed the surrounding communities.

Entire communities — or remains of communities — are under the control, so to speak, of gangs representing one or the other of the warring parties, and even for "civilians" trying desperately not to be involved, being caught on the wrong side of a demarcation line can cost a life. More than sixteen thousand people were killed in the East Rand during the first half of the nineties. Even now, courageous Peace Committee mediators, absorbed since 1994 by Mandela's all-encompassing Reconstruction and Development Program, do not pretend that peace has been achieved — only that there is a tense and fragile kind of stability in the conflict zone.

Official violence and its legacies have been addressed, albeit delicately, by the new government's Truth and Reconciliation Commission. Delicately because many perpetrators of official violence have been grandfathered into their military and security forces positions and might still strike back somehow. Delicately also because anti-government violence, of which some prominent ANC members stand accused, was being addressed by the same commission. And delicately because there is a certain inherent instability in a reconciliation between the armed and the unarmed, the abuser and the victims.

Perhaps the weightiest "truth" is that, as in the cases of some supposedly "re-democratized" Latin American governments, the beasts of the *ancien régime* have yet to be defanged. Almost everybody is betting on the survival of the new social truce, but few are anxious to up the ante.

Like many other institutions that had served the apartheid regime so well, violence is now being privatized. The fact that the new, privatized kind of violence is more pervasive and less predictable does not make it more reprehensible than the more familiar, official kind, but it does make it an awful threat to the young vulnerable democracy. Such street-level anarchy is as certain as tyranny to dissolve community and to recreate apartheid, but an apartheid of the sort more common elsewhere in the world — an apartheid of many dimensions, based primarily on income inequality, or class, but also on language and culture, even on age and lifestyle. Finally, lacking inhabitable public space, we may come also to lack shared goals and visions and so increasingly to withdraw, each into his own physically and psychologically fortified enclosure.

# Notes

1. As in so much of the rest of the world, economic growth is proving to be a mixed blessing. *The Economist* (12/13–19/97) reported that a 3 percent GDP growth rate for 1996 was accomplished by a 1 percent shrinkage in the number of jobs in the formal sector. In late 1998, after hot money jitters had ricocheted from the collapsing markets of Asia to "emerging markets" elsewhere, including South Africa, it was estimated that one-third of the South African workforce was unemployed.
2. The worst was yet to come. Armed robbery was up 71 percent in 1996 over the previous year.

## Chapter 20

# Food Security: The Bottom Line for Africa's Front-line States

*In the Global Village real prices are international, real wages are local.*

"*THE WATER IS* coming down," an old man said, gazing across the bone-dry bed of the Okavango River. Since it clearly was not about to rain, my husband and I had trouble grasping the concept. Most of the flow of the Okavango, voluminous as it departs Angola, fans out and disappears into the delta in Botswana a few hundred miles north of the town of Maun. But this was an exceptionally bad year for Maun, and both the river bed and the town's reservoir had been dry for more than six months. In fact, rainfall had been low in much of the region for thirteen years, and some scientists were predicting that the drought would assume catastrophic proportions.

A bespectacled and pin-striped gentleman at Harry's Bar shoved his newspaper over to us with apologies that it contained no news. The headline announced a record-breaking drought — hardly news there at Riley's riverside hotel. Our companion, an employee of the postal service, speculated that this year's extended drought was a plot by Angola to squelch Botswana's burgeoning tourism industry. But travelers arriving from the north insisted, accurately as it turned out, that the water was coming down now from Angola and should reach Maun in a couple of days.

## Dealing with Drought

For much of the region's wildlife, the water was coming too late. The decaying carcasses of zebra, a half dozen of them within yards of each other in what was supposed to be a game preserve near Maun, was stark evidence of the severity of the drought; dry river beds, parched fields, and dusty roads were the rule rather than the exception all across southern Africa in the mid-1990s.

Some of the supposed wildlife across the way in Zambia and Zimbabwe had come up with their own ways of dealing with the drought — and perhaps also with the onslaught of tourists. When the tourists headed for the bush, the animal safaris headed for the resort hotels. We found elephants drinking from the swimming pool and romping over swings and slides in the playground at our hotel at Lake Kariba. Around Victoria Falls, the monkeys and baboons had become hooked on junk food — sandwiches and chips stolen from stunned guests at poolsides and patio restaurants.

The not-so-wild life has not fared so well. International organizations and bilateral agencies were at the ready in Harare, prepared to transfer large amounts of food aid at a moment's notice, but under their own laws and regulations they could not do so until President Mugabe declared a drought emergency. And that he was not prepared to do. A frustrated official of the UN Population Fund suggested that Mugabe's reticence stemmed from fears that a declaration of emergency might scare off foreign investors or even set off a stampede of fleeing capital, thereby undermining the currency and perhaps destabilizing the whole economy.

Drought is only one of several torments that have given rise to the peculiarly African issue of food security. Food security is also about civil strife and displaced populations, land tenure patterns and squatter's rights, agricultural productivity and crop diversification, trade, transportation, and comparative advantage, food prices and distribution systems. It is an issue at once infinitely complex and pristinely simple; it is about not starving.

## Land Tenure Problems

Adamson, at sixty-six a very senior citizen in his Ndebele village in northern Zimbabwe, sat quietly carving the wooden pieces of a traditional instrument while his wife and daughter replastered one of the round thatched huts in the family compound. The mud plaster is made from what appears to be the most durable prefabricated building material on the continent: termite hills. The women dig out chunks of the almost impenetrable stuff from the ruins of ancient termite cities, break it up and moisten it with the scarce water. Women are also responsible for making and maintaining the thatch roofs. And along with cooking, cleaning, and child care, they gather grasses for thatch and wood for fire and they haul water — in seasons like this from ever more distant places.

The compound had raised bins and round huts for storage. There was a separate hut for Adamson's married son and one for cooking during the rainy season. Cooking is usually outdoors and dishes are dried and sterilized in the sun. A covered hole in the earth handles garbage disposal, but there isn't much to dispose of. Life is low-impact and there is no litter to be seen. Unlike the teeming cities, traditional villages of southern Africa tend to be neat, clean, and orderly — and threatened with extinction.

Adamson was not worried. He had a broad, toothless, contagious smile; and of late he had something to smile about. His family was among the fortunate ones selected by the local Ndebele chief to receive land under the Mugabe government's land resettlement program. On ample plots villagers will grow corn, a traditional mainstay, and relatively drought-resistant millet, for local consumption.

Land reform or resettlement was taking place under one formula or another across much of southern Africa in the mid-1990s, but results were not always as intended. South Africa's ANC government let it be known early on that sharecroppers on large estates were to gain ownership of the land they worked. But implementation had been delayed and in the interim peevish landlords had been preemptively ejecting tenants from their land.

Namibia's independence struggle, against white-ruled South Africa, had most of the characteristics of a social revolution. The museum of the revolution in Windhoek is so like its counterparts in Havana and elsewhere that one is left to wonder if the archetype of revolution is really found in nature or only in the neatly structured minds of historians and social scientists. Even so, the country's new land tenure law falls far short of the revolutionary pattern.

Redistribution is to be undertaken only in cases of absentee-owned farmland and then only into the care of farmers with proven track records. Thus, it will benefit mid-level farmers rather than the landless. André De Pisano, an academic consultant on legislative matters, said there was no margin for error on production. As it is, only about 5 percent of the land is arable, and 90 percent of the food must be imported. Therefore the main consideration must be food security.

If food insecurity in Namibia can be blamed on the stinginess of Mother Nature, scarcity in Mozambique must be blamed on the folly of man. Land that was once sown with maize and manioc is now strewn with land mines — toxic residue of a decade of struggle against South Africa's RENAMO mercenaries — and resettlement proceeds with due caution. But in Mozambique even more than in most of southern Africa, scarcity and recovery are unevenly distributed.

## Pricing out the Hungry

Traditional markets in Mozambique are only now beginning to recover. But modern supermarkets are well stocked with foreign delicacies, processed and packaged goods offered at international prices. Elizabeth Sequeiros, offspring of Portuguese settlers and director of an NGO devoted to basic education, says there used to be money but nothing to buy. Now there is plenty to buy, but it is affordable only to those who have access to dollars. Mozambicans still call each other *irmão* (brother), but as Nicaraguans and others have learned, revolutionary comradeship is difficult to maintain in counter-revolutionary times — when jobs are scarce and one needs three of them just to make ends meet. (The theorists who tell us that the purpose of a globalized marketplace is to maintain competitive prices must not do their shopping in the Third World.)

Unaffordable food is imported with the foreign exchange proceeds of cash crops that have been exported — that is, with what remains of such proceeds after foreign debts have been serviced, or with additional borrowings premised on further "structural adjustment." The debt burden makes it ever more essential that what remains of arable land be devoted to export crops, though exporting more does not necessarily bring in more foreign exchange; since all less developed countries are induced to pursue the same strategy, world market prices for primary products they export continue to drop relative to imported manufactured goods.

Professor Naomi Wekwete, at the University of Zimbabwe's Institute of Development Studies, investigates the consequences of the structural adjustment programs that are the price of hard currency credit, the ante for staying in the global market poker game. She finds that even as the economy grows at an impressive clip, the standard of living of the majority deteriorates. Privatization, especially of public utilities, has generally meant the same lousy service at higher prices. Government services have deteriorated as well, due to budget shrinkage and downsizing, known in Harare as retrenchment.

In Africa, as elsewhere, the new burdens fall disproportionately on women. The services that for a time some women were paid by the government to provide to others — i.e., care for the young, the old, the sick — each must now provide unassisted to her own family and community while trying also to scare up new sources of income. The burden of increased responsibilities imposed by the downsizing of governments has been compounded by the scourge of HIV-AIDs. The epidemic that has put a whole planet at risk is at its most threatening in Eastern and southern Africa. Infection rates in 1998 in South Africa, Botswana, Zimbabwe, Kenya, Uganda, and Zambia ranged between 10 and 25 percent. Almost all of those infected were expected to die within ten years. The kind of campaign that might stem the spread and deal humanely with the sick and the orphaned remains a pipedream while international financial institutions keep the pressure on governments to cut social services in order to service debt. Most African governments were allocating less than $6 per person annually to health care, while basic life-extending drugs for AIDS victims cost more than $15,000 per patient per year.

Even the basic nutrition that might have strengthened resistance to more familiar diseases and more traditional threats to health becomes ever harder to come by as debt service needs and global investment prospects destine an ever greater portion of the arable land to serve as plantations for export crops. Those crops edge out food crops grown for local consumption, displacing families, dissolving communities, or at the very least driving the women, who have primary responsibility for food crops, to less fertile land farther from home and village. Returns from exports must be allocated first to foreign creditors and are not necessarily redistributed in any form to general populations, while import-derived inflation most assuredly is.

The ultimate Catch-22 with respect to food security is that the more African and other poor countries acquiesce to demands of creditors, the less they are able to meet their own basic needs on their own terms and with their own resources. And the more dependent they become, the harsher the blame and the penalty for that dependence. Austerity, viewed once as the problem, is touted now as the solution. But just as the debt crisis ceased to be a crisis once the banks' needs were being met, perhaps the issue of food security will lose its salience once police security becomes advanced enough to keep the hungry at a safe and respectable distance, out of sight of the shoppers at the well-stocked supermarkets.

## Recycled Poverty

*Jan Knippers Black*

Out of the bush in a distant land
A tiny ragamuffin band
Lunged at our car with outstretched hand
Beseeching gimmemoni

Back in the town, a well-dressed chap
Expressed chagrin at this mishap
Must be a generation gap
How crude to ask for money

Then after oh so brief a pause
He's looking for a Santa Claus
To make donations to his cause
In urgent need of money

There is a need that's now unmet
Some budget cuts we all regret
Drained services to deal with debt
The creditors want money

The president, with hat in hand
Has gone abroad to take a stand
In line to plead with the Big Man
The IMF has money

The IMF then looks around
To see where riches now abound
That's where the suckers can be found
To cough up lots of money

"The bankers backed a losing horse."
"Trade will suffer, jobs perforce."
Taxpayers see the need, of course
For shelling out their money

The IMF, if it comes through
Soon comes again to take its due
To the president, it says anew
Now you must gimmemoni

The president then takes his cue
And turns again to folks like you
"It's in the short-term bills come due
You have to gimmemoni"

IMF bailouts have their price
They call for all to sacrifice
Pay more for fuel, milk and rice
For wages, take less money

As for the kids, that wasteful bunch
The world of finance has a hunch
They can just wait to have their lunch
Or they can beg for money

# Part VI: Security States and States of Insecurity
## Suggested Readings


Athanasiou, Tom. *Divided Planet: The Ecology of Rich and Poor.* Boston: Little, Brown and Co., 1996.

Bello, Walden and S. Rosenfeld. *Dragons in Distress: Asia's Miracle Economies in Crisis.* San Francisco: Food First, 1992.

Carey, Peter, ed., with a foreword by Aung San Suu Kyi. *Burma: the Challenge of Change in a Divided Society.* London: Macmillan Press, Ltd., in association with St. Antony's College, Oxford, 1997.

Galtung, Johan. *The True Worlds: A Transnational Perspective.* New York: The Free Press, 1980.

Goulet, Dennis. *The Cruel Choice: A New Concept in the Theory of Development.* New York: Atheneum, 1973.

Khor, Martin. *The Future of North-South Relations: Conflict or Cooperation?* Penang: Third World Network, 1992.

Maniruzzaman, Talukkder. "Arms Transfers, Military Coups and Military Rule in Developing States," *Journal of Conflict Resolution.* 36(4), 733, 1992.

Marshall, Judith. *War, Debt and Structural Adjustment in Mozambique: The Social Impact.* Ottawa: The North-South Institute, 1992.

Mitchell, Donald O., Merlinda D. Ingco, and Ronald C. Duncan. *The World Food Outlook.* Cambridge: Cambridge University Press, 1997.

Nef, Jorge. *Human Security and Mutual Vulnerability: An Exploration into the Global Political Economy of Development and Underdevelopment.* Ottawa: International Development Research Center, 1995.

Salinger, Pierre. *The Secret Dossier.* New York and London: Doubleday, 1991.

Schoultz, Lars. *National Security and United States Policy Toward Latin America.* Princeton: Princeton University Press, 1987.

Silverstein, Ken. "Privatizing War," *The Nation* 265, No. 4, July 28–Aug. 4, 1997, pp. 11–17.

Stepan, Alfred. *Rethinking Military Politics: Brazil and the Southern Cone.* Princeton: Princeton University Press, 1988.

"Tempering Collaboration: UN Task-sharing with Regional Arrangements and Non-Governmental Organizations for Security and Services." *Third World Quarterly,* 1997 Special Issue, Vol. 18, No. 3.

Willetts, Peter, ed. "The Conscience of the World: The Influence of NGOs in the United Nations System." London: C. Hurst and Co., 1996.

Sana'a, Yemen

# Part VII

# When All Else Fails: Engendering a New Order

*History is all about gods and kings*
*and warriors; the rest is women's studies.*

*IN THE PURSUIT* of social change, burnout, buy out, and blast out are all too common, so that there is necessarily a frequent turnover in the personnel "manning" the forward barricades. In decades past, that position had been held, in turn, by organized labor, broadly based political parties, ethnic minorities, university students, even ironically, by organized religion. In the 1990s the charge, such as it is, is being led by a new genre of non-governmental organizations, most prominently those promoting ecological and feminist agendas.

To the extent that sectoral or issue-specific groups are able to sensitize and mobilize previously non-participant populations, their efforts can be expected to have a democratizing effect on society in general — all the more so in the case of women, since they, as more than half of the population, are no ordinary "interest group." And the society in question — now more than ever — is a global one.

For the organizers of the Fourth UN World Conference on Women, seeing the multitude descending on Beijing in August 1995, the burning question was whether the fruits of this conference would be sufficient to justify siphoning off the energies of the women from less glamorous but more immediately demanding tasks. For those watching from the sidelines, however, larger questions arose. How is one to explain such a massive mobilization? Why women? Why now? Why global?

# Why Women?

Because, as the Chinese proverb goes, "women hold up half the sky." That's on a good day. On a bad day, women hold up considerably more than half. But they receive far less than half of the material and psychic rewards and scarcely enough of the power to keep the whole sky — in the worst of times — from crumbling. Men have assumed responsibility (as religious leaders) for life after death and (as the anti-abortion lobby) for life before birth; the rest is up to women.

In the slums and shantytowns from Santiago to Shanghai, Memphis to Madras, wherever communities are most oppressed or desperate, community leadership is most likely to be provided by women. When all else fails, as it so often does, women are most likely to be the economic mainstays as well as the care-givers of their families and the organizational glue of their communities. This is partly because men can, and often do, flee from their responsibilities to another place or another mate, or perhaps just into a bottle. Women cannot.

In so many of the world's traditional societies, women grow most of the food, yet are landless. They work longer hours, from an earlier age, for less pay, and they do so with less nourishment because they must feed the men first. One might hope that modernization would improve the situation of women, but that is not necessarily the case. In much of Africa, Asia, and the South Pacific, women remain obliged to engage in subsistence farming while the land available to them is being shrunk, eroded, and degraded by the encroachment of cash cropping, logging, and mining; and the cash acquired in such pursuits is earned and controlled almost entirely by men.

The women of Papua New Guinea have long suffered abuse in the home and subordination in public affairs. Clan leadership in PNG is exercised by a chief, or *bigman*, who presides over village meetings and interprets customary laws. Clans are male-dominant; women have generally been excluded from participation in political and religious affairs. In fact, they have often been prohibited from speaking at public meetings. Wife-beating has been common, and commonly assumed by men to be among their rights. Even so, prior to Western colonization, women's roles in economic life were complementary to those of men and recognized, by men and women alike, as important. In fact, women had considerable autonomy in economic affairs, including control over their earnings.

European colonialism and, more recently, the influence of Western missionaries, diplomats and development advisors, and multinational corporations and financial interests has reinforced preexisting male dominance in politics and religion and undermined the position of women in the economy as well. In effect, the formal sector, from which women are excluded, is no longer limited to the rituals of politics and religion, but now has parallels in the economy and in virtually all aspects of society. The rights newly attributed to women through the constitution and national legislation remain unenforceable so long as women's status in the economy is being eroded.

Like so much else in India, abuse of women is a long-standing tradition. The growing problem of dowry abuse, however, a relatively recent phenomenon, appears to be a product of modernization. The trend is attributed in part to the new materialism infecting the urban middle class. The dowry, conceived traditionally as a daughter's inheritance, has come to be seen as a means whereby the bridegroom's family can acquire expensive consumer goods, over an indefinite period, at the expense of the bride's family.

## Why Now?

If the modernization occurring over the last couple of centuries has been for women a mixed blessing, the post-Cold War order has been, at least in economic terms, an unmitigated disaster. As we have seen in the extreme case of Albania, the new global village is a boys' town, wherein social responsibility is held in disrepute and self-indulgence is prized, admired, and rewarded.

The situation in the Caribbean has been less extreme but more typical. After achieving independence and limited economic self-assertion in the sixties and seventies, most Caribbean states have been re-absorbed by a now globalized neocolonial system. The "structural adjustment" exacted in the process has exacerbated hardship and inequality generally and has been particularly hard on women. It has deprived them of resources and authority gained through public service sector jobs, while requiring them to assume on an unpaid basis service and welfare responsibilities being abandoned by the state. As male unemployment rises, more women are working longer hours for less in new *maquiladora* industries, leaving children unattended and endangered.

Nor have the ravages of structural adjustment been limited to the Third World. Europe had seen a pronounced trend to feminization of the workplace during the last half of the twentieth century, but that has not countered the trend to the feminization of poverty. Whereas women constituted only about 30 percent of Europe's working population in the 1960s, they made up almost 43 percent by 1996. While the number of men in the workforce remained steady between 1975 and 1995 at about eighty-six million, the number of working women soared from forty-five million to sixty-one million. But as employment of women was growing, so too were unemployment and underemployment.

In 1996 only 9.8 percent of the men in the European Union were listed as unemployed, compared to 12.4 percent of the women. Working women, in Europe as elsewhere, were highly concentrated in the jobs that were short-term or part-time or otherwise low in security and pay and lacking in benefits. Eighty-one percent of the European Union's part-time workers in 1998 were women and, although wage figures were unreliable, it was clear that hundreds of thousands of women were working for less than the basic minimum wage.[1]

It was reported in 1998 that the gap in pay between men and women in the United Kingdom had widened for the first time in ten years. Analysts attributed the shift in this case to downward pressure on public sector wages. The professions hardest hit in Britain as elsewhere have been the nurturing ones, such as teaching and nursing. Some in Britain are calling it gender discrimination, but perhaps that misses the point. The degradation of public service and particularly of the "caring" professions constitute discrimination against everybody except males in a certain age bracket (i.e., between sixteen and sixty), stuck in an overextended process of reaching the age of responsibility.

What has been lost in this "boys' town" is not only attention to the needs of women and children but attention to the needs of society, including future generations. The values and strategies that inform a feminist agenda are crucial to the survival of the young and thus to the survival of the species.

## Why Global?

For women, as for other categories of people who have suffered discrimination, exploitation, and repression, there is no gain without political struggle. And for women even more than for other such categories, the price of liberation is constant vigilance. The gains achieved through organization and mobilization are all too soon eroded as organizations are co-opted and mobilization, once initial goals are met, begins to dissolve. Feminist leaders find themselves forced to choose between, on the one hand, trying to maintain their own separate organizations representing primarily women's interests and perspectives and being marginalized from the central political arena and, on the other, mainstreaming — integrating male-dominant parties and institutions only to lose their voice within them.

In fact, despite all the obstacles and dilemmas, women have made remarkable progress over the last couple of decades, and particularly over the last decade, in gaining political representation. Globally women's representation in national legislatures increased from 7.4 percent to nearly 11 percent between 1975, the beginning of the U.N. Decade for Women, and 1995. In the developed West representation doubled during that period.

Progress was particularly dramatic between 1987 and 1995. Representation in the United States rose from 5 percent to the global average of 11 percent, still no more than one-third, however, of the average in the Nordic countries. According to the Inter-parliamentary Union, there were only nine countries in the world in 1995 having no female representation in their legislatures. Twenty-four of the thirty-two women who have served as presidents or prime ministers during the twentieth century were in power in the 1990s.[2]

Even so, like other groups that must look to the political process to bring about urgently needed social and economic change, to protect hard-won rights and to reverse devastating trends of recent years in income, employment, and service delivery, women are finding that participation, even effective participation, in national politics is not enough if the decisions that most affect their lives are not being made at that level. The 1995 UN Conference in Beijing, along with so many other recent transnational gatherings, represented the recognition that women must work collectively at all levels to achieve political change at any level.

## Notes

1. Margaret Maruani, "Hard Times for Working Women," *Le Monde Diplomatique,* Nov. 1998, p. 16.
2. Jane S. Jaquette, "Women in Power: From Tokenism to Critical Mass," *Foreign Policy,* Vol. 108, Fall 1997, pp. 23–37.

Chapter 21

# Dowry Abuse: No Honeymoon for Indian Brides

*As masters of the spiritual realm,*
*men have assumed responsibility for life after death and before birth;*
*Women only have to worry about the part in between.*

*When two become one, it's generally one or the other.*

*ONE SUNNY AFTERNOON,* Usha, twenty-six, a trained chemist and a bride of seven months, slipped silently away from her workplace in a Bangalore pharmaceutical plant and did not return. Colleagues found her some while later, unconscious, in the restroom. She regained consciousness at the hospital and, before she died, let it be known that she had intentionally consumed sodiumarsenate and phenobarbitone.

Usha's husband Eshwar, who ran a tutorial service, was arrested shortly thereafter on charges of dowry abuse. In accordance with legislation passed in 1986, the death of a bride in the first seven years of marriage automatically calls for a post-mortem report and a coroner's inquest. Were Eshwar to be found guilty of driving his wife to suicide, he might be sentenced to two to seven years in prison; but while apparent dowry deaths become more and more common, convictions remain rare.

Like most marriages in India, even among the urban affluent, that of Usha and Eshwar was arranged. Usha's father, a government geologist, had met Eshwar through a relative, and the young couple were betrothed before they ever met. The betrothal ceremony, five months before the wedding, was an elaborate affair with some two hundred guests. The wedding was even more elaborate, with three thousand guests entertained at a cost to Usha's father of 100,000 rupees; or about 8,000 dollars.

At the time of the betrothal, Eshwar's family had demanded from Usha's father a dowry amounting to some 60,000 rupees. Along with a cash "gift" of 10,000 rupees, itemized demands included a dozen pieces of jewelry in gold and silver.[1] The gifts listed as being for the bride in fact had to be turned over to Eshwar's father, and additional gifts were demanded during the period between the engagement and the wedding. Furthermore, some of the original gifts were rejected and had to be replaced by finer ones. Meeting these demands, along with the cost of the wedding itself, drove Usha's father deeply into debt.

Following Indian custom, the new bride moved in with her husband's family, into a household that included Eshwar's two brothers and their wives. The abuse began almost immediately. Even though she was the only daughter-in-law employed outside the home, Usha had to prepare her own breakfast and lunch, and after returning from work in the evening, she had to wash the entire family's dishes. She was neglected when she was sick, and she was rebuked by her husband on a monthly basis for not having conceived a child. She was, in fact, continuously taunted and insulted by the entire family. And the demand for gifts from her family to his continued.

In December, in a letter to a friend, Usha wrote of feeling trapped in a loveless marriage, of her chagrin over the endless claims of her in-laws against her parents and of the impossibility in her society of divorce. She intimated that, seeing no other way out, she was contemplating suicide.

## Tapping Tradition to Feed Modern Materialism

The custom of dowry dates back many centuries in India, as does the casual abuse of women. The disturbing and puzzling thing about dowry abuse, however, is that it is a relatively recent phenomenon. It is most prevalent among the urban middle class, and it is spreading fast. Registered cases of dowry death, about one thousand in 1985, had doubled by the end of the decade and were reaching more than five thousand a year by the late 1990s. Moreover, those registered were assumed to be only a small fraction of the actual cases. An attorney serving India's Supreme Court estimated in 1996 that there were eleven thousand to fifteen thousand such deaths each year. In 1997 hundreds of thousands of cases involving alleged assault or torture over dowries awaited trial in courts across India. Perpetrators are very rarely punished.

The dowry system came about, in Hindu custom, because real property could not be passed to a daughter. As the daughter would be relocating to her husband's household, she could inherit only moveable goods. The dowry, then, was simply the daughter's inheritance, passed to her at the time of her marriage. The interest of the in-laws were irrelevant to the transaction.

The potential for abuse in the system was officially recognized, however, and proscribed by the Dowry Prohibition Act of 1961. The act was almost universally violated; but it was not until the 1970s that accounts of brides being killed in bizarre accidents, particularly kitchen fires, became so common as to demand the attention of researchers and law enforcement officials. The concept of "bride-burning," once a reference to the practice of *sati* (the immolation of the bride on the husband's funeral pyre), has since taken on a new meaning. The real story behind the fatal kitchen fire has all too often turned out to be that of a husband or mother-in-law spilling kerosene over the bride's saree and striking a match to it. Along with such "accidents," there has also been an upsurge in suicides. A great many brides have apparently seen suicide as their only acceptable escape from the incessant pressure to drain the livelihood of their parents to satisfy the whims of their in-laws. In 1986, India's penal code was amended to identify dowry death as an offense. But the legislation is loopholed and enforcement is lax.[2]

Sociologists and others who have studied this trend tend to attribute it in part to the new materialism and consumerism infecting the middle class. For the bridegroom and his family, marriage may become a means of acquiring the shiny new toys — stereos, VCRs, motorcycles, even cars — that they could never afford on their own salaries. And the extortion may go on long after the wedding, as brides rarely feel that they have the option of leaving their husbands. It is socially unacceptable for a bride to return to her parents' household. Indian women are expected to marry and stay married and, apart from a few shelters established by charities or women's groups, there are virtually no alternative living arrangements. Even for female professionals who could afford to rent their own apartments, there are few landlords who would rent to single women.

## Dowry and the Depreciation of Women

Formerly prevalent only among Hindu middle class families in the northern states, dowry demands — and dowry deaths — have spread across lines of geography, class and caste, and even religion. The practice is now common throughout the country, even in areas of Moslem or Christian settlement. In a region where women have traditionally been undervalued, at least in modern times, the steady inflation of dowry demands has led many parents to see female offspring as a distinct liability. Thus the dowry system has exacerbated the problems of female infanticide and, where amniocentesis is available, feticide. A study of 8,000 abortions carried out after amniocentesis in Bombay showed that 7,999 of the fetuses were female. Sex determination tests were banned by law in 1994, but they continue unabated. It has also contributed to the neglect and ill-treatment of female children. The ratio of females to males in the population has been dropping steadily for at least a couple of decades. From a ratio of 972 females per 1,000 males in 1901, the ratio dropped over a ninety-year period to 927 per 1,000. Furthermore, India is one of the few countries where women's life expectancy is markedly shorter than men's.

The only good news with respect to this grim topic is that recognition of the seriousness of the problem has served to mobilize women. Indian women are better organized now and more active politically and socially than they had been at any time since Mahatma Gandhi tapped their energies for the independence movement. Constitutional revision in 1994 provided that one-third of India's local council seats should be reserved for women. The impact will be felt far beyond the local level, because it means that some 800,000 women will enter the pipeline to leadership at state or national levels.[3] The increasing political clout of women has also been reflected in new legislation to address birth imbalance and the undervaluing of women. Timed to coincide with the birthday of Gandhi, the government launched a 720 million rupee (£12.4 million) scheme to offer incentives to low-income families to give birth to daughters and to send them to school.[4]

In the aftermath of Usha's death, more than five hundred women, representing six women's support or solidarity organizations based in Bangalore, led a march to the residence of Usha's husband. The local Lions Club also participated in the demonstration, as Usha's brothers and cousins were members. The demonstration was an impressive event and, I suspect, a fairly effective one in consciousness-raising. Protesters carried placards with such slogans as "Usha Was Murdered," "Down With Dowry Murder," and, for good measure, "No More Police Atrocities Against Women." They sang and chanted, pounded on doors and windows, and swore they would not leave until members of the family made an appearance. In time the mother-in-law came to the door and conceded that family pressures might have contributed to Usha's suicide. The media covered the scene, as did a contingent of police, who only stood back and watched. Before it was over, a great many neighbors had joined in the clamor to ostracize Usha's in-laws.

Usha's own family remains inconsolable, but determined that the story of her loss should bring other families to their senses. Her brothers declare that when they marry they will not demand, or even accept, dowry. Her younger sister simply vows never to marry.

## Notes

1. This information was offered to me by Usha's parents, who wanted her story to be told in the hope that other brides and their families might be spared such anguish.
2. Kathleen Koman, "India's Burning Brides," *Harvard Magazine,* Jan.–Feb., 1996, pp. 18–19.
3. UNDP *Human Development Report 1997.* Oxford: Oxford University Press, 1997, p. 31.
4. Peter Popham, "Parents Are Paid to Have the Daughters India Lost," *The Independent,* Oct. 3, 1997, p. 5.

## Chapter 22

# Doing More with Less: Structural Adjustment in the Caribbean

*The greater the risks and the smaller the rewards, the more likely it is that leadership roles will be held by women.*

*VISITING WITH BRENDA* Hood in 1994 in the offices of Save the Children in the Grenadian capital, St. George's, it was easy to believe what so many had said, that she was the mainstay of the country's nonprofit sector. It was also easy to see that she needed help.

The service retrenchment and social dislocation implicit in "structural adjustment" had struck earlier in the Caribbean than in other parts of the world because it came in the guise of a Reagan Administration aid and trade package, the Caribbean Basin Initiative. Brenda noted that pressure to reduce public deficits — so much a part of CBI and subsequently of structural adjustment — had meant that services previously offered by the government were being left to the nonprofit sector; but the funds that had underwritten them were not. In fact, general public sector retrenchment meant that there would be less public support for the nonprofit sector just as the demands placed on that sector were swelled by needy people being abandoned by the government. In short, there were more organizations but also more needs chasing fewer funds, which meant, among other things, that funds that might have been used directly and immediately to address the needs of children would have to be drawn off into appeals for donations.

Grenada, of course, as the last-but-one Caribbean country to be invaded by the United States, is a special case.[1] The Reagan Administration, having "rescued" the country in 1983 from what it portrayed as a Communist threat, had allowed that private investment and US aid and technical assistance would pour in, creating jobs and generating widespread prosperity.

By the end of the decade, Grenada was deeper in debt that ever before. The budget was badly out of balance, the tax system in disarray. Agricultural productivity was in decline; the manufacturing sector was small and stagnant; unemployment was pushing 30 percent, an all-time high; and USAID was withholding promised grants to the Grenadian government to leverage compliance with structural adjustment conditionalities. Meanwhile street crime, previously rare in Grenada, had come to be common.

The Grenadian difference, however, among Caribbean states, was more of degree than of kind. After a decade of US "assistance" through the Caribbean Basin Initiative, the Caribbean countries as a whole were deeper in debt and more economically and politically dependent than they had been at any time since independence movements began to gather steam in the 1960s. The credit conditionalities that accompanied the deeper globalization of the 1990s only exacerbated that dependency.

Given these circumstances, it is not hard to understand how women in the Caribbean as elsewhere have come to dominate the nonprofit sector. Women have never been denied responsibility; what they have lacked is authority and resources.

## Responsibility without Authority or Resources

The economic restructuring that has been under way since the early 1980s, and accelerating in the 1990s, has placed enormous strains on family life in the Caribbean. It has had the effect of marginalizing men and of heaping new responsibilities, both for "bread-winning" and for care-giving, on women whose time and resources were already stretched to the limits.

The social and economic hardships that have accompanied the thoroughgoing reabsorption of the Caribbean into a First World-centered global system have been particularly hard on women. In general, the long-term trend toward global economic integration, with its accompanying rollercoaster of economic growth and decline, has had the effect in the Caribbean as elsewhere of exacerbating inequality — of widening gaps between rich and poor countries, between rural and urban communities, between classes and sectors, and between men and women. Moreover, the economic hardship that accompanies modernizing trends has the effect of stripping women of resources and authority even as it heaps upon them greater responsibility. The particular nature of the structural adjustment programs of the past decade or so and their CBI precursors has required women to assume greater responsibility for family financial support at the same time they must shoulder the burden of service and welfare previously borne in part by the state.

While the men have long been dominant in politics and religion, Caribbean women have traditionally had important roles and rights in economic affairs, including control of food markets and of their own earnings. But those markets are being marginalized by food imports. Meanwhile women continue to raise food crops, but the land available to them is subject to the encroachment of cash cropping. The woman's plot might at least have fed her children. The cash, controlled almost entirely by men, is more likely to feed the bartender. Several studies from various regions have shown that, compared to men, women spend more of their incomes on meeting family needs and less on personal gratification.

About half of the households in the Caribbean are headed by women. At any rate, child-rearing in the Caribbean is almost exclusively the responsibility of women. A participant in the Third International Caribbean Women Writers' Conference, convened in Curaçao in 1993, noted that even married women were, in effect, single mothers. Such women have no choice about entering the wage labor force if, in fact, there are jobs to be found. For the less well educated, such jobs as are available are likely to be in the low-wage informal sector or in export-processing industries — in either case beyond the reach of organized labor and, in large part, beyond the protection of labor legislation.

As economic crisis deepens, even women who had been able previously to count on male support are pushed into the labor force as men lose jobs and wages lose purchasing power. Meanwhile, even as the less skilled, newly wage-dependent work longer hours under more hazardous conditions for less pay, experienced women are disproportionately victimized by corporate "down-sizing" and public sector shrinkage. Loss of income and autonomy in turn diminishes the influence women exercise over the allocation of resources within households and communities. Thus, confronted by men rendered dangerous by loss of jobs and self-esteem, women are subject to more frequent episodes of violence in the home as well as on the street.

In the English-speaking Caribbean, while women constitute only 40 percent of the labor force, they account for 50 to 60 percent of educators and civil servants.[2] Between 1981 and 1985, the number of women employed by the public sector in Jamaica dropped by fourteen thousand. In Jamaica, female unemployment, at 36.6 percent, was over twice the rate of male unemployment in 1985. Average weekly earnings stood at J$68.3 for women that year, compared to J$86.9 for men. In 1987, 38 percent of the employed women, compared to 12 percent of the men, worked in the informal sector, where average wages were less than half those in the formal sector. Thirty-nine percent of the Jamaican households were headed by women, and three-fourths of them had weekly incomes of less than $J100, or less than US$18, compared to 39 percent of male household heads at that income level.

Similarly in the Dominican Republic, unemployment was higher among women, and there were major wage differentials between men and women, especially in urban areas. In 1980, women's earnings were just about 60 percent those of men. Average income for urban female heads of household was less than half that of male bread-winners. For men and women alike, real wages dropped by 30 percent in the Dominican Republic between 1980 and 1987, at the same time that the weekly cost of a basic family food basket more than doubled. In fact, the cost of that food basket in 1987 was higher than the minimum wage.

Meanwhile government services, including public health care, were being slashed. Repercussions for the health of women and children were predictable. Prenatal clinics screening pregnant women reported an increase in cases of anemia from 23 percent in 1981 to 43 percent in 1985. The major maternity hospital in Santo Domingo reported an increase in maternal mortality during that period from fifteen to twenty-two per 100,000, and rates were much higher in rural areas. Infant mortality increased from sixteen per one thousand in 1980 to eighteen per one thousand in 1987.[3]

In sum, the "adjustments" that have drawn the Caribbean ever more tightly into the global market have made the region more attractive to creditors and investors by shifting resources and rewards, including returns on labor, upward in the social pyramid and outward to high-stakes players in the global arena, while socializing costs and losses and shifting burdens — attention to human, as opposed to financial, resources — downward. At the bottom, where both exploitation and responsibility are greatest, one still finds women.

For women, structural adjustment has meant being forced out of positions at higher pay and status, particularly in the public sector, and being forced into working longer hours for less pay under conditions of greater hardship in the informal sector or in export-processing industries. At the same time, such adjustment has meant paying higher prices for essential commodities now imported and assuming greater responsibility for services, such as the care of the young and the old and the sick, previously shared by the state. But Caribbean women are elaborating new collective strategies for coping with this crisis.

## Coping Collectively

Women's coping mechanisms, in the worst of times, have always been collective. The extended family system, which had always provided a measure of security, is less secure now as urbanization and emigration limit the accessibility of family members and, in general, weaken family ties. But women are finding new ways to pool resources, nurture souls, and regenerate energies through communal living.

Collective strategies for coping with the new hardships and responsibilities have included communal laundries, kitchens, and child care facilities and more nearly systematized barter-type exchanges of goods and services. They have also included organizing for cultural preservation and artistic expression. The most notable innovation, however, has been the emergence of a new category of women's organizations, one that focuses explicitly on the empowerment of women. Unlike traditional religious, social, or task-oriented organizations, international networks such as Development Alternatives for Women in a New Era (DAWN) straightforwardly challenge the assumption of male dominance from the home to the workplace to the halls of government and set forth alternative agendas based on women's strengths and priorities.[4]

Both the new set of government agencies addressing women's concerns and the network of feminist NGOs that grows ever more dense in the Caribbean were inspired in part by the United Nations Decade for Women. The Women's Bureau established by the government of Prime Minister Michael Manley of Jamaica in the mid-1970s was copied throughout the English-speaking Caribbean, so that by 1980 each of the CARICOM governments had one.

The Women and Development Unit of the University of the West Indies, now located in Barbados, emerged from a 1977 initiative of Jamaica's Women's Bureau, with funding from UNICEF, to implement regional plans for the UN Decade for Women. Also important in the English-speaking Caribbean have been Jamaica's SISTERN Collective, which seeks to energize and empower women through community theater and Grenada's Grenfruit cooperative; established in 1982 as an income-generating project, it has since taken on a broader range of functions.

Other income-producing co-ops in the region that have been particularly empowering women include the Dominican Republic's Mujer y Desarrollo (MUDE), or Women and Development, and Dominica's Program for Better Nutrition. Labor unions as such in the Caribbean remain heavily dominated by men, but a number of women's NGOs, like Haiti's Centre de Promotion des Femmes Ouvrières (Center for the Promotion of Working Women) have sprung up around the region to address workers' legal rights and to provide training in job skills and literacy.

The Dominican Republic's Centro de Investigación para la Acción Feminina (CIPAF), or Center for Research for Women's Action, is one of a number of organizations devoted to research, public education, and political action. Regionwide, the Caribbean Association for Feminist Research and Action (CAFRA), founded in 1985, serves a similar purpose; its members in Jamaica and in Trinidad and Tobago, for example, have organized to protest the extension of export-processing zones in their countries.[5]

# Notes

1. The US invaded Grenada in 1983 and Panama in 1989. For more information on the invasion of Grenada, see Jan K. Black. "The Selling of the Invasion of Grenada," *USA Today Magazine,* May 1984, reprinted in *World Politics, Annual Editions 1985/86,* Chap. 2, pp. 11–13.
2. Sally W. Yudelman, *Hopeful Openings: A Study of Five Women's Develop-*

*ment Organizations in Latin America and the Caribbean* (West Hartford, CT: Kumarian Press, 1987), pp. 61–87.

3. Carmen Diana Deere et al., *In the Shadows of the Sun: Caribbean Development Alternatives and US Policy* (Boulder, CO: PACCA Books, Westview Press, 1990), pp. 51–85.
4. Kathy McAfee, *Storm Signals: Structural Adjustment and Development Alternatives in the Caribbean* (London: Zed Books, and Boston: Oxfam America, 1991), p. 199.
5. Deere et al., *In the Shadows of the Sun,* pp. 106–117.

## Chapter 23

# Globalizing Popular Organization: The Old Girls Network

*How many women does it take to change a lightbulb?*
*About one-third.*
*For women to change anything,*
*they must constitute at least one-third of the decision-makers.*

*A meaningful life is the kind you get crucified for.*

*IN 1980, HSIU-LIEN* (Annette) Lu was in a dark and musty prison cell in Taiwan, suffering from ill health, feeling utterly alone and in deep despair, when the guards brought her a package, delivered, they said, by the Mayor of Albuquerque, from her friends in New Mexico. Her first thought was, "*What* friends in New Mexico?" But then she realized what it meant, and it made a world of difference. It meant that her case had been adopted by Amnesty International.

More recently a member of the Taiwanese Yuan, or parliament, representing the opposition Democratic Progressive Party, and co-chair of the Yuan's Foreign Affairs Committee, Annette Lu has become one of the most respected and most promising leaders of a democratizing Taiwan as well as a driving force in the political mobilization of women around the world. In opening the 1994 global Summit of Women in Taiwan, which she chaired, Lu commented that she might not have been there, addressing the several hundred women political leaders from some eighty countries — or anywhere else for that matter — had it not been for the persistent efforts of Amnesty International, particularly of the Albuquerque, New Mexico, adoption group, and of Dr. Jan Black, who was present that evening. For the duration of the Summit, I was treated by all in attendance as if I walked on water; unaccustomed as I am to such strolls, I occasionally got my feet wet.

Amnesty work is always rewarding, in that the cause of human rights is so basic and so important and the need for protection so urgent, but the rewards are rarely so immediate and personal. It was a humbling experience to be reminded that for the most part all we, in Amnesty International and other human rights organizations, generally try to do is to be there, in the safety zones, for the real players on the field. Theirs is the vision and the courage, the risk, and all too often the terrible price. And yet, their prospects of success against tyranny, even perhaps of survival, and ultimately of keeping hope alive, are utterly dependent on having support groups — groups that by the nature of the struggle must be global in purview — who will back them in the worst of times.

## Women at the Summit

The Global Summit, convened first in 1990, was only one of a growing number of regular international or transnational gatherings of women. The UN Decade of Women, declared in 1975, closed with a meeting in Nairobi in 1985; but unwilling to settle for a single decade, women who have monitored programs on behalf of the United Nations organized yet another set of international and non-governmental conferences, the biggest ever in 1995 in Beijing. The International Interdisciplinary Congress of Women, drawing academicians, development professionals, and grassroots activists, which has met in a different country every three years since 1981, will have its Seventh Assembly in Norway in 1999. The decennial UN Conference on Population, mainly a women's affair, had its third meeting in Cairo in September of 1994. Many less ambitious gatherings of membership organizations, such as the Association of Women in Development, take place each year.

The special niche of the 1994 Global Summit in Taiwan was expressed in its theme "Women and Political Leadership." The Summit drew some 450 delegates from eighty countries, most of whom were parliamentarians or other elected officials, including a dozen or more cabinet members. Participants also included a few scholars and many prominent leaders of women's movements, from a tree-planting initiative in Kenya to peace movements in Cambodia and Northern Ireland. The summit gave rise to a new organization, the International Alliance of Women Politicians, which continues to meet biennially. Its first meeting took place in Barcelona in 1996.

Along with the chair, Hsiu-Lien Annette Lu, organizers of the 1994 Global Summit included former Prime Minister of Lithuania Kazimiera Prunskiene and Anne Summers, former editor of *Ms.* Magazine; the late US Congresswoman Bella Abzug, an organizer, was also among the speakers.

## Consciousness-raising and Mobilization

Addressing the summit's opening banquet, former French Prime Minister Edith Cresson noted that as a rule it is only in the event of disaster that women show their true potential. It was political disaster that inspired some courageous Taiwanese women to launch a democratic movement. At the insistence of Madam Chiang Kai-shek, the Constitution drawn up in 1947 in China by the Kuomintang (KMT) provided that 10 percent of all legislative seats would be reserved for women. But such guarantees were meaningless when the KMT government was imposed on Taiwan, leaving the islanders — male and female alike — unrepresented and repressed. The movement launched in the 1970s by Annette Lu and others began to sensitize and mobilize women in defense of human rights in general and women's rights in particular, ultimately building a new constituency for a remarkably successful democratic opening.

In the United States, it was to some degree the economic disaster of the 1980s — the feminization of poverty — along with the concurrent exaggerated machismo in both domestic and foreign policy that began to generate a cleavage between male and female voting patterns during that decade. However, the abortion and "family values" (in fact, patriarchal values) issues, given prominence by anti-feminists, had put the women's movement on the defensive and divided female voters by class, generation, and region.

The episode that provoked a climate change for feminism, that brought angry women to the polls in droves in 1992, was the testimony and treatment of Anita Hill at the US Senate confirmation hearings for Supreme Court nominee Clarence Thomas. Relatively few women had faced the agonizing decision of whether or not to seek an abortion, but there was hardly a woman drawing breath who had not fallen prey to some sort of sexual harassment.

## Shaping the Policy Agenda

Bella Abzug, who said her motto was "speak softly and carry a lipstick," was in fact soft-spoken, at least off-podium. When she first ran for the US Congress in the 1970s, however, the fact that she was running as a feminist — seeking to represent women as such and to promote a women's agenda — was a shock to the system. The media caricatured her as a brassy broad, a development she says she did not resist because it gave her the attention necessary to get her points across. There has been since then very considerable change in the political climate in the US, as in many other countries, and running as a feminist is no longer an oddity. But the media continues to resist such change.[1] Ignoring our issues and policy recommendations, they much prefer to engage in gossip about our hair and our clothes, our families and our intimate relations.

In part because the media has insisted on trivializing our concerns as well as our candidacies, women have found it difficult to place our own interests and the public interest as we see it on the policy agenda. The problem has been most pronounced in the areas of foreign affairs and security. The prevailing mindset has held that affairs of state, along with theology, scholarship, sports, and war-making, must be left to men while women tend to the humdrum business of ensuring the survival of the species. The management of conflict thus has enjoyed more prestige than its resolution and punishing has been more popular than nurturing. The challenge, then, is not simply to convince the gatekeepers that women can be as "tough-minded" as men, but rather to get across the message that the species and its habitat can no longer afford wasteful and dangerous contests of machismo. Recent surveys have shown women to be, on balance, skeptical about defense spending, deregulation and global competitiveness, and "market reforms"; they are more concerned about peace, about fairness and social equity, about home and family, community and environment. The global village needs women in positions of leadership, not because they are the same as men, but precisely because they are not.

Women politicians at this summit reported no credibility problem with respect to environmental issues. Since cleaning up messes has always fallen to the lot of women, it is not so difficult to persuade electorates that planetary housekeeping may also be our responsibility. The challenge is to persuade men to share responsibility for both planetary and domestic house-cleaning.

It was also clear that the ongoing battle would have to be fought on many fronts simultaneously.

1. Constituencies. We will have little success in promoting the candidacy of women unless there are organized and mobilized constituencies of women seeking representation.
2. Candidates. It is not enough to launch the candidacy of women if we cannot fund their campaigns and attract fair and serious-minded media attention.
3. Electorates. It is not enough to get women to the polls if they are not politically sensitized, prepared to support women and a women's agenda.
4. Support networks. It is not enough to elect women to office if we do not provide the ongoing support essential to enable them to enact new legislation.
5. Results. If women's organizations and women voters do what is necessary to elect women and to support their legislative efforts, then we must insist on collecting on the promises that have been made.

**FIGURE 23.1: Percent of Women in National Legislatures, by Region, 1975–97**

**Percent of Women in National Legislatures**

| | 1975 | 1987 | 1997 |
|---|---|---|---|
| Arab States | 3.5 | 2.8 | 3.3 |
| Asia | 8.4 | 9.7 | 13.4 |
| (Asia excluding China, Mongolia, N. Korea, Vietnam) † | (3.8) | (6.2) | (6.3) |
| Central and Eastern Europe and Former Soviet Union | 23.3 | 23.1 | 11.5 |
| Developed countries (excluding East Asia) | 5.1 | 9.6 | 14.7 |
| Latin America and the Caribbean | 6.0 | 6.9 | 10.5 |
| Nordic Countries | 16.1 | 28.8 | 36.4 |

* 1997 statistics for lower houses and single house systems. (Mongolia scheduled.)
† women's representation under party control
*Sources: Democracy Still in the Making: A World Comparative Study* (Geneva: Inter-Parliamentary Union, 1997) and *The World's Women, 1970–1990: Trends and Statistics* (New York: United Nations, 1991).
Reprinted with permission from *Foreign Policy* 108 (Fall 1997), Copyright 1997 by the Carnegie Endowment for International Peace.

Monica Barnes, former member of the Irish parliament and at the time of the summit a candidate for the European parliament, warned that for women, even more generally than for men, the route to public office is an arduous and frustrating one. It cannot be worth the struggle unless we undertake it on behalf of a cause much larger than ourselves and larger even than the welfare of women. We have no doubt that a larger voice for women would make the world a more congenial place for men as well.

## Converging on the Challenge: Beijing and Beyond

At the end of August 1995, tens of thousands of women, representing thousands of NGOs and speaking scores of languages, descended upon the long isolated, if not altogether "forbidden," city of Beijing. The Fourth UN World Conference on Women, with its accompanying NGO forum, was both a logistical wonder and a logistical nightmare. It was hoped that a solid, democratically conceived, officially sanctioned document would emerge from the chaos. But the usefulness of the conference did not hinge on such an outcome. The most important work of the conference — the mobilization and networking and idea exchange in anticipation of it — had already been done.

What had once been thousands of agenda items had been screened and massaged and squeezed into a dense, weighty mass of a few dozen demands by a barrage of preparatory meetings taking place over the previous several years all around the world. In the fall of 1994, the process had been gathered into four sets of regional preparatory meetings — NGO Forums feeding into official meetings of the UN Regional Economic and Social Commissions in Austria, Argentina, Jordan, and Senegal.

In all, 163 countries were represented. The largest of the meetings, that of the African Women's NGO Forum in Senegal, drew some four thousand women. No one suggested this time around, as some had in the case of ECO '92, the ecological conference in Rio de Janeiro, that the official conference was needed to "legitimate" the NGO Forum. It was crystal clear this time that the legitimacy issue cut the other way.

While government delegations at the official conference meeting in downtown Beijing argued earnestly over the wording of documents, NGO delegations that were transnational and cross-cultural from the outset slogged through the mud in the maze of the satellite city of Huairou, marching, singing, swapping information, ideas, and inspiration, planning projects, and building even wider and denser networks. For any participant, trying to describe the world's largest ever gathering of women would be rather like a blind person trying to describe an elephant by touch. It was a world's fair, a theme park, a street theater, a rally, an academic conference, a women's political caucus. With some thirty-five thousand women, twelve thousand of them giving presentations on three thousand panels, the miracle is that so much of it actually went as planned.[2]

## What the Media Missed

It seems that media coverage in the US generally missed the significance of the event. The focus on logistics, on mud and heat and overcrowding, on Chinese security measures, and on already overplayed, reliably controversial issues like abortion, tended to trivialize the gathering and to distract attention from the real issues engaging the participants.

The fact that there was an army of well-trained and enthusiastic Chinese students trying their best to be helpful was missed by journalists looking for flashpoints. The problem of overzealous security was not so much a matter of the hassling of visitors as of the effort to limit spillover of this effervescent, celebratory indiscipline to the Chinese population.

For those who had friends there, as I did, whom they were trying to visit or to involve in the conference, such visits became more difficult than they should have been, and conference participation for Chinese citizens who were not officially sponsored was almost out of the question. The other matter particularly troubling to me with respect to the hospitality of the Chinese government was that of the women who were not officially there, most prominently the Taiwanese and the Tibetans.[3]

## The Women's Agenda

Media coverage of the conference tended unsurprisingly to seek out issues that were seen as polarizing. But the conference agenda was far broader and more serious than generally portrayed. It was after all the culmination of efforts dating back at least to the United Nations Charter and the Universal Declaration on Human Rights to identify obstacles to women's advancement and strategies for overcoming them. Attention was focused, in particular, on prompting ratification and adherence to the Convention on the Elimination of All Forms of Discrimination Against Women (CEDAW), adopted by the United Nations General Assembly in 1979. By late 1997 it had been ratified by 160 member states.[4] But it was also made very clear that the women's agenda is not simply about women's needs, but rather about human needs.

For those who have been involved in the processes of consciousness-raising, winnowing, and seeking consensus, the question now is whether this dense mass of select concerns will be weighed in when crucial policy decisions are being made. Many of those who converged on Beijing express frustration that the hard-won right to be heard does not necessarily translate into a voice in policy-making or implementation.

True, such conferences do not constitute real popular representation at the global level; but for the time being, except at the grassroots where resources are not, virtual representation may be the best most people — men or women — can get anyway. If the global arena is where the decisions that count are to be made, then it is there that we must take our stand. To those who ask why we are there, rather than in our kitchens and courtyards, we might respond as British outlaw Willie Sutton did when asked why he robbed banks: "Because that's where the money is."

# Notes

1. Some years later US representative Patricia Schroeder (D-Colorado) was asked by a slow-learning press if she was "running as a woman." She responded, "Do I have an option?"
2. In fact, I had expected much worse. I had been traveling for three months, out of contact with conference organizers, and I arrived in Beijing alone, from Tibet, at a domestic airport where there were no guides or interpreters for foreign guests. I had no hotel assigned and did not even know when or where my panels were to convene. "*Ni hao*" exhausted my Mandarin. To present to a taxi driver I had only the name of a hotel where friends were to be staying, and it had been transliterated back and forth several times between the Roman alphabet and Chinese characters. (It might have been more reassuring if when I showed the driver whatever I had scratched in Chinese characters on a scrap of paper he had smiled and nodded. Instead, he just shook his head and smirked.) It was fortunate enough, then, that I was able to find my contacts and my panels and to have a roof over my head, and sheer marvel that in that surging, chaotic crowd I kept stumbling into old friends from here and there around the world.
3. In fact, just a few weeks before the opening of the conference, the Chinese were lobbing missiles into Taiwanese waters, and while Tibetan women holding US or European passports were staging a protest demonstration on the grounds of the NGO Forum, the Chinese government was staging in Lhasa a very high-profile and high-security celebration of the fortieth anniversary of the annexation of Tibet.
4. The US is the only developed country that has failed to ratify. The Convention was signed by President Jimmy Carter in 1980, but ratification has since been stalled by Republican presidents or congresses and particularly, of late, by Senate Foreign Relations Committee Chairman Jesse Helms.

# Part VII: When All Else Fails: Engendering a New Order
## Suggested Readings


Afshar, Haleh, ed. *Women and Politics in the Third World.* London: Routledge, 1996.

Agarwal, Bina. *A Field of One's Own: Gender and Land Rights in South Asia.* New York: Cambridge University Press, 1994.

Anand, Sudhir and Amartya Sen. "Gender Inequality in Human Development: Theories and Measurement," Human Development Report Office Occasional Paper 19, New York: UNDP, 1995.

Bose, Christine E., and Edna Acosta-Belén. *Women in the Latin American Development Process.* Philadelphia: Temple University Press, 1995.

Boserup, Esther. *Woman's Role in Economic Development.* London: Allen and Unwin, 1970.

Chatty, Dawn and Annika Rabo, eds. *Organizing Women: Formal and Informal Women's Groups in the Middle East.* Oxford and New York: Berg Press, 1997.

Dankelman, Irene, and Joan Davidson. *Women and the Environment in the Third World: Alliance for the Future.* London: Earthscan Publications, Ltd., 1988.

Eisler, Riane. *The Chalice and the Blade.* Cambridge, MA: Harper and Row, 1987.

Inter-American Development Bank. *Women in the Americas: Bridging the Gender Gap.* Washington, DC: IADB, 1995.

Jacquette, Jane. *The Women's Movement in Latin America.* Boston: Unwin Hyman, 1989.

———. *Trying Democracy: Women in Post-Authoritarian Politics in Latin America and Central and Eastern Europe.* Baltimore: Johns Hopkins University Press, 1998.

Kardam, Nuket. *Bringing Women In: Women's Issues in International Development Programs.* Boulder, CO: Lynne Rienner, 1991.

Karl, Merilee. *Women and Empowerment: Participation and Decision-Making.* London: Zed Books, 1995.

O'Sullivan, Helene. *Silk and Steel: Asian Women Workers Confront Challenges of Industrial Restructuring.* Hong Kong: Committee for Asian Women, 1995.

Patterson, Maggie, ed. *Shadows Behind the Screen: Economic Restructuring and Asian Women.* Hong Kong: ARENA, June 1995.

Pettman, Jan Jindy. *Worlding Women: A Feminist International Politics.* New York: Routledge, 1996.

Scott, Catherine V. *Gender and Development: Rethinking Modernization and Development Theory.* Boulder, CO: Lynne Rienner, 1996.

Sen, Amartya. "More than 100 Million Women Are Missing." *New York Review of*

*Books*. 37(20): 61–66, 1990.

Summerfield, Gale, and Jiyang Howard. *Women and Economic Reform in China.* London: Routledge, 1998.

Tinker, Irene, and M. Bramsen. *Women and World Development.* Washington, DC: Overseas Development Council, 1976.

United Nations Development Program. *Human Development Report*. New York: United Nations Development Program, 1995.

United Nations. "Report of the Fourth World Conference on Women." Beijing, Sept. 4–15, 1995.

Waylen, Georgina. *Gender in Third World Politics.* Buckingham: Open University Press, 1996.

Witt, Linda, Karen M. Paget, and Glenna Mathews. *Running as a Woman: Gender and Power in American Politics*. New York: The Free Press, 1994.

# Chapter 24

# Conclusion: Back to the Future

*The future is not what it used to be*
*because the past keeps changing.*

*It doesn't matter where you start;*
*What matters is which way you're headed.*
*No matter where you're headed,*
*you have to start from where you are.*
*Having to start from where you are means*
*having to recognize where you are.*

*IT SEEMS THAT* somewhere along the route to a civilized twenty-first century we got waylaid and pulled back into the nineteenth. The equilibrium or social contract that had been achieved in the most advanced of the European social welfare states and that had been since World War II for so much of the world at least a distant goal has been severely eroded since the beginning of the 1980s and might even be said to have fallen into disrepute.

Both in terms of social relationships and of the belief and value systems that legitimate them, Second-Coming Capitalism is a throwback to the cruder Dickensian years of the industrial revolution or, at the latest, to the roaring twenties — before the global great depression, the American New Deal, the European Great War, and Third World decolonization and nationalism inspired a change of course and generated constituencies organized and able to confront the raw power of money.

Second-Coming Capitalism has built-in contradictions but no built-in symbiosis and no readily visible exit. Even as debt becomes the prevailing mechanism of social organization or reorganization, collective default seems no more likely than collective debt forgiveness, and since sheltered banking has gone global, even the idea of a revolution in Switzerland has lost its promise.

While the way back may not be clear, it should be clear enough that it is not to be found in the extremes of recent experience of either East or West. The "worker's state" was in a sense achieved, but applying only to the workplace, it turned out to be, in effect, a conspiracy of workers against themselves as consumers. But the US model of each against all — of Americans as individuals against America as a society — is no solution either. The next model of popular self-defeat toward which we appear to be headed, a feature of the casino economy, pits everyone as "investors" against themselves as wage earners and taxpayers.

As pension plans, including social security systems, are privatized and drawn into stock markets we lose even the option of frugality. The system will have turned all of us into gamblers. And the highest rollers will have us truly cornered. While collecting on the "house advantage," they will be able to tell us that we must not demand higher wages as that would only unsettle the stock market and thus threaten our pensions. Nor, they will argue, do we dare to demand government services in exchange for our taxes; all of us will be said to have a stake in the expansion of the "free market" at the expense of the public sector, because our pensions are sloshing around out there.

## The Trouble with Miracles

In 1997, before the onset of Asia's financial meltdown, the World Bank released an upbeat report to the effect that economies were growing in every region of the world. This felicitous turn of events was attributed to market reforms and public sector spending restraints that have drawn foreign investment to the developing world — 100 billion US dollars in 1996 alone.[1] Could this be the same World Bank that at its 1997 conference, meeting in Montevideo, urged Latin American countries to reduce unemployment, increase public investment in health and education, and shrink the gap between rich and poor?[2] Yes, of course, though comments came from different quarters within the bank.

A struggle as important as that for the general direction of reallocation of resources and opportunities — from richer to poorer to vice versa — and for the theoretical high ground explaining and justifying directional signals goes on continuously within major institutions as well as among them and among regions and states, political parties, and even non-profit organizations. The same World Bank that particularly since the early 1980s had used its credit to leverage policy changes punishing to the poor has in the 1990s rediscovered charity and in the new millennium might even rediscover development. Meanwhile, as the twentieth century draws to a close, a major struggle is already under way for the soul of the United Nations.

The economic miracle of the 1990s is the old-fashioned kind — of economies rising from the dead. It happens that those now claiming credit for the miracles are the same doctors whose prescriptions brought on the fatalities. But growth is an aggregate accounting device. A closer look shows clearly that in most of those restored economies the resurrected sectors and populations are a minority. Most victims of the restructuring are still dead.

It is not exactly news that a people made desperate enough by the stripping of their currencies, the loss of jobs and incomes, pensions and services, in some cases land and homes and habitat, will sell cheap what they prize most, including their time and labor. Such bargains attract carpet-baggers — i.e., foreign investors — whose capital translates into growth. The UNDP and other agencies have noted that in this sellers' market for capital, much of the growth of the 1990s has been jobless growth, as cheap imports have eliminated more domestically generated jobs than the new, often foreign-based, export industries could replace.

Such externally generated growth has reduced inflation, in some cases quite sharply, but it has not reduced insecurity. Many of those fortunate enough to have jobs in the restructured economy will have part-time or temporary or contingent ones and will need three of them just to make ends meet. They will be driving on toll roads, paying for services that once were free, and praying that they do not get sick, in which case they'd be on their own.

Growth so engendered demands human sacrifice, most often of the helpless and the selfless. In the former Soviet sphere, the elderly are undergoing transitional sacrifice for the second time. The first time around it was possible for many of them to believe that their generation was being sacrificed for its children. There is no such illusion this time because the children are being sacrificed too.

A 1997 UNICEF report on the status of children in the former Soviet Union, Central Europe, and the Balkans paints a dismal picture of poverty and disease, family breakdown, sexual abuse, petty crime, murder, and suicide. In Central Europe, the number of children living in poverty had more than doubled in the 1990s to 2.5 million. In the region as a whole the number of children living in orphanages or other group homes had grown in the 1990s to more than a million, the numbers having grown by 76 percent in Estonia and about 40 percent in Latvia, Romania, and Russia since 1990.[3]

Such insecurities are not limited to the countries caught on the wrong side of the Cold War. In Chile where, following the deep depression of the mid-1970s and early 1980s, growth has been sustained for more than a decade and where an elected civilian government has sought, after the devastating years of dictatorship, to rebuild social infrastructures and safety nets, the incidence of clinical depression and suicide remains extraordinarily high.

In the United States, some five years of steady growth has reduced unemployment but not inequality. Ninety-seven percent of the income gains in the US since 1980 have gone to the richest 20 percent of the population. The richest one percent of the population has as much income as the bottom 35 percent, and the gap is still growing. While the average US employee enjoyed a 3 percent raise in 1995, the "layoff leaders" among corporate chief executive officers averaged 67 percent pay raises. Nor has such growth relieved insecurity. A 1997 Washington Post-ABC News poll indicated that most of the public believe the country is headed in the wrong direction and that among Americans under thirty-five there were more who believed in UFOs than in the likelihood of receiving social security.[4]

Insecurity, even in times of economic growth, turns citizens against immigrants and immigrants ultimately against each other and even against themselves. Increasing rates of homicides in the last two decades have almost been matched by increasing suicides. Nor is individual insecurity a trade-off against national or regional security. When depletable resources are depleted or social organization threatens to change the balance of power between capital and labor, capital can be expected to pick up and move on to the next desperate place.

## Economic and Ecological Limits

Is there a limit to the predations of such a system? Yes, in relatively contained national systems limits to exploitation appeared when scarcity of disposable income left production to outstrip effective demand or when growth tightened labor markets to such an extent as to enhance labor's bargaining power. Capital escaped those constraints by going global and by eliminating competition among economic systems in the global arena.

The constraints that at times and places operated effectively at the national level might ultimately come into play at the global level, but that would assume a drop in population growth achieved in the past only through famine, epidemic, war, or generalized and equitable prosperity. At any rate, waiting for such constraints to come into play may represent a five-hundred-year plan.

Limits might be found simply in the manageability of the international financial house of cards. An exceptionally greedy or panicky move on the part of a limited number of players might trigger a crash that would make the depression of the 1930s look like a tremor instead of a quake. The East Asian financial meltdown of late 1997 ought at least to sound a warning.

There is even the possibility that Keynesianism might be rediscovered — that the business community in general would realize that widespread prosperity based on growing effective demand (fair wages, disposable income) served them better than a brutalizing race to the bottom-line of profit margins and stock values in which winners are ever fewer and larger. But even in that unlikely event there would remain the limits to the growth model posed by the carrying capacity of a finite planet.

Ecological limits have already begun to constrain growth in some areas and industries. Rio Plus Five, the second world environment summit, meeting at the United Nations in New York City in June 1997, was not a happy campsite. Greenpeace representatives noted that the world's environmental record following up on the commitments made at ECO '92 in Rio de Janeiro amounted to a U-turn. Virtually every target had been missed, and most problems identified in 1992 had gotten worse.

More than 130,000 species have become extinct since 1982 as logging firms have plundered forests everywhere almost at will. Even as the forests that might have absorbed some of the carbon dioxide are being destroyed, emissions, both from motor-vehicles in the First World and from dirty industry in the Third, are increasing. Trends in almost every country are such as to accelerate global warming.

The water crisis is worsening. In 1995, one-fifth of the world's population lacked access to potable water and two-thirds will face serious problems if current patterns of use and management continue. In poor countries, 90 percent of urban sewage is released untreated into rivers, lakes, or oceans.

Meanwhile oceans are threatened by the increasingly ambitious operations of oil and gas companies, and fish stocks are being overfished. Even the prized salmon of the US Northwest coastal regions are becoming endangered.

Most of the seventy heads of government and others gathered in New York to take stock of progress or retrogression in dealing with environmental threats concluded, however, that the greatest threat to the planet's natural resources lay in the mistreatment of its human resources. Poverty was found to be at the root of the worst failures of commitment. Rising debt and unfair terms of trade leave bankrupt governments unable to resist the propositions of investors.

According to the UNDP's 1997 *Human Development Report* the poorest 20 percent of the world's population, which in 1960 received only 2.3 percent of global income, now receives only 1.1 percent. The combined wealth of the world's three richest individuals is greater than the combined GDP of the forty-eight poorest countries — a quarter of all the world's states. At ECO '92, the rich nations had promised to increase aid for sustainable development from 0.33 percent to 0.7 percent of gross domestic product. In fact, they have cut it by 20 percent to only 0.27 percent.[5]

It may be that there will be no planned transformation of this system, only its collapse when producers run out of consumers, when share traders in stock markets run out of new issues, when down-sizing corporate chiefs run out of "Indians" to do the work, when the financially comfortable have plenty of VCRs and computer games and cellular phones but no breathable air and drinkable water. If that's the case, the arguments about the extraordinary rational power of homo sapiens can be no more than speciesist arrogance.

## A Challenge of Political Will

If you have concluded after reading thus far that I am a pessimist, you have missed the point. Why would I bother to write such a book if I saw this state of affairs as inevitable, this direction of trends as immutable? Why wouldn't I be scuba-diving or playing tiddlywinks instead?

Utopias aside, the idea of a social system that is relatively open and democratic, fair and equitable, and at the same time creative and productive is no pipe dream. We have seen many of them at local and national levels in the past and a few, the Scandinavian countries for example, are holding on despite all odds even now. Moreover, many of the trajectories of global trends cited in Chapter 2 suggest that we could in time eradicate mass poverty and achieve a more hospitable world.

The good news is that we can get there from here. The bad news is that we are headed the wrong way. Getting there need not be so hard. The hard part is negotiating the U-turn.

The obstacles to civilization are not to be found in a lack of technical or economic know-how. We know how to produce and conserve, to regenerate and recycle essential goods. We know how to recycle and redistribute money and opportunity, how to provide for what we euphemistically call human resource development and how to care for those with special needs. The resources are not lacking; they are simply maldistributed. What is most sadly lacking in this equation is political will. But the black-hole density of the current concentration of economic power and the technological sophistication with which it is continuously reconcentrated make the political task an awesome one.

We escaped the nineteenth century once; we can do it again. But we cannot do it in quite the same way. All the tactics we have used in the past we will continue to need and to need in more effective form than what we now see: the organization of labor, across all the categories now used to divide; the breakdown of barriers to recognition of common interest and reorganization and mobilization of non-elite groups along lines that recognize common need and stress common purpose; the aggregation of interests by mass-based multiclass parties; and the communication of ideas and options in clear enough form to dissipate the fog spread by corporate-controlled media. But we no longer have what came to be in many cases the advantage of the confines of a national system.

The central problem and challenge as I see it is that of limiting the mobility of money or globalizing the popular regulation of it; and I can see no means of doing the former without first achieving the latter. The worst of the traps we now find ourselves in is that if we are able to elect progressive governments and then bring such pressures to bear on them as to inspire more equitable policies — e.g., progressive taxation to fund public parks or health services — capital will streak away to some other place where the population is less able politically, or more desperate, or governments are more corrupt.

I am not suggesting that we cease to support progressive candidates or that we absolve them when they lose heart or nerve and shrink from their commitments to the public. But to limit participation to election day and then to stand idly by blaming one leader after another for selling out is something of a cop-out. Popular participation must be day in and day out and it must not be limited to national electoral arenas. I can see no alternative to the outrageously ambitious task of popular organization at the global level, though some progress might be achieved in smaller bites of transnational organization in regional markets on the order of the European Community.

The organizations most successful at the regional and global levels will not necessarily be the same ones that have shown the greatest promise at the national level. In fact there are even now a multitude of organizations old and new operating transnationally that have come to be known simply by what they are not: the non-governmental organizations or NGOs.

## The Promise and the Limitations of NGOs

The NGO denomination provides categorical cover to a great congregation of saints and sinners. Technically the category includes the private, for-profit sector, and First World government agencies have been known to slip a little help past taxpayers to their business cronies in developing states under that guise. NGOs are also contracted directly or indirectly, wittingly or unwittingly, by government agencies whose ultimate motives may be less than fully aired.

For the most part, however, the tens of thousands of NGOs funded by government agencies, private enterprises, religious denominations, and individual givers, which in turn support the efforts of millions of popular organizations at the community level, are non-profit, non-elite organizations conscientiously engaged in programs of charity, relief, development, conservation, human rights monitoring, and policy advocacy. Many of them engage in policy or program implementation and in policy advocacy at the same time, supporting efforts in many countries and lobbying national governments as well as international and transnational organizations.

Non-profit organizations and, in general, the ideal of volunteerism now have the advantage of political support (rhetorical, that is, not necessarily material) from both ends of the political spectrum. This offers some advantages for those who would promote the interests of the unpowerful, but it should also raise concerns. Bipartisanship is generally a conspiracy of the elected against the electorate. In this case it represents for governments good cover for making a great escape from responsibility. But the non-profit sector is not and cannot be a substitute for government services. Government down-sizing, in fact, has meant retreat not only from services provided directly but also from crucial support for the non-profit sector.

The maintenance of a strong non-profit sector in fact requires the support of a strong government. In addition to the necessary allocations from the public budget, donations from the private sector will not be forthcoming in adequate amounts unless tax and other incentives are established by governments and unless the threat of regulation inspires big business to cultivate an image of social responsibility. Finally, if governments are unable to protect the non-profit sector, those aspects of it that might be seen as competitive with business will come under attack. That is, if business can see profit potential in a service offered on a non-profit basis, it will move to eliminate the competition. The strategies employed by US health maintenance organizations like Hospital Corporation of America-Humana to eliminate both public and private non-profit hospitals and clinics are a case in point.

A great deal has been written about the potential of and the challenges faced by NGOs in their ameliorative and developmental grassroots endeavors and in their mobilization of particular communities (e.g., women) for local or global campaigns; but such organizations also have considerable potential in policy advocacy. Even presidents and prime ministers who seem genuinely committed to a course of action favoring the nonpowerful may be unable to move, to risk the displeasure of companies or agencies with interests or prejudice at stake, in the absence of a vociferous display of public support. Thus, even though the roles of non-governmental organizations and other nontraditional actors cannot be expected to be strong enough in themselves to redirect the general course of policy, their participation may in some cases be critical. That is, the mobilization of public support by NGOs may be a necessary enabling factor, if not in itself a sufficient cause, for policy reversal.

Lacking the resources available to public and for-profit sectors, NGOs are in a sense handicapped players, but they are not without their strengths. NGOs play a liaison role, linking people in bureaucracies and even in elective office with like-minded people on the outside. Even governmental officials at fairly high levels perceive themselves as having far less power and less voice than outsiders might imagine. Thus it is often the case that only through helping NGOs to mobilize support on the outside are some government officials able to acquire voice on the inside. Also, it often happens that NGOs in themselves having limited budgets and memberships are able to tap into strongly held but poorly articulated public opinion and give it resonance. Human rights organizations have been particularly effective in drawing upon and channeling the largely untapped wellspring of human compassion and empathy.

## Collective Security: It Takes a Community

Many of us who regularly celebrate Human Rights Day, the anniversary (in 1998, the fiftieth) of the adoption on December 10, 1948, of the UN Universal Declaration of Human Rights, have seen years when "celebrate" would have seemed a peculiar term — when it seemed that in country after country we were losing the battle to the perpetrators of official terror, the torturers, executioners, and death squads and their employers. In much of the world we have come a long way since those years in winning official respect for human rights.

But those rights so hard won for some people and classes and nations may soon be lost again if they are not extended to all peoples, and if they are not embraced in an extended family — a closely knit community — of related and mutually reinforcing rights. Amnesty International, the flagship organization of human rights monitors, was born in 1961, when a British lawyer was moved by the plight of Portuguese students imprisoned by the autocratic regime of Salazar. Since that time the organization has helped bring about resolution of the cases of more than forty-five thousand political prisoners. And many other creative, courageous, and effective organizations have joined the endeavor.

Concern for human rights gained momentum in the United States when Congress belatedly, in the mid-1970s, withdrew US military aid from some of Latin America's predatory military regimes. The congressional response came in part because victimization was no longer limited to the anonymous poor. It had been extended to leaders in politics, religion, academia, and the media, people with whom prominent foreigners could identify.

The cause advanced further when it was adopted by the Carter Administration. It was in fact a good fit with the ideological ambivalence of that administration because there were plenty of abusive regimes to be targeted on both Right and Left extremes of the political spectrum. The initiatives of the Carter Administration and of like-minded governments and NGOs in Europe and elsewhere emboldened would-be democrats and wilted the will of oppressors.

The social truce of the late twentieth century, however, remains a tenuous one. The worst of the abusers have not been defeated, only displaced. And while the affluent have for the most part gained relief from torment by armed and uniformed thugs, the poor, as always, remain vulnerable.

## Reconciliation without Atonement

The rituals of democracy that have reappeared in so much of the world in recent years have, in many cases, rested on the principles of reconciliation. But it is a reconciliation without atonement, a reconciliation of the privileged and the wretched, the armed and the unarmed, the abusers and the abused. Victims not only fail to feel vindicated; they find it difficult to exercise freely their hard-won civil rights when perpetrators enjoy impunity, free even of open condemnation of their misdeeds. Like battered wives, battered populations, having no clear alternative, choose to try to believe the protestations of abusers that it will not happen again; but lacking full confidence, they temper their words and their actions.

Even if policy options in the 1990s were more clear, it is not clear that battered populations would be prepared to pursue them in the free-wheeling style of the politics they once knew. At any rate, options with respect to the policy issues that matter most are by no means clear, since economic decision making has been out-sourced.

## Redefining Human Rights

Apart from the newly assertive Orient, human rights are more likely to be respected in the 1990s than in decades past, so long as eating is not one of them. In general, the national security state, constructed in response to the insecurity of national and neocolonial economic elites, is no longer needed. The threat of accountable democracy, wherein economic decision making might be responsive to the interests of the non-affluent majority, has abated. The armed forces that once occupied their own countries as if they were on enemy turf have been replaced as guardians of elite interests by a dense global concentration of money managers — in effect, a global creditor cartel. The gray eminence looming over each President and Prime Minister is no long the commander of the Armed Forces, but rather the Minister of Finance. Defiance of authority is anomic and apolitical and handled by police (who incidentally occupy troubled neighborhoods as if on enemy turf).

In Indochina in the 1960s, South America in the 1970s, and Central America and South Africa in the 1980s, great battles raged within and at times among states as have-nots found hope and haves found threat in the prospect of social change. The threat of imprisonment, torture, execution, and "disappearance" was so urgent that human rights, as monitored by Amnesty International, Human Rights Watch, and other groups came to be defined in terms of such politically motivated, physical threats by official or officially tolerated thugs. The definition was elemental also because the deluge of cases deserving attention necessitated a kind of triage.

But as human rights organizations expanded, incorporating more chapters based in the Third World, pressures mounted for extending the parameters of the mandate. Surely, it was argued by Africans and South Asians who had suffered famine, there is a human right to eat. And by extension, there must be a right to clothing and shelter, medical attention and literacy. And if these are rights, must they not be available to and affordable by all?

The list of rights lengthened with the growth of new categories of victims, new constituencies and new support groups: women, environmentalists, indigenous peoples, refugees and immigrants, the homeless and the stateless. If people should be protected from abuse by governments, should not women be protected from abuse by their husbands? If there is a right to food, is there not also a right to drinkable water and breathable air? What about a right, in this age of ethnic cleansing, to preservation of language and culture? Does not human dignity rest on having a culture one can call one's own? There must also be a right to citizenship (in places of birth and/or extended stay), without which no rights are enforceable, and to political participation, without which no claim is sustainable.

Of late the most vociferous right-to-life debate has been about life only until birth. If there is a right to life after birth, is there also a right to some means of earning a living? The question is by no means a frivolous one in this age of down-sizing and out-sourcing; of asset-stripping and plant-closing; of resource pillaging and habitat trashing; of near disappearance of subsistence farming and fishing; of shrinkage of public sectors and fraying of safety nets.

Some might argue that the concept of human rights has become too broad to be addressed effectively, but Amnesty International, which now has more than a million members and chapters in 150 countries, assumes the contrary. To be effective, human rights advocates must address a broad range of interrelated problems and defend a community of rights. Should all of this be the domain of human rights agencies and activists? Of course not. Not ours alone. But is it our business? You bet. Because rights are a seamless web, and the more we concede, the harder it becomes to defend what we have left.

## Notes

1. The International Bank for Reconstruction and Development (IBRD — World Bank), "Global Economic Prospects and the Developing Countries, 1997," Washington, DC: IBRD, 1997.
2. "Recomienda el BM, Reducir la Brecha Entre Ricos y Pobres en America Latina," *Excelsior,* Mexico City, 1 de julio de 1997, p. 2F.
3. Ian Traynor, "Children Pay Price for Democracy," *The Manchester Guardian Weekly,* London, April 27, 1997, p. 4.
4. "Why All the Pessimism in Such Good Times?" *San Francisco Chronicle,* Sept. 7, 1997, p. 8.
5. David Harrison, "Turning a Blind Eye to a Plague of Pollution," *The Manchester Guardian Weekly,* June 29, 1997, p. 12.

# Index

# About the Author

JAN KNIPPERS BLACK is a professor in the Graduate School of International Policy Studies at the Monterey Institute of International Studies in California. Formerly she has been a senior associate member of St. Antony's College, Oxford, a faculty member on the University of Pittsburgh's Semester at Sea, a research professor at the University of New Mexico, and a research team supervisor at American University. She has published more than a hundred articles and has authored or edited and co-authored eleven books.